CROSSING THE GULF

CROSSING THE GULF

LOVE AND FAMILY IN MIGRANT LIVES

PARDIS MAHDAVI

STANFORD UNIVERSITY PRESS ▮ STANFORD, CALIFORNIA

Stanford University Press
Stanford, California

Printed in the United States of America on acid-free, archival-quality paper

Library of Congress Cataloging-in-Publication Data

Names: Mahdavi, Pardis, 1978– author.
Title: Crossing the Gulf : love and family in migrant lives / Pardis Mahdavi.
Description: Stanford, California : Stanford University Press, 2016. |
   Includes bibliographical references and index.
Identifiers: LCCN 2015050234 | ISBN 9780804794428 (cloth : alk. paper) |
ISBN 9780804798839 (pbk. : alk. paper) | ISBN 9780804798846 (electronic)
Subjects: LCSH: Immigrants—Family relationships—Persian Gulf States. |
   Women immigrants—Family relationships—Persian Gulf States. |
   Immigrants—Persian Gulf States—Social conditions. | Women
   immigrants—Persian Gulf States—Social conditions. | Persian Gulf
   States—Emigration and immigration—Government policy.
Classification: LCC JV8750 .M34 2016 | DDC 305.9/0691209536—dc23
LC record available at http://lccn.loc.gov/2015050234

Typeset by Bruce Lundquist in 10/14 Minion

For Shayan and Raami

CONTENTS

PROLOGUE

"WHY HAS IT TAKEN YOU SO LONG TO COME BACK?" asked Noor. The question hung in the air between us that had thickened with the anticipation of two close friends who haven't seen each other in far too long. I had returned to Dubai after more than three years, and Noor was one of the first people I called upon my return. A thirty-nine-year-old woman of mixed Iranian and Arab descent, Noor first migrated from Iran to Dubai in 2004 when her then husband got a job with Microsoft Middle East in Dubai. Not three months after their arrival in Dubai, Noor's husband filed for divorce and left the country.

Noor decided to remain in Dubai because she was afraid of the shame of returning to Iran as a divorcee. "I couldn't even tell them, couldn't even form the words, they were stuck in my throat," Noor had said to me back in 2008 when I first met her. Unable to face her family back home, Noor stayed in Dubai working illegally as a nanny, beautician, and at some point as an escort in the sex industry. As an escort she met Waleed, an Emirati young man who fell in love with Noor almost immediately. The two moved in together, Noor stopped working, and a year later Noor became pregnant. Upon hearing of Noor's pregnancy, Waleed admitted he was actually engaged to another woman, but he promised to continue supporting Noor through her pregnancy and beyond. For the first three years of their son's life Waleed kept his promise, furnishing an apartment for Noor and their son and visiting on occasion. Once Waleed's new wife discovered the existence of Noor, however, all contact—and all financial support—was severed. Unsure of how to make ends meet, Noor decided to return to the sex industry in order to support herself and her son. After a few months of working as an escort, however, Noor said that she found the work exhausting when coupled with single parenting. "It's like I'm up all night, then I have to come home, and he (her son) needs love from me too, so I'm always giving love. But eventually, you start to feel you can't keep going. It's not like it was when it was just me. I feel like a car trying to drive fast without any gas," she had said to me back in 2009. Noor attempted to find work as a nanny and searched for work that could be done during daytime hours when she could more easily find child care for her son, but to no avail. "It was bad, and I was falling low," she explained. "You have to know how desperate I was because I decided to go back to Iran. To face the shame of everything, divorcee, sex worker, single mom, all of it, just to go back home to my family." But days after Noor made this difficult decision she was told that she could not return to Iran so easily. Worse yet, she was told that she had overstayed her visa illegally for many years and would have to pay a high fine (in the sum of USD$20,000), likely face imprisonment, and almost certainly face deportation—without her son. Determined to fight the charges, Noor called on her previous boyfriend, Waleed, for help.

Involving Waleed was both a blessing and a curse, according to Noor. He was able to prevent her being imprisoned and assisted in paying some of her fines, but his coming forward aroused suspicion on the part of the authorities. Emirati laws regarding custody are stringent. If a child is suspected of having Emirati fatherhood, the mother will not be able to leave the country with the child unless she has permission from the child's father. In Noor's case, Waleed had never explicitly acknowledged paternity, and now Noor, who herself had become an illegal migrant when she overstayed her visa, was unsure how to obtain legal status for her child. Unable to leave Dubai without her son, Noor remains immobilized—by the bonds of love she has for her son—in Dubai. She has been embroiled in long and bitter court disputes in order to gain full legal custody of her son. She has begged Waleed to come forward, acknowledge paternity, and give her permission to leave the country with their son. While she is frustrated with her immobility, she remains terrified of the possibility of forced mobility, or deportation, should she not get the outcome she hopes for in the Emirati courts or with her ex-boyfriend.

I first met Noor when she was a volunteer working at an informal shelter for trafficked women. It was during this time that I got to know her and her son, Waleed (named after his father). We became good friends and had stayed in touch over the years. Her story was one that I had continued to grapple with. I had worked with some lawyer friends in Dubai who were kind enough to represent Noor on a pro bono basis, but even they felt that they were running out of options and time. I had often worried that if and when I returned to Dubai I would not be able to find Noor. I wondered if she would be imprisoned or deported to Iran. I knew that her deportation, particularly without her son, would be excruciatingly painful for her, and I also knew that she would face extreme hardship if she returned to Iran. It seemed doubtful that she would survive the ordeal. In the months before my arrival in Dubai I had written to Noor many times, but she had stopped answering. When I asked my lawyer friends if they had heard from her, they too had no news. As soon as I arrived in Dubai, I dialed her number with trepidation, almost certain she would not pick up. When I heard her voice on the other end of the phone, I was overcome with emotion. Excited to connect after such a long time, we agreed to meet at one of our favorite cafés on the boardwalk of what used to be referred to as "New Dubai."

When I first walked into the café, I hardly recognized the somber woman sitting in the corner, staring out the window with a cigarette in her right hand. Noor had aged nearly a decade since I had last seen her three years prior. She now sat hunched over, her hair graying at the temples, her eyes ringed with dark circles of fatigue. When she saw me she stood up slowly, and we embraced for a long time. With Noor at the café, I looked out across the Dubai Marina that had developed so rapidly, and I remembered the many conversations that we'd had about life, love, and the future. When I didn't answer Noor's initial question, she repeated it. "Come now, why has it taken you so long to come back to Dubai?" I wasn't sure how to answer, but I decided to be completely honest with her as she had always been with me.

I told her that I had been having some troubles of my own; personal and familial challenges that made me see her life in a whole new light. Noor looked at me quizzically. "What happened, *habbibti**?" she asked. I settled in to tell her my story, as she had told me hers some years ago. I felt compelled to tell her everything, even though I felt ashamed, frightened, and angry. Her story and the many stories I had heard during my fieldwork had always stayed with me during my challenging experiences. And it was their stories that I kept thinking of in order to put my own turmoil in perspective. But I knew I had to tell Noor what had happened to me, as I had known it all along.

I I I

* *Habbibti* is an Arabic term of endearment, roughly translating as "dear."

In 2010, just after completing a draft of my previous book, I gave birth to a little girl. Through a series of high-level conflicts with my daughter's father, I ended up as a single parent shortly after she was born. After many months had passed and I was in a new relationship, my ex-husband emerged, threatening to take away my daughter for good. This led to a long and litigious struggle to keep custody of my daughter. Owing to the seemingly unending legal proceedings and the fact that in the United States, if a parent wants to leave the country, the other parent must sign a letter of consent (which my ex-husband refused to do), I was not permitted to leave the state of California with my little girl. I became immobilized—by the bonds of love for my daughter—in Los Angeles.

After over two years of conflict and litigation, in April of 2013, my ex-husband decided to sever all contact with my daughter and me, finally giving us some peace. He even signed paperwork that allowed me to take her out of the country so that I could do some fieldwork, though I later learned that this was only a brief break in the turmoil. That was how I had returned to Dubai at last. My ex-husband, who would not give me permission to leave the state of California with my daughter, had held me hostage for almost three years. I was immobilized because I refused to travel without her. And at the same time, I feared my daughter's forced mobility in the form of kidnapping.

ı ı ı

As I told the full story to Noor, she listened quietly, tears coming to her eyes. "I knew something was wrong," she said, placing her hand on mine across the table at the café. She wiped the tears that streamed down her face, causing me to cry as well. "I can't believe what you have been going through. And to think, this is what you write about, abuses to women, kidnapping, all of it, and now you are living it." I was amazed. I hadn't put it all together until that point. I knew that I had become interested in migrant mothers, and I knew that my passion for understanding immobility and mobility as co-constitutive factors was related to my own situation, but I couldn't put all the pieces together until that day.

Noor let me sit in silence awhile before continuing. "You must write about this. You must write of what you have lived. It is your life, it is your struggle, but that is what connects you to us." I told her I was hesitant about writing my own story, fearing the consequences of baring the intimate details of my life. "But you always say that people are more than what they seem, you say that we have to tell our stories," said Noor. I shrugged and looked out over the Marina. "For so long you have been the voice of other people; now it is time you find your voice." In that moment, I knew she was right. That summer, I conducted several months of fieldwork, focusing exclusively on migrant mothers and their children. I was inspired and saddened by the stories I heard, and I returned to California only to face more hardship in my own life.

The legal struggles continued as soon as I returned, and each day as I walked into the courthouse, surrounded by law enforcement and bureaucrats, I found myself having to take deep breaths just to steady my nerves and myself. As I sat in the courtroom, silenced and terrified by the judge and lawyers, I couldn't help but think of Noor and my many interlocutors who had had to stand trial in countries where they hardly spoke the language, much less understood the reasons for which they were standing trial. I suddenly saw my fieldwork in a whole new light. I empathized with the unending sense of doom, the feeling of liminality, and the sense of paralysis that comes with being involved in a trial that may have no end in sight. As difficult as it was for me, I imagined how much more fearful I would be if I were in a different country where my citizenship afforded me no rights and where there was no support system in place to get me through each day. I was fortunate enough to have family members, my partner, and my closest friends accompany me to court to soften the hard edges of what I faced, but I thought of my interlocutors, most of whom had stood trial alone.

Throughout this process, I was frustrated with my own immobility, but I increasingly thought about how people are bound by love for their children, parents, or families. I came to see how people might choose mobility for the very same reasons that they choose immobility. I started to see the connections between mobility, immobility, and the family. And I began to understand that immobility and mobility are two sides of the same coin. It is true I could have left the state, leaving my daughter behind. It is also true I could have reached a settlement, which would have helped minimize my stress, trauma, and legal fees. But my daughter's safety and well-being means everything to me. And though I had many more options than most of my interlocutors, my experiences affected my positionality. In those months I finally started to see Noor's decisions in a whole different way, and I thought deeply about those who have found themselves in precarious situations just to remain connected to their family members and to provide for and keep their children safe.

All of that time spent in court and immobilized because of my daughter inspired me to write this book. As I sat in that tense courtroom, I thought about the many women whom I had met in the Gulf, women like Noor, whose experiences were so much worse than my own. It was painful to have to relive events, perform for the judge, withhold or dole out affect at just the right time, but at least I understood the legal system in which I was entrenched. At least I was a US citizen with an excellent command of the language in which my trial was taking place. Many of the women I knew had not been so fortunate.

Throughout my legal struggles, I maintained constant contact with other mothers who were in similar but worse situations across the globe. I had regular phone and Skype calls with mothers who had been deported, some of whom had been forced to leave their children behind, while others had been fortunate enough to return home penniless but with their children in their arms. Women told me their stories of falling in love, getting pregnant, and falling in love again with their children. Children left behind spoke of their anguish and desperation to find their departed mothers. While these stories broke my heart, they also kept me going. When things got really bad for me, I thought of these families, separated because of policies and laws that were supposed to protect them. I was inspired by the women who had become activists in this process, drawing on their own intimate lives and telling their stories, so that they might transform the policies that had failed them. I watched women stand up, claim the violence and challenges they faced, and use their bonds of love to mobilize. I watched them fight for and against both their immobility and their mobility. I saw them contemplate their limited options, factoring in mobility, distance, and heartache. I watched them drawing strength from their intimate lives to go on.

ı ı ı

I have never felt as connected to any project as I have to this one. My first book was about young people in Iran, and many assumed I had written *Passionate Uprisings* as a way to explore my own identity. And maybe I did. But there has never been a project that has been as close to my heart as this one. This book got me through the worst time in my life. I found solace in some state officials and hostility in others, and this helped me see the role that "the state" plays in migrants' lives in a whole new light. As I typed the pages of this manuscript, more often than not I didn't know if I was crying for my interlocutors, for myself, for my daughter, for the daughters and sons of my interlocutors, or for their parents. There were so many occasions during which I found myself wiping away the tears. Some of my interviewees spoke of an emptiness that they felt when they were separated from family members. For many years, I couldn't really understand the contours of the emotions they described and couldn't conceptualize this emptiness—and then one day I could. I remember feeling as if a black hole was occupying my house whenever my daughter was away. Other interlocutors talked about the pain of separation or the anguish of having to make untenable choices. Though my choices were not nearly as restricted as those of my interlocutors, my limited experience gave me a new-found empathy such as I had not had before.

Each of my interlocutors' experiences is unique and complex. Every person is different. Every story speaks of a different journey. But the connections and intertwining of mobility and immobility in these stories is strikingly similar. Ties to families, the difficult decisions people must make, and the encounters individuals have with different personifications of the state speak to some commonalities. I do not mean to trivialize, valorize, or demonize any of my interlocutors' experiences by telling their stories. I also do not mean to equate my own story with what they have experienced, as I am painfully aware every day how fortunate I have been—if anything, my experiences have helped me to see how much more complex the challenges of my interlocutors really are. My goal in presenting my story is to help the reader understand my positionality as I explore, reflexively, what it means to write about a topic that is so close to my heart in deeper ways than I would have imagined. The men and women whose stories animate this book have lived through and endured far more than I ever could, and my admiration for them is unending. I will always owe them my sanity.

1

IM/MOBILITIES AND IM/MIGRATIONS

DAISY SITS AT THE INDIAN EMBASSY IN KUWAIT, waiting for her paperwork and a plane ticket home. "I would do anything to stay here, to stay in Kuwait. I don't want to go home," she says, clutching a brown paper bag that contains all of her belongings. One of the Indian officials motions her over to explain the deportation procedures as they take her fingerprint. She begins to cry and asks to see the labor attaché one more time. "Please, let me see him, maybe he can help me get my baby back." She is told to wait while the attaché is located. Her plan is to ask him for a white passport so that she may take her eleven-month-old son back to India with her.

Daisy migrated from India to Kuwait to work as a domestic worker for a local family. Like many other women, she made a difficult decision to leave her daughter in India with her mother in order to support her family. Unlike some women from her village, she did not have to pay a recruiter, and her migratory journey was "pleasant" as she describes it. Upon arrival, Daisy was placed in the home of a local family who were very kind to her. "They were the best family, they became like my family. I was so happy with them," Daisy says. She describes missing her daughter and mother back home tremendously, but adds that "my daughter is my jewel, so I want to work hard to give her jewels."

Daisy's employers regularly gave her two days off per week. During her days off, Daisy would go to the bazaar or visit the Hindu temple nearby. It was during one of these visits to the temple that she met Deepak, an Indian migrant worker who worked as a security guard for a Kuwaiti bank. The two began meeting regularly on their days off, and before long Daisy became pregnant. By this time Deepak's contract was nearly up, and he was sent from Kuwait back to India. Daisy never heard from him again.

Fortunately, her employers were supportive of her pregnancy and provided her additional days off and assistance with prenatal care. As time passed, the female head of household promised Daisy that she could keep her job and the baby if she wanted to. "They were so kind to me, I will always remember their kindness," Daisy says. She was given a larger room and several boxes filled with hand-me-downs for the baby on the way.

During her days off, Daisy would take advantage of the cooler temperatures at dusk to walk along the water at the edge of Kuwait City. As her belly expanded, however, these walks became more and more difficult. One evening, when Daisy was seven months pregnant, she was stopped by a local policeman, who asked to see her working papers as well as proof of marriage. Daisy had neither. She was arrested and put in a detention center on the spot; she was told that she would be on trial for the crime of *zina* (or sex outside marriage). Distraught, Daisy begged the police to call her employers, but they refused.

Daisy was kept in detention for the next fourteen months. She was permitted to leave for a few days to give birth but was then returned to the detention center when her son was only three days old. She joined several other women who were being detained with their children. When her son was ten months old, Daisy was told that the *zina* charges were being dropped but that she would be deported immediately. Because she had no proof of paternity, however, her son would not be permitted to travel with her and would remain in Kuwait at an orphanage.

"My heart broke that day, that day when they tell me he can't come home with me," Daisy says. Because of complex citizenship laws whereby citizenship passes through the father in Kuwait, as well as increasing pressure to deny Indian citizenship to the children of migrants born abroad, particularly migrant women who have been criminalized by the legal system, Daisy's son will be stateless. On the eve of her departure, Daisy begged the labor attaché to permit her to return home with her son. Her request was denied.

ı ı ı

Saleema does not know the whereabouts of her mother. Like Daisy, Saleema's mother was deported when Saleema was only twelve months old. Saleema is a seventeen-year-old young woman who has spent her life in hospitals and orphanages in Kuwait. She doesn't know much about her mother or the circumstances of her birth; what she does know is that she was born to an unmarried Sri Lankan domestic worker who was brave enough to go to the hospital in Kuwait City to give birth after being raped by her employer. The day after Saleema was born, her mother was sent to prison, where the baby was brought to her five to seven times a day so that she could nurse. "It's hard to think that all those days I saw my mother, but I don't remember," says Saleema. "I never knew her. I don't remember her smell. No one even thought to take a picture of her for me."

The doctors and nurses who raised Saleema described her mother as brave and headstrong. When offered the chance to return to Sri Lanka, Saleema's mother had declined, reasoning that she preferred to remain incarcerated if it meant that she could at least have contact with her daughter. She had been told that because the baby's father was unknown (and this was how it was written in the chart because the male head of household would not claim paternity), the baby was considered stateless and thus could not leave Kuwaiti borders. "But she didn't want to leave without me. She really wanted me. She wanted to be with me, and I know I wanted to be with her. But they wouldn't let us." Saleema's mother begged the authorities to allow her to stay in prison with the baby as long as possible. When Saleema turned one, however, her mother was deported, and to this day Saleema does not know where her mother is or how to contact her. "I don't even know if she is alive," Saleema says.

After her mother was deported, Saleema remained in the hospital, cared for by doctors, nurses, and other hospital staff. After ten years had passed, she was transferred to a local orphanage, where she was told she would likely remain until someone was "brave" enough to marry her. When she asked if she could work or leave the country to find her only parent, she was told, at the age of thirteen, that she had no legal papers. "That was the first time I know that I'm really different. That is the time that I know that my life will be sadness and darkness. It doesn't matter how I am in school. Doesn't matter that I do well at maths. None of it matters. I'm stuck. I can't leave. I can't even go to my mother. No one wants me here. My mom wants me there. But I can't even try to find her." On account of laws in both Kuwait and Sri Lanka concerning the transfer of citizenship, Saleema remains stateless and cannot leave the country. Last year, she attempted suicide on three separate occasions out of frustration with her immobility.

ı ı ı

Anita moved to Dubai in search of economic opportunities to support her two daughters and ailing mother back in the Philippines. When her husband left her for another woman, Anita moved in with her mother and attempted to find work in their local village. She had dropped out of high school when she became pregnant with her first child at the insistence of her then boyfriend. This was a decision she regretted, as it significantly limited her options for finding employment that would allow her to support her family. Anita's mother had been working as a seamstress and was able to help support her daughter and granddaughters, but when she fell ill one year after Anita moved in with her, Anita knew that supporting the family would fall upon her shoulders alone. Anita had found informal work selling sweets on the street and occasionally helping to clean clothing stands in the village, but this did not bring in enough money. In addition, Anita's ex-husband had moved in with his former mistress, and the visibility of his romance with another woman weighed heavily on Anita, causing her to fall into a depression.

When she learned of a possibility for employment as a domestic worker in the Gulf, Anita jumped at the opportunity. With the help of some family friends, she borrowed enough money to pay her recruiter and secure passage to Dubai in early 2010. When she arrived, she was placed in the home of a British couple who had recently moved to Dubai themselves. Her first year in Dubai was "difficult," as Anita described it, because the female head of household was very strict and demanding. She mandated that Anita could not leave the apartment, would not permit her a cell phone, and ensured that Anita worked long hours without any days off. Though this was a challenging period, Anita said that she was "tired, but happy" because her salary was much higher than she had anticipated and the money she started sending home allowed for her mother to receive treatment, her daughters to enroll in a private school, and later enabled her mother to move to a more prominent neighborhood in Manila. Though Anita herself was restricted to the home of her employer, she said she felt "her heart soar" during her biweekly conversations with her mother when she would hear news of how well her family members back home were doing.

After a year of working for her employers, the British couple divorced, and the female head of household returned to England. Anita was left working for the male head of the house, who was much more lenient and generous. He bought Anita a cell phone, moved her into a larger room in the apartment, and gave her regular days off. A year later, Anita and her employer began sleeping together. Anita said that she was not sure if she was in love with him but felt "so happy in Dubai, working for him, living with him, and living my life" that she was overcome with emotion when he expressed his love for her. Moreover, Anita said, for the first time in her life she felt sexually free and was enjoying her romance. Before long, Anita became pregnant and decided that she wanted to return to the Philippines to have the baby. Her boyfriend/employer insisted that she remain in Dubai and promised he would support her, but Anita was determined to return to the Philippines so that she could be reunited with her family. This caused a rift between Anita and the father of her baby, and Anita resolved to move out as soon as possible.

Shortly after deciding to return to the Philippines, Anita discovered she had overstayed her visa and was now living and working in the UAE (United Arab Emirates) illegally. Uncertain of how to resolve her legal issues and unwilling to ask her boyfriend/employer for help, Anita approached the labor attaché at the embassy of the Philippines in Dubai. As soon as she entered the labor attaché's office, however, things began to spiral downward. Despite Anita's insistence that her pregnancy was not a result of rape and that she had voluntarily engaged in sexual relations with her employer, the staff at the office insisted that she had been "trafficked." Reflecting on this nomenclature, Anita said, "It was the first time I hear this word: 'trafficked.' What does it mean? Why they are assuming that I was raped? Why they are assuming all bad things?" Anita was quickly transferred to a shelter where she was told all "victims of violence and trafficking" were to be held. Though she was emphatic that she did not fit this description and was simply looking for assistance in returning home, the employees of the shelter, as well as those working with the labor attaché, insisted that she needed to remain in the shelter to be "rehabilitated." Anita was unable to contact her former boyfriend/employer (who was referred to later in court over Anita's protestations as her "trafficker") or her family back in the Philippines while her "case" was pending. She gave birth to her son in the shelter in Dubai and spent six months in court insisting that she was not "trafficked" and just wanted to go home. Finally, after many long months in the shelter and in and out of court, on Christmas Eve of 2014, Anita returned home with her son.

ı ı ı

This is a book about immobilities and mobilities, migrations and immigrations. A focus on the intimate lives of laborers and their kin reveals the interconnections between movements, emotions, and destinations. Migrants become both mobilized and immobilized because of their families and the bonds of love they share across borders. And just as mobility or migration can lead to immobilities, immobilities or immobilizations can lead to mobility. Mobility and immobility are mutually reinforcing and mutually constitutive forces impacting the intimate lives of migrants and their loved ones. But rather than focus on ways in which intimate subjectivities are produced and explored in and through migration, conversations about gendered migration in the Gulf have recently been couched in the inadequate framework of human trafficking. Were these individuals trafficked? Would or should someone like Anita, Daisy, or Saleema be considered a "victim" of human trafficking? And what would be the outcome of their trajectories if they were? These questions and the flawed framework of "human trafficking" have problematically come to overshadow the intricacies of migrants' lives and adversely impact the lived experiences of migrants and their loved ones.

Many migrants in contemporary Asia are caught in the web of laws and policies on migration and human trafficking. Migrant women who become pregnant in some host countries can be forcibly detained, deported, and separated from their children. Children of migrants may live and/or become immigrants in countries where they do not have citizenship. Nonetheless, women and men frequently remain in challenging situations because of their own intimate lives. These aspects of their stories are rarely heard.

Migration or the migratory experience is often contoured by the intimate lives of migrants moving across borders. Individuals may choose to migrate in order to honor, support, or escape family and loved ones. They may choose to stay abroad for similar reasons, or their movements may change as their affective lives transform. Similarly, migration affects the intimate lives of laborers and can be experienced as a major interruption, not just for the migrants but also for their families across borders. Intimate and family lives are altered when loved ones are separated, while migrants may be immobilized and altered by the bonds of love that they share with their families.

But policies—especially policies pertaining to human trafficking—rarely acknowledge migrants as multidimensional beings with intimate lives. Therefore laws and policies pertaining to migration, citizenship, and labor that are meant to protect migrants actually increase the challenges faced by migrants and their kin, precisely because they are couched in a human trafficking framework inspired by a type of moral panic (Cohen 1972). In some cases, these very laws produce situations of illegality or statelessness for migrant mothers and their children. In other cases, antitrafficking policies that inspire rescue rhetoric increase surveillance and policing, which result in higher rates of deportation, detention, and abuse. These policies have the added effect of flattening the lives of migrants and their families by focusing exclusively on the conditions of their labor or migration. Bad policies have the effect of creating worse problems.

When the focus shifts to the intimate lives of migrants and their intimate im/mobilities, lived experience is brought to the foreground and shows the mutually transformative effects of migration on the state, as well as on migrant subjectivities. The sphere of the intimate is a space where migrants assert their agency and citizenship in the absence of their ability to do so vis-à-vis the state (Giddens 1990). Many migrants draw on their intimate experiences as a source of inspiration for their activism in fighting for social change. State officials in both sending and receiving countries are often moved to action by the lived realities of migrants' lives. State policies that do recognize migrants as multidimensional beings are typically more robust than knee-jerk policies on human trafficking, inspired by moral panic rather than attention to lived reality. Policies that affect migration and the lives of migrants and their kin must be grounded in data generated by those who have lived the experience.

The stories of migrants illuminate the messy intersections of human trafficking, parenthood, statelessness, citizenship, and migration in migrant sending and receiving countries. Ethnography is needed to bring migrant voices and stories to the table, complicating the presumed picture of human trafficking or forced labor. Trafficking, as a framework and discourse, has generated a series of responses ranging from policies to NGO-type intervention. Perhaps most damaging is the fact that trafficking as an overdetermined discursive category is not only disconnected from lived realities but has erased the complexity of lived experiences altogether. However, very little qualitative research focuses on the negative impact of trafficking policies, especially as they erase the migrant experience. Indeed, the moral panic that infuses the trafficking discourse has obscured both the texture of migrants' agency as well as the domino effect of challenges on migrants' families. Data generated by lived experience directs attention to how financial pressures, a sense of familial duty, and citizenship and reunification laws place many migrants in challenging situations that have been exacerbated by the rescue industry born from trafficking discourses.[1] Categories of stateless, trafficked, or deportable persons are socially constructed (often by structures such as laws, policies, and discourses) and run the risk of eclipsing the identities of persons experiencing challenges within migration.

Academics from disciplines such as sociology, legal studies, criminology, anthropology, geography, gender studies, and political science have deconstructed the term "trafficking," questioning its construction, weight, and capability for doing significant damage. But "trafficking" as a framework blurs the lines of conversations, policies, and research on migration writ large. Some academics, such as Denise Brennan, Carole Vance, Sealing Cheng, Dina Haynes, Svati Shah, Nicole Constable, Alicia Peters, and others, have even pointed to the ways in which "trafficking" as a framework inspired by moral panic has led to policies and responses that do more harm than good.[2] This moral panic leads to media portrayals of survivors that are disconnected from lived experience. Furthermore, this type of panic inspires policies that seek to restrict the movements of or immobilize those who need to migrate to make ends meet or, as in Anita's case, be reunited with their families. But it is important to recognize that human trafficking as a framework has contoured much of our understanding of (gendered) migration to the Gulf and has been a major focus of NGOs, embassies, and those seeking to provide outreach to migrants living in places such as Dubai and Kuwait City. As such, the discursive weight of trafficking has eclipsed the many layers of migrants' intimate lives and reduced them to their circumstances or the products of abuses within labor migration.

The many layers of the stories of people like Noor, Anita, and Daisy would typically be erased by the trafficking portraiture painting them as victims in need of "rescue." But it is within the many layers of their stories that migrant subjectivities and the complexities of their situations can be observed. Noor is not looking for "rescue," and while at times she wishes to return "home," at other times she feels that Dubai *is* her home and that returning to Iran is decidedly undesirable. Anita did not undergo "trafficking" because she became pregnant, though her experiences with her female employer were at the level of abuse. But could, or rather *should*, these experiences be considered trafficking? From the outside, some might gloss Noor's story as a typical trafficking story because of her involvement in the sex industry. Her pregnancy might be taken to be the result of a rape on the part of her employer (if the rescuers are generous), or it might be taken as proof of her status as a sex worker, given the ways in which pregnancy makes women's sexuality immediately visible. And what of Daisy's experiences? Does her pregnancy result in her being presumed to be trafficked? What is evident is that when someone is considered "trafficked," as in Anita's case, their trajectory spirals out of their control, and in many instances being labeled a "victim" further restricts one's mobility and migration. It is in cases like these that the inadequacies of the human trafficking framework, as well as the impact of this framing on the lived experiences of many of my interviewees, can be observed.

A closer look at migrant interactions with various arms and personifications of the state, particularly in the UAE and Kuwait, complicates the imagined "victim"/"villain" dichotomy. Looking at how migrants often work with their employers and are aided by various personifications of the state further highlights the shortcomings of the trafficking framework. Looking at migrants' intimate lives, their connections with their families, and the challenges to their mobility that fall outside the typical imaginings of nefarious smugglers, recruiters, and "evil" employers allows for more honest conversations about the challenges and transformations taking place for migrants, employers, service providers, and various arms of the state. These conversations may help to focus attention on the shortcomings of policies regarding human trafficking that seek to restrict the mobility of migrants (women in particular) and place blame on certain receiving states and their citizens. The consequences of migration can be harrowing both for migrants and for members of their families. But there are instances of migration wherein individuals find the space to explore their subjectivities and intimate selves. It is also important to remember that the impetus to move, whether in search of love, adventure, or the possibility of making a better life for oneself and one's family, is something to which almost everyone can relate. Understanding migrants as people and exploring the role of intimacy in their migratory journeys emphasizes how the discursive weight of the human trafficking framework has done more damage—whether to the perceived "victims" or the "villains"—than good. Significantly, focusing conversations about migration to the Gulf on human trafficking functions to legitimate problematic rescue and development approaches to curbing migration that are disconnected from the real needs and desires of migrants, their families, and their loved ones.

A Note on "Family" and "Kin"

The study of what constitutes the "family" has a very long lineage in the field of anthropology. Indeed, kinship studies formed one of the earliest cornerstones of anthropological inquiry by scholars seeking to understand different cultural notions of the family. Throughout this text I am mindful of this important body of literature and take the analyses of anthropologists who preceded me as a starting point for conceptualizing the family.[3] However, my use of the term "family" follows the work of scholars who look at the family within migration, including Rhacel Parreñas, Geraldine Pratt, and Leisy Abrego. Specifically, following a feminist methodological framework, I understand family as defined by my interlocutors. I allow my interviewees to decide what constitutes family for them, and I aim to understand familial duty through their own narrations of what this concept means to them. Like other family and migration scholars, I seek to follow the flexibility of my interviewees, recognizing the changing nature of the term "family" and the changing nature of who or what constitutes "the family."

Scholars such as Rhacel Parreñas have written extensively about the problematic aspects of employers referring to intimate laborers as "members of the family," a phrase that erases the labor performed by domestic workers and ignores the obvious power dynamics at play between employees and employers (Parreñas 2001b). Furthermore, narrating intimate laborers as "members of the family" has been a tool deployed by employers to blur the boundaries of work and personal life, while ignoring the fact that intimate laborers typically have intimate lives of their own. For this reason, it is important to have an understanding of the family that comes from employees rather than employers, and one that recognizes the contours of power dynamics and lived realities inside the home as work space.

It is true that there are many power dynamics at play between various members of the family as defined not by employers but by migrants themselves. Many of my interlocutors lamented the power that their family members had over them, even when they were thousands of miles away. Some had been compelled to migrate by family members and were resentful of this type of familial pressure. Others felt that they gained power over their families by migrating and becoming breadwinners. The act of migration was also an avenue of familial escape for some of my interviewees, who found a new sense of freedom in severing familial ties. For virtually all of my interlocutors, their families—with family members as defined by them—were an important aspect of their migration. The intimate lives of laborers reflect the complexity of migratory journeys and challenges and therefore must be recognized through their own lived experiences.

Theorizing Im/Mobility and Im/Migration

The migrants I met all depend on mobility and migration for their well-being—emotional, physical, and/or financial. They desire the flexibility to move across borders and between industries. And their families must be flexible as well. Children may go years without seeing one or more parents, while grandparents, aunts, and uncles might raise children other than their own.[4] But the very same reason they must be flexible and mobile can also lead to immobility, and vice versa. Mobility and immobility are mutually reinforcing and co-constitutive forces, supporting my use of the trope of im/mobility. It is in the intricacies of and connections between mobility and immobility that the complexity and strength of the migrant experience can be observed.

Migrant workers can become immobilized through the bonds of love that they share with kin and community. These bonds may take the form of feelings of obligation toward familial duty and self-sacrifice, a desire to make kin proud, or a desire to make a better life for loved ones. The immobility that migrants experience can result from their perceptions that they cannot leave the working situation they are in, however good or bad. This is heightened for migrants because they are often working in places far from home, without the support of loved ones. Some of the domestic workers I met emphasized that while their working conditions abroad were acceptable to them, they would still have preferred to obtain employment at home. They remained abroad, torn between feelings of sadness at being separated from family members and a desire to financially support the family. Others found themselves in deplorable working conditions but stayed with their employers in order to pay off familial debt. Though not physically immobilized by any locks or laws, these migrants felt their movements restricted.

Similarly, while the family can be a source of immobility within migration, family and intimate ties can also be a major factor encouraging mobility or migration. Yes, many migrants move in order to support their families, but others move in order to explore their own subjectivities away from their families. There is no doubt that many people's migratory journeys are motivated by economic factors. Some migrants, however, seek to move for other reasons, tied to emotional and social mobility. Much of the literature and research on low-skilled migrants in particular focuses on "migrating out of poverty."[5] Contrary to common frameworks of migration that focus on poverty and other economic reasons as "push" factors, some of my interlocutors narrate social and intimate reasons for wanting to leave home. Specifically, young women and men describe wanting to migrate not away from poverty but away from their families and communities—away from unwanted or arranged marriages, familial pressures, or social contracts that require them to perform within communal expectations. Some migrate in search of love or adventure abroad, hoping to form new intimate bonds away from the watchful eyes of their social communities. Others feel that they will only be able to express their sexualities, which may be immobilized at home, when they are not in a space where they might bring shame upon their families. Migrants thus move seeking emotional and social mobility, which may also result in upward class mobility for families back home. Some seek and attain economic success, which can enable other types of mobility—such as movement out of undesirable work situations—or can lead to a greater sense of self and self-worth through economic success and an increased ability to support family. While economic success does not always lead to class mobility, all of my interviewees who achieved economic success experienced a shift in their subjectivity, especially vis-à-vis their families and intimate lives. A framework that recognizes the intimate lives of laborers and their loved ones is more robust in understanding the many layers of complexity and ambivalence with which migrants contend in their efforts to navigate and negotiate their migratory journeys.

Migration is a strategy not just for class mobility but also for social and emotional mobility, which for some may be hampered or challenged when they are in their home communities. The desire to migrate, not just to make ends meet but also in search of love, adventure, or "freedom," can be just as salient a "push" factor as economic motivations.[6] It is impossible to artificially categorize migrants based on who migrates for what particular reason. Many people may migrate for multiple reasons that include economic, social, *and* intimate mobility. My aim here is not to say that economic migration is not a factor but rather to ask that we understand the role of other (intimate) reasons for migration and the impact these decision-making processes have on the experiences of im/mobility and im/migration. I argue that attention to these complex decision-making processes will help us understand the role of migration in producing or challenging subjectivity, masculinity, and femininity for many individuals.

While migration and mobility produce situations of immobility, feelings of immobility can produce the desire and impetus for movement. Caroline and Filippo Osella have written extensively about the interconnections among migration, subjectivity, and social/economic/class mobility. In an article titled "Migration, Money and Masculinity in Kerala," they describe how migration becomes a major aspect of shaping identities and subjectivities of male migrants from India to the Gulf States (Osella and Osella 2000). They describe different types of masculinity that emerge through migration, some related to newfound income-generating potential (economic mobility), others tethered to new relationships and definitions of the self in the migratory journey. Specifically, they show how masculinity, which may be challenged in the home country, may find an avenue of expression (mobility) within migration. The work of the Osellas on these topics has been groundbreaking and frames my own work on many levels. They argue that migration becomes a formative aspect of the journey into manhood for Keralan male migrants and show how new identities are found and forged through migration. One segment of the construction of new migrant subjectivities is tied to economic prosperity, but the "money" part of their argument is only one aspect of the construction of identity. Most of the Osellas' interlocutors are not "migrating out of poverty" per se but rather migrating *in* to new positions of power, new identities, and new subjectivities; money is only one small part of a much larger and more intricate picture. In addition, the important work of Neha Vora on Indian middle-class migrants in Dubai demonstrates the changes in migrant subjectivity that take place when migrants settle and remain in a locale for generations (Vora 2013). Vora points to the many reasons behind migration, but also shows how subjectivity is navigated and mobilized differently in the host country. I build on the work of Vora and the Osellas to argue that while migration shapes subjectivity, subjectivity can also shape migration and the connected mobilities. Migrants often make decisions about when, where, and how to migrate and when, where, and how to work as a result of changes in subjectivity, thus emphasizing the multidirectional effects of migration on subjectivity and vice versa. Migrants' intimate lives, as well as their intimate subjectivities, are not only affected by migration but also shape migratory decision making and the attendant mobilities that accompany changes in subjectivity through migration.

There is no doubt that laws, poverty, and economic and working conditions do immobilize some migrants. Migrants such as Daisy can become incarcerated (immobilized) when they become pregnant or deported (forcibly mobilized) shortly thereafter on account of host country laws. Migrants who have moved across borders illegally or have chosen to work in industries considered by the state to be illegal may become incarcerated (immobilized) when they are caught, or they may choose to restrict their own movements out of fear of arrest and prosecution. Many people may wish to remain in the home or host country so that they are not separated from their kin; others may be forcibly deported. In deploying the theoretical trope of im/mobility, I wish to focus on the intimate forces and choices that also affect the migratory experience and decision making. While migrants certainly experience the pressures of policies, the weight of poverty, and the challenges of labor conditions as powerful factors in their lives, they also contend with their intimate lives and choices, perhaps on a more daily basis than with larger, macrostructural factors. Thus, while the state, as operationalized in laws and policies and through employers, forms one layer of challenges to migrants' mobilities, their intimate lives structure their daily experiences and decision making.

In addition, the framing of im/mobility allows for a recognition of often simultaneous challenges or opportunities experienced by both migrants and their transnational families. In other words, im/mobility is a framework that foregrounds instances where mobility (physical, social, economic, or otherwise) may result in a type of immobility back home; or as is more often the case, immobilities experienced by migrants abroad (owing to their working conditions or some other constraint) may lead to mobility (class or otherwise) or immobility back home for the transnational family, as was the case for Anita and possibly Daisy.

In this book, when I discuss mobilities and immobilities, I am referring to both physical and emotional restrictions and opportunities experienced by migrants and their families. I use the concept of im/mobility to emphasize the interconnections between mobilities and immobilities that are brought to the fore when looking at the intimate lives of laborers. Physical immobility or mobility may be a product of emotional bonds of love, fears of deportation, or the physical restrictions placed on mobility by laws or law enforcement—and vice versa. The im/mobilities I write about are experienced on many levels and for many reasons. Foregrounding im/mobility as a messy concept, an emotional state, and a physical experience begins to address the messy but complex lives of migrants and those they love. But policies that don't recognize these messy intersections and complexities only further exacerbate challenges that migrants and their families experience.

The trope of intimate im/mobilities, then, refers to the ways in which the intimate lives of migrants enforce and challenge their mutually constitutive mobility and immobility. In her pivotal book *Intimate Migrations: Gender, Family, and Illegality among Transnational Mexicans* (2012), Deborah Boehm chronicles the impact that family lives have on shaping migration. She argues powerfully that migrants often make the decisions they do based on their intimate ties and lives. Conversely, Clare Holdsworth, in her book *Family and Intimate Mobilities* (2013), and Andrew Gorman-Murray, in "Intimate Mobilities: Emotional Embodiment and Queer Migration" (2009), an essay about mobilizing the sexual self, focus on the production of family and intimate lives in and through migration. These authors astutely point to ways in which intimate lives are mobilized by physical movement. My use of intimate im/mobilities as a ground plan builds on these important works by bringing them into conversation with one another, as well as introducing the possibility of immobility as a factor sutured with mobility in shaping both migration and the intimate lives of migrants. I look at how mobility and immobility are affected by and affect both the intimate lives of laborers, as well as the migratory experience as a whole. In this way, I see intimate im/mobilities as allowing for a theorization of migration that understands the mutually constitutive effects of mobility and immobility on migration and vice versa. Rooted in ethnography at the local level, intimate im/mobilities can be used as an instance of grounded theory for speculating about the effects of intimacy, mobility, migration, and love on migrants in various situations across the globe.

Similarly, my use of the term "im/migration" is an attempt at contouring the messy and liminal space in which many individuals find themselves while in a country where they do not have citizenship. When discussing the situations of noncitizens in the Gulf, the term "migration" might be more accurate legally, because attaining permanent residency or citizenship rights in countries such as the UAE and Kuwait is virtually impossible for noncitizens. Sponsorship laws in the form of the *kefala*, or guest worker system, result in noncitizens' almost complete dependence on their citizen employers or sponsors, resulting in a situation of precariousness for those whose employers might exploit their status.[7]

And yet many of my interlocutors were born in the host countries of the Gulf or have lived there for the majority of their lives, even if they do not carry Emirati or Kuwaiti citizenship. Young people like Saleema or the children of migrants who have been living in the Gulf for generations can be termed "foreign-born natives."[8] Despite repeated denials of the right of permanent residency, many migrant communities have spent over two decades in the Gulf and have birthed multiple generations of noncitizen children. These children are not migrants per se, but they are not immigrant children either. And though their parents are technically migrants, and though their parents' intention or the intention of their sponsors may have been that they migrate to the Gulf on a temporary basis, many have remained for over half their lives in these host countries. Saleema's case provides a particularly clear demonstration of the liminality between immigration and migratory statuses in the Gulf. Saleema and other children in her situation do not carry citizenship of any country. They are not migrants or immigrants, nor are they citizens; and thus they exist somewhere in between.

My use of the term "im/migrations" is meant to highlight the ambiguity that inheres in artificially assigning status categories to individuals living, residing, and in some cases born in countries where they are not recognized as citizens or permanent residents. It is also meant, like my use of "im/mobility," to enable me to chronicle the ways in which migrants' consciousness moves across statuses and borders, where their emotional states sometimes collide with their legal status. Though official immigration may be a goal for many of my interlocutors, the path to immigration in legal or bureaucratic terms is long, complicated, and fraught with difficulty. Nevertheless, many have lived in these countries, betwixt and between statuses, for many years. These individuals, though not legally recognized as such, see the Gulf as their home and thus identify as immigrants. I use the term "im/migration" in order to avoid falsely placing migrants in dichotomous categories that may not reflect their lived realities.

Furthermore, it is important to emphasize that many migrants' sense of self and home changes in and through the migratory process. They may feel disconnected with the home they left behind, or they may feel that they no longer have a home to return to. Some identify with the host country as their home, not necessarily because they were born there or because they have spent significant portions of their time there, but because they feel the host country is the first place to allow them the "space" to explore their intimate subjectivities. For this reason, they identify with the host country as home. Still others feel liminally caught between home and host, even as their understandings and notions of home are changing. Many migrants are would-be immigrants, while others are content to remain migrants yet emotionally identify with their new homes. Much of the migratory experience is about redefining and reconstituting the notion of "home" while in motion. Thus the deployment of the term "im/migration" reflects the liminality many migrants feel and grapple with as their bodies, minds, subjectivities, and intimate lives move and take shape across borders.

Trafficking in Binaries

Several problematic, false binaries emerge in regard to the economies or migratory schemes within which migrants operate. These binaries have become objects of concern and inquiry and have been reified as a result of the trafficking moral panic that colors conversations about migration. The binaries "legal/illegal" and "formal/informal" have both been used frequently, neither of which capture the gray areas of lived experience. Many of my interlocutors migrated "legally" (i.e., through state-sanctioned visa entry processes) but then worked in the informal (or unregulated, untaxed) economies of care work or sex work. Others came illegally (were smuggled or engaged in the ever-popular "visa trading") but work for companies in the formal economy. Still others migrated legally but then overstayed their visas or absconded from their employers, thus rendering them "illegal" in terms of their visa status. What it means to migrate or work legally or illegally and where the formal economy ends and the informal economy begins encompass many shades of gray. The terms "illegal" and "informal" carry some pejorative weight, and for this reason some have used the terms "regular" and "irregular" migration, not to dichotomize the two but in an attempt to find more neutral terminology.

Migrants themselves have also been placed in categories of labor as a stand-in for their identities. These fixed categories do not recognize the ways in which migrants move with great fluidity between artificially imposed identities—for example, for women in particular, wife versus worker or domestic worker versus sex worker. As Piper and Roces and later Friedman, Yeoh, and Hsia have documented across Asia, today women traverse the categories of wife and worker with greater frequency, moving in both directions.[9] Similarly, women move frequently between domestic work and sex work, often engaging in both at the same time.[10] What is worse, the categories created by language that is couched in false binaries lead to policies, such as antitrafficking policies aimed at abolishing sex work altogether, that often do more harm than good. Discourses couched in artificial binaries obscure the complexity of reality, for example, that people could actually experience their families as a locus of force or constraint. Yet most of the stories that animate the rich ethnographic accounts of forced labor and migration are more complex than simple categories of victims and villains allow for.

The discourse around trafficking is the most extreme form of a discourse that rests on a series of binaries that obscure more than they reveal. For instance, when discussing trafficking and migration, hard distinctions are made between force and choice, free and unfree labor, and structure and agency. The reality, however, is that most migrants are forced to choose from a series of limited options wherein their own intimate lives operate as major sources of constraint (Doezema 1998). Christine Chin uses the term "creativity" to "emphasize the complex and even contradictory ways in which the exercise of human agency shapes and is shaped by structural forces," thus highlighting the interplay of structure and agency (Chin 2013, 15). To dichotomize migrants as either those who choose (and by extension are free to exercise complete agency) or those who are forced (tricked, kidnapped, or unfree) is to elide the majority of migrants who exist somewhere in the middle. It is more accurate to say, then, that migrants find themselves challenged by both ends of the spectrum (force/choice, freedom/unfreedom, structure/agency) on a continuum basis. It is also more accurate to say that migrants may experience *degrees* of freedom or unfreedom (Fernandez 2015).

One of my goals in writing this book is to highlight the shortcomings of the human trafficking framework and the resulting set of policies for addressing the issue of (gendered) migration to the Gulf. I do this not only by describing the negative impact of human trafficking policies but also by showing the inadequacies of a framework that has been constructed and operates with such great disconnect from lived experience. Policy makers and advocates with very little on-the-ground experience have crafted a large majority of the human trafficking policies that affect migrants and their loved ones today.[11] Most notably, trafficking policies have been written predominantly by and in the global North but are having adverse effects throughout the world. Significant antitrafficking legislation includes the Trafficking in Persons Report (TIP), written and operationalized by the US Department of State, and the UN Protocol to Prevent, Suppress, and Punish Trafficking in Persons, Especially Women and Children, which was heavily influenced by member states from the global North. Noticeably absent from these discussions were activists and scholars with qualitative experience and research to share.

Policies to address human trafficking create some of the largest obstacles facing migrant workers in the Gulf because they seek to put migrants into artificial categories that function to erase their lived realities. It is virtually impossible to write about the fate of migrants in the Gulf without understanding the morally infused panic around trafficking. The issue of human trafficking has taken center stage in the past few decades through Hollywood films, journalistic exposés, corporate investment, and local and global policies. There have also been a number of policies and legal categories created to address and combat what is loosely defined as "trafficking," rendering the term opaque and leading many to question the utility of the category or term entirely. For migrants and laborers, not only is the ongoing trafficking discourse damaging, but so too are the overwhelmingly negative effects of migration policies and the resulting outreach strategies that take a "raid and rescue" approach, sometimes in the form of forced raids, abuse, detention, and deportation.[12]

The official definition of "trafficking" as stated in Article 3, Paragraph (a), of the Protocol to Prevent, Suppress and Punish Trafficking in Persons prepared by the UN Office on Drugs and Crime (UNODC; note the disjuncture in regard to the UN agency designated to monitor human trafficking—an agency dedicated to organized crime and the movement of drugs rather than the human rights arm of the UN) is as follows:

> The recruitment, transportation, transfer, harbouring or receipt of persons, by means of the threat or use of force or other forms of coercion, of abduction, of fraud, of deception, of the abuse of power or of a position of vulnerability or of the giving or receiving of payments or benefits to achieve the consent of a person having control over another person, for the purpose of exploitation. Exploitation shall include, at a minimum, the exploitation of the prostitution of others or other forms of sexual exploitation, forced labour or services, slavery or practices similar to slavery, servitude or the removal of organs.

That this policy has been constructed within a framework of criminalization (rather than a framework of rights) is just one aspect of the problem.

On the basis of the definition of trafficking given in this protocol, it is evident that trafficking in persons has three constituent elements:

1. *The act (what is done):* recruitment, transportation, transfer, harbouring, or receipt of persons

2. *The means (how it is done):* including the threat or use of force, coercion, abduction, fraud, deception, abuse of power or vulnerability, or giving payments or benefits to a person in control of the victim

3. *The purpose (why it is done):* possible categories here are for the purpose of exploitation, which includes exploiting the prostitution of others; sexual exploitation; forced labor, slavery, or similar practices; and the removal of organs.

While this is the definition used by the international community, the Protocol has built into it a passage that makes the state the ultimate investigator and enforcer of these crimes. Toward the end of the protocol this is highlighted in the following passage:

> To ascertain whether a particular circumstance constitutes trafficking in persons, consider the definition of trafficking in the Trafficking in Persons Protocol and the constituent elements of the offense, as defined by relevant domestic legislation.

This is the agreed-upon definition of trafficking in the international community and is broad enough to encompass a variety of abuses to migrants in a variety of sectors. The functional definition of the term as produced and perpetuated by the discourse, however, has focused the issue on sex work. Moreover, each state has its own interpretation of "trafficking," and more important, in deciding who "counts" as a trafficked person. The colloquial version of the definition adopted by scholars, policy makers, and activists has been shortened to describe instances of "force, fraud or coercion."

The discourse on human trafficking oversimplifies complex decision-making processes. The ideal "victim" cannot (and must not) have had any agency in his or her circumstances. Either he or she was forced, and therefore trafficked, or he or she chose to migrate and therefore was not trafficked. But this simplification extends further. "Victims" are most often women who have been forced by a particular trafficker. In some forms of legislation, such as laws concerning the provision of trafficking visas (t-visas) in the United States, the awarding of a t-visa is predicated on the "victim's" willingness and ability to testify against his or her trafficker.

In this way, the trafficking framework seems to depend on the question of blame. This blame is further localized in the form of the trafficker, or villain. With an office focused on criminalization (UNODC) as the home of trafficking policies and with a focus on prosecution, the stereotypical victim must be able to point a finger at a particular person or set of persons who resulted in his or her "victimization." But what of a person who cannot point to a single villain as the source of his or her problem? What if someone consented to migrate, even sought out employment abroad, possibly encouraged by family members, and then did not receive his or her pay? What happens to the migrant who does not know whether it is his or her manager denying the funds or a recruiter or even family members taking the money? And what of the wife who remains abroad in the home of her husband but can't leave out of fear of losing her children?

Not only is the focus on individual villains unsupported by data, but it obscures the complex strategies and decisions migrants work through in order to make better lives for themselves and their loved ones. Many migrants made the difficult choice to migrate (or remain in trafficking-like situations) because of poverty or other structural conditions in their home countries that have made supporting family members at home impossible. Some are fleeing war or conflict, while others migrate because their home economies have become almost entirely dependent on remittances. Others are not fleeing their home countries but looking for mobility. Still others do not wish to return home under any circumstance. Without looking at the complexity of lived experience and the intimate lives of laborers, the picture remains half formed.[13]

In addition to the trafficking framework's functioning to overshadow and obscure the complexities involved in migration and the intimate lives of laborers, antitrafficking policies often produce results that in turn create more problems than they solve. Raid and rescue, increased deportation, and policies designed to prevent women in particular from migrating are all examples of knee-jerk responses on the part of both sending and receiving countries to the worldwide moral panic over human trafficking.[14] Trafficking as a global phenomenon occupies opaque and contested terrain. That such a widely debated concept has formed the basis of immigration policies worldwide has resulted in devastating consequences for thousands of migrants and their families. Trafficking focuses on the conditions of migration or labor exclusively and places the migrant in a one-dimensional frame. Not only do trafficking policies not recognize the complexities of real life, they have actually created more challenges in the real lives of migrants and their loved ones.

Transforming Intimacy, Transforming the State

Bad laws and policies increase challenges for migrants and their kin. What is interesting to note, however, is that the very same migrants who were adversely affected by problematic policies are now drawing on their own experiences and intimate lives to change existing regulations. Grassroots activism has become the most powerful force fighting for political and social change in the realm of migration, leading to policies such as the Domestic Workers Convention, the California Clean Supply Chain Act, and the ratification of treaties such as the Convention on the Rights of the Child.

Policies—notably, antitrafficking policies—that obscure the intimate lives of laborers are especially problematic because the realm of the intimate has the potential to transform migrants, the state, and migrant-state encounters. Migrants' intimate lives inspire them to activism. In instances where migrants encounter the state, whether through law enforcement, detention, regulation, or circumvention, the intimate lives of laborers serve as a catalyst for change. Throughout this book I refer to "the state" through the eyes and experiences of my interlocutors. Though not necessarily conceived of as the state in international relations literature, the noncitizen employees and their children who live in the UAE and

Kuwait experience NGOs, employers, and even aid workers as the state. Many migrants see their employers as extensions of the state because their movements within the host country are dependent on these employer/sponsors. NGO workers and those who implement antitrafficking raid and rescue campaigns are also experienced as the state by migrants who are forcibly "rescued" or deported or whose movements become regulated by these agencies.

While migrants experience the state in challenging and restrictive ways, many of my interlocutors have been able to draw on their intimate lives in order to effect change within their encounters with the state—whether home or host country. For example, the Malagasy state had enacted a series of laws in response to panic over trafficking between 2008 and 2014, intended to prevent Malagasy women from migrating to the Gulf to work as domestic workers or nannies. In order to make ends meet, however, women continued to migrate into these industries in the Gulf at an estimated rate of 17,000 migrants per year.[15] When a series of Malagasy women were imprisoned in Kuwait and Saudi Arabia together with their children born abroad, the state was moved to action. The stories of these Malagasy women and their children detained in Kuwait attracted the attention of state officials, who began working to amend migration laws.

In receiving countries such as Kuwait, state officials have also been responsive to concerns regarding migrants' children. When I relayed the stories of stateless children to labor attachés in Kuwait, they were surprised. Few of them knew that children such as Saleema existed, much less that these children were stateless or that their mothers wanted the children to return home with them. These conversations about the children, in particular, prompted efforts toward the revision of the Kuwaiti family law. As of today, officials are in dialogue about issuing white passports so that the children may return home with their mothers. While this does not solve the problem of citizenship and much of it may be connected to the status of children in the eyes of the state, it is an important starting point for activism.

The most important work that has been done to counteract the damaging effects of antitrafficking and other migration policies has been inspired by migrants' intimate lives.[16] By looking at the intimate lives of migrants who enter countries under a range of statuses, a continuum of relationships with the state as well as with the self comes into focus. Anthony Giddens has described the realm of the intimate as a space wherein individuals can navigate and negotiate agency. More specifically, Giddens argues that in the absence of the ability to negotiate their identities and citizenship vis-à-vis the state, individuals increasingly turn to intimacy and their intimate lives as a platform from which to assert their rights (Giddens 1993). The sphere of the intimate, therefore, both is affected by the state and at the same time provides a space in which to renegotiate agency within various structural constraints.

ı ı ı

Rather than delving into the intimate lives of laborers, the literature and discourse on migration tends to focus on migrants solely within the framework of the type of labor they engage in or the circumstances of their migration, which flattens migrant identities by reducing them to their employment or locale. This flattening often occurs through hegemonic state discourses and policies such as those pertaining to human trafficking or labor regulations. Characterizations of migrant workers even in the rich literature on gendered migration range primarily from their roles as caretakers to those of sex workers (Boris and Parreñas 2010; Hondagneu-Sotelo 2007; Thai 2008).

Scholarship on both intimate labor and gendered migration in Asia has resulted in an exciting body of literature that points to the commodification of intimacy and the body, the role of productive and reproductive labor, and the question of privacy, the home, and economic regulation of intimate spaces (Boris and Parreñas 2010; Chin 2013; Bernstein 2007). In their volume titled *Intimate Labors: Cultures, Technologies, and the Politics of Care*, Eileen Boris and Rhacel Parreñas define intimate labor as encompassing "a range of activities, including bodily and household upkeep, personal and family maintenance, and sexual contact and liaison. It entails touch, whether of children or customers; bodily or emotional closeness or personal familiarity, such as sexual intercourse and bathing another; or close observation of another and knowledge of personal information, such as watching elderly people or advising trainees" (Boris and Parreñas 2010, 2). Intimate labor, therefore, encompasses the fields of domestic work, care work, sex work, and productive and reproductive labor both inside the home and on the street. Boris and Parreñas point to the gendered nature of intimate labor as it engages the work typically presumed to be within the realm of "women's duties" and thus rendered invisible or devalued. The ethnographers who populate Boris and Parreñas's volume and scholars such as Sara Friedman, Christine Chin, and Lieba Faier have highlighted the difficult working conditions in which women in realms of intimate labor must persevere. They have documented the complexities of navigating a sphere of labor presumed to be private and marginalized as gendered, raced, and classed.

There is also a smaller, though no less influential, body of literature on challenges that migrant women face in parenting their children transnationally. While some scholars have homed in on the effects of absentee parents on the lives of children left behind,[17] others have focused on the challenges that migrant women themselves face.[18] Geraldine Pratt and Nobue Suzuki have engaged the question of what happens when these women are reunited with their children, either when returning to their home country or in the host country. These studies, with their emphasis on how migration affects parenting, provide an important lens through which to examine the effects of parenting on migration.

While the body of work on intimate labor and the commodification of intimacy has been groundbreaking in asking us to rethink our understandings of the messy intersections of work, space, race, class, and gender, it remains focused on the type of labor women engage in. I take the important work of these scholars as a starting point from which to look beyond the question of intimate labor and rather to emphasize the intimate lives of laborers. When the nature of the work performed within intimate labor is the focus, the intimate lives of these laborers are eclipsed, even though it is their intimate lives that structure their capacity for decision making within their work space. By understanding the contours of the experiences of those working in spheres of intimate labor, I believe we can better engage the multidimensionality of migrants' lives.

ı ı ı

Foregrounding experiences of love, kinship, gender, and sexuality within analyses of migration highlights the agency of migrants and their families. Specifically, attention to love and the intimate details of choices migrants must make brings subjectivity back into both kinship and migration studies. The family itself is simultaneously a site of pleasure, intimacy, sharing, exploration, oppression, and inequality (Padilla et al. 2007). Movement across borders for extended periods of time heightens migrants' experiences with love, intimacy, and the complexities of family ties. Looking at their choices and decision making within the confines of political-economic structures in addition to familial infrastructures complicates understandings of the migration experience and can contribute to the creation of more robust discourse and policy regarding migration.

A Global Anthropology

In this project, I follow Aihwa Ong (2006) in engaging in what she calls an "anthropology of the global." A global anthropology is one in which the focus of the ethnography is not a single site but rather an idea, concept, or phenomenon that is followed across a series of sites. Ong defines her anthropology of the global as one in which she poses "big questions through an ethnographic investigation of the lines of mutation that shape diverse situations of contemporary living" (Ong 2006, i). The contemporary problems I investigate ethnographically center on the intimate lives of migrant laborers moving to and from the Gulf. It is important to draw connections between multi-sited fieldwork involving ethnographic research in multiple locales and fieldwork that is "global." A "global anthropology" is an approach that not only makes connections across physical field sites but also examines the intersections between the micro-lives of interviewees and larger macrostructural forces. This ethnographic approach requires an awareness of factors, forces, ideas, discourses, choices, and relationships that cross borders. Thus my fieldwork is multi-sited, in that it is conducted in both the "home" and "host" countries (and I am aware of the artificial nature of categorizing countries as such, if for no other reason than the challenges involved with im/migrations outlined above) between which my interlocutors move physically as well as in their imaginations. The fieldwork is also global in that I aim to make connections between the physical spaces and borders across which my interlocutors move, as well as larger discursive connections that seek to answer more global questions.

I have been conducting ethnographic research with migrant workers in various parts of the Persian Gulf, also referred to as the Gulf Cooperation Council (GCC), since 2008. This research has led me to form relationships with migrants, their families, activists, and state officials in the host countries of the UAE, Kuwait, and Qatar. While I conducted fieldwork in Dubai and Abu Dhabi in 2008, 2009, and 2013, my fieldwork in Kuwait was limited to 2013. I was not able to follow up on fieldwork that I had commenced in Qatar in 2010 after my initial visit. Thus, while some of the experiences narrated here could be generalized to the entire GCC, it is important to stress that I'm focusing on three main Gulf cities: Dubai, Abu Dhabi, and Kuwait City. Through my encounters with migrants, I began to see the importance of "following" them back home. Thus, I myself moved with migrants to interview them in both sending and receiving countries, all the time rethinking the globally interconnected ways in which migrants move physically and in their consciousness through different spaces, encountering multiple layers of challenges and opportunities.

Much of my work centers on experiences in the two migrant receiving countries of the UAE and Kuwait, but I also touch down in the sending countries of the Philippines (2009), Indonesia (2012, 2014), Malaysia (2014), South Africa (2014), and Madagascar (2014). I conducted participant observation by spending days, weeks, and sometimes months with migrants and their families as they moved across borders. I talked with migrants from a wide array of cultural, religious, and socioeconomic backgrounds. I also spent extensive time with their families, from children born in the receiving countries to families back in the sending countries. This work was complemented by ethnographic engagement with activists, health professionals, and state officials in both sending and receiving countries—though it is important to note that many of my interviewees traversed these artificial categories.

In the end, I interviewed 147 individuals for this project. Some were migrants who became activists in sending or receiving countries. Some were health professionals who were also activists and then became migrants. Some began as family members of migrants and then became state officials and/or activists. The messiness of these artificial categories that people move through reflects the messiness of real life that ethnography has the power to capture so well.

I conducted participant observation at specific locales such as malls or churches, but also by following migrants through their daily routines, both in their home and host countries. Some of my observations were made at local orphanages—one in Kuwait City, two in Dubai, and one in Ras-Al-Khaimah. I also spent time at embassies, at shelters, and in faith-based organizations. Fridays are typically a day off for migrant workers in the GCC, so on Fridays I would go to various places where groups of co-ethnics would mingle, such as grocery stores, bazaars, temples, mosques, and churches. Much of my time was spent walking along boardwalks with my interviewees or meeting them for a meal or tea.

Most of the migrants I interviewed in the Gulf spoke enough English, Farsi, French, or Arabic that I was able to converse with them without a translator. There were fourteen migrant men and women that I interviewed through a contact at the Indian embassy in Kuwait. Since these interviewees were more comfortable speaking in Hindi or Tamil, my friend at the embassy generously provided translation. I also interviewed twenty-two women from Ethiopia, fifteen of whom spoke enough English that we were able to get by. For the remaining seven, Abiba, an Ethiopian woman with whom I had become quite close, provided translation. Most of the interviews took between one and three hours, but in many cases I got to know the individuals outside the context of the interview as well.

In this project I found myself up against the "documentary risk":[19] the risk that in rendering with vivid immediacy the contours of lives otherwise invisible and in celebrating the outlaw inventiveness that makes these marginal lives manageable, they and their identities will be exposed. I struggled to find a way to present the rich stories I heard and to offer Geertzian "thick description" while at the same time preserving the right to privacy of individuals and families. The beauty of ethnography is that it can delve deeply into the lives of people and show the complexities of the human experience. The drawback is that maintaining confidentiality and in some cases anonymity becomes a significant challenge.

My response was the same as that of many anthropologists before me. In order to maintain confidentiality, I had to weave the stories of multiple individuals into one person. Like a surgeon, I had to cut people up, to change their body parts as well as their names and identifying information, while struggling to keep the story and the soul intact. In some cases I give only limited information about the background of an interviewee—referring only to his or her country rather than city, state, or province, for example. The names of most officials and activists have been changed, as have those of all interviewees unless they specifically asked that their real names or the names of their organizations be mentioned. This is not ideal, but I am committed first and foremost to protecting those who were kind and brave enough to open their hearts and souls to me.

Rather than excerpting quotes from my interviewees, I have tried, when possible, to provide their life stories in context, so as to keep them whole despite the surgical dismemberments employed to protect their anonymity. In some cases there were contradictions or loose ends in the stories my interviewees told me. Some contradicted themselves in telling their stories, while in other cases various family members or social workers or law enforcement personnel contradicted their narratives. Still others left loose ends or holes in their stories such that things didn't quite add up. But unlike judges, lawyers, and state officials, I saw my role primarily as a listener, providing support and an empathic ear rather than judging them or forcing them to rethink their narratives in a different way. If some of the stories presented here exhibit contradictions or loose ends, this has been done intentionally to preserve the stories as I heard them.

Because the fieldwork was multi-sited, I struggled with where (geographically) to begin in contextualizing the research. Though I was interviewing migrants from different parts of Asia and Africa and often followed them home, the one thing all of them—state officials, activists, health professionals, and migrant family members—had in common was the Gulf. All of them were either working in various parts of the GCC or working with or caring for people living there at one time or another.

Locating the GCC

The six Gulf Cooperation Council (GCC) countries—comprising Bahrain, Kuwait, Oman, Qatar, Saudi Arabia, and the UAE—are the largest per-capita recipients in the world of temporary labor migration. As of early 2015, they have a total population of 48 million, 46 percent of whom are migrant workers (Reijenga, Brückner, and Meij 2013). These nonnationals constitute a significant part of the Gulf states' populations, ranging from 25 percent in Saudi Arabia to 66 percent in Kuwait to over 90 percent in the UAE and Qatar (Ahmad 2012, 32). Additionally, four of the GCC countries are among the top ten countries in the world in terms of migrants as a percentage of total population: Qatar (1st), UAE (3rd), Kuwait (5th), and Bahrain (10th) (Naufal and Termos 2009).

The early years of labor immigration into the GCC were replaced in the 1970s by tighter controls and restrictions in the management of immigration across the GCC. As GCC governments became increasingly concerned about the permanent settlement of immigrant workers, formal policies became increasingly restrictive. In Kuwait, for example, policies enacted in 1985 included minimum income requirements for family settlement, prohibition of establishing a business without a Kuwaiti partner, and severe restrictions on participation in trade unions (Baldwin-Edwards 2011). The control of the presence and movement of the overwhelming majority of noncitizens rests on two primary foundations: the preference for non-Arab, short-term workers and the sponsorship, or *kefala*, system, which will be discussed in detail in the next chapter.

The greatest increases in foreign labor in the GCC countries occurred in Qatar, the UAE, and Kuwait because they benefited from an increase in oil and gas revenues, as well as from the expansion of their non-oil sectors, mainly tourism and the real estate and construction industries. Rapid economic growth also led to an improvement in living standards, which in turn led to an increase in the employment of foreign workers. Along with economic growth came the desire and ability to bring in the flexible labor of foreign workers with inflexible citizenship, which helps maintain and produce the "good life" for citizens (Agamben 2013). The new economic world order—heavily dependent on a flexible oversupply of "cheap" labor—disallows noncitizens from reaping the benefits of capitalist development that they, as migrant workers, have helped create, while at the same time preserving these benefits for citizens. I had originally intended to focus my fieldwork on Qatar, Kuwait, and the UAE specifically because these three countries were experiencing the greatest boom in migrant labor. After my initial contact with interlocutors in Qatar, however, it became clear that I would be unable to follow up with many of my interviewees, who had either moved on or with whom I had unfortunately lost touch. I then decided to focus the bulk of my fieldwork on Kuwait and the UAE, both being countries where the population of noncitizens is staggeringly high and diverse. I also decided to focus on life for migrants in the largest cities in these countries, namely, Dubai, Abu Dhabi, and Kuwait City, because these had the highest concentration of migrant workers and were locales in which I had made contacts through universities, informal NGOs, and friends and colleagues.

In 2011, Kuwaiti demographics included a population of 3.63 million residents, 67.9 percent of whom were nonnationals. Among these second-generation nonnationals, 17.9 percent were born in Kuwait, 80 percent (352,962) were of Arab origin, and 18 percent (79,536) were Asians (N. Shah 2013). The rules of migration do not entitle children born in Kuwait to non-Kuwaiti parents to become citizens, regardless of how long they have lived in the country. Thus, a substantial proportion of Kuwaiti-born persons have been living in Kuwait as foreigners, even though this may be the only country they have resided in most or all of their lives.

Migrant workers in the UAE constitute a staggering 90 percent of the labor force. According to estimates in 2009, the population consists of 1.75 million Indian migrants (30%), 1.25 million Pakistanis (21%), more than 700,000 Filipinos (8.47%), 500,000 Bangladeshis (8%), and 300,000 Egyptians ("United Arab Emirates" 2015; Salama 2012b). As in Kuwait, children born in the UAE to noncitizen parents are not entitled to citizenship, and thus a large number of locally born "foreigners" reside in the UAE without Emirati citizenship.

Mapping the Journey

The following chapters focus on ethnographic case studies in order to foreground migrants' lives, their families, and the complexities of the choices they have made and pathways they have navigated in the shadows of the state. The impact of the intimate lives of laborers as well as larger political, economic, and legal structures on lived experience is explored through the ethnography. The goal is to show how im/mobilities, and specifically, intimate im/mobilities—or a framework that foregrounds the intimate lived realities of migrants and their loved ones—can provide a more robust understanding of migration than the current human trafficking framework. I work through the trope of intimate im/mobilities in order to highlight an important way of conceptualizing migrants' experiences that may be more in line with their daily challenges and struggles. In so doing, I hope to use these theoretical frameworks in combination with ethnography to show emphatically that human trafficking discourses and policies are not only inadequate, but also dangerous. Trafficking will not take center stage throughout the journey, but it will be there in the shadows as an inflexible opposition to data grounded in the fluidity of lived realities. The stories of children like Saleema who have been born into situations of statelessness, prevented from crossing borders or entering the labor sector, complicate the half-formed picture of statelessness and the results of human-trafficking policies. The stories of their parents, migrants like Daisy and Anita, also demonstrate the ways in which migrants deal with legality and illegality, giving texture to the constraints they face. And ethnographic accounts of the children of migrant workers who were once left behind, swore they would never end up like their parents, but are now working, sometimes side-by-side, with the previous generation of migrant workers, add the intergenerational aspect of migration that is so often missing from conversations about love, labor, and the law.

Chapter 2, "Love, Labor, and the Law," looks at how experiences of migration are affected by the intimate lives of women who become mothers during the migratory journey. Through their experiences I examine how immobility and mobility are co-constitutive forces when migrant mothers find themselves compelled to remain immobilized in the host country while living in fear of forced mobility or deportation back "home." Chapter 3, "Inflexible Citizenship and Flexible Practices," looks at how the intimate lives of families are affected by the experience of migration. Drawing on the experiences of various family members and the flexibility they must employ in the face of inflexible laws and regimes, I explore the ways in which migrants and their kin grapple with citizenship, identity, and the formation of subjectivity in the host country. Chapter 4, "Changing Home/s," sutures together the themes of im/migration and im/mobility by looking both at young people who undertake migratory journeys in order to distance themselves from their families and at children of migrants born in the host country who choose to remain there after their parents return home. The stories of these young people challenge the notion of what it means to be an im/migrant, as well as complicating the links between immobility and mobility and asking us to rethink the concept of home. Through their stories, the notion of "rescue," born of antitrafficking legislation, is also complicated when it becomes clear that "going home" is a more complex notion than it is presumed to be. Chapter 5, "Children of the Emir," focuses on the children of migrant women born in Kuwait who are "native born foreigners." Some of these children become incorporated as citizen-like subjects, while others face the challenges of statelessness in the absence of their parents. In particular, Chapters 4 and 5 highlight the malleable desires of migrants and their kin, who are often caught between wanting to move and wanting to belong.

According to the global anthropology approach, the aim of ethnography is to integrate the micro and the macro. With this in view, through a series of case studies, Chapter 6 ("Transformations and Mobilizations") and Chapter 7 ("Negotiated Intimacies and Unwanted Gifts") examine the transformative effects of migrants' lives on the state, and vice versa. The discussion then turns to policy reform, focusing on legal productions of illegality, statelessness, and abuse. Specific instances of laws created to stem illegality and trafficking are presented, showing how they have produced more situations of abuse and herded more people into the shadowy realms of illegality and informality. I revisit the question of binaries and how these artificial dichotomies, combined with a lack of data, have been the Achilles heel of conversations about forced labor, illegal migration, and trafficking.

2

LOVE, LABOR, AND THE LAW

"WHAT IS *ZINA?*" someone asked. The question hung in the air as the various women in the jail cell looked at one another. I was conducting fieldwork during the summer of 2013 at a women's detention center in Ras-Al-Khaimah, an emirate in the United Arab Emirates (UAE) located just forty miles north of Dubai. Most of the women in the cell were imprisoned with their babies. "I don't understand, it shouldn't be *zina* if it is love case or rape case, no?" said an Indian woman who was sweeping the hallway outside the jail cell. "My case is a love case, so I don't know why I'm in here," said Nargis, a twenty-two-year-old woman from Nepal who was living there with her three-month-old son. Nargis and her co-inmates were engaged in a larger discussion about what it meant to be charged with the crime of *zina*, or sex outside of marriage, as codified by some interpretations of Islamic law. One of the women who shared the jail cell was adamant that her case was definitely not *zina* because she was a domestic worker who had been raped. With her limited understanding of Islamic law, she felt that a rape survivor should not be charged with *zina*. Some women agreed but noted that it was difficult to prove their "rape" cases before the judge.

"Now, how, why I'm in jail?" asked an Ethiopian woman who was nursing her six-month-old daughter while seated on the toilet in the corner of the room. "It's him who [should be] in jail. Him [referring to man who raped her]. Him here. Me home. My baby home," she said emphatically, gesturing with her free hand for effect. This woman, whose name I later learned was Diana, had migrated to the UAE to work for a family as a domestic worker in 2011. When she arrived, her employers confiscated her passport, made her work long hours, and told her they would take money out of her wages for every meal she ate. After some months the male head of household began making advances toward Diana. She was afraid but felt she had nowhere to turn. If she absconded, her recruiter told her, he would collect her debt from her family. She would also be rendered illegal, be deported, and would likely be unable to return to work in the Gulf for many years. Before long, Diana's male employer began raping her regularly. Diana cried and prayed for help, but things continued to get worse. When Diana was visibly pregnant, the female head of household began beating her. Finally, her male employer took Diana to the police, accusing her of *zina*, which, she was told, put her in breach of contract. She was arrested and gave birth to her son in jail.

"If it's rape, is it *zina*?" someone asked Nargis, who was the only inmate in the cell who regularly read the Koran. Nargis put down her baby to search out her Koran, shaking her head. "I don't know. I don't understand *zina*. And for me, it's a love case. We wanted to be married, so I don't know why for me it's *zina* too?" Nargis had encountered the negative pitfalls of "preventive pathway switching" policies, which prevent women who migrate on worker visas to switch to wife or spousal visas. These "categorize and control" policies, which force women to stay with either worker or wife visas, lead to challenging situations for women around the world.[1] Women like Nargis who migrate as workers but then fall in love are unable to switch from worker to wife and must live with their partner as his employee rather than his spouse. As a result, if their partners are citizens and decide to end the relationship, the worker/wife is rendered illegal in the country. To add to these many layers of complexity, if the woman becomes pregnant and the couple is not married, the mother has no rights to her child. Worse still, if the father does not acknowledge paternity and the mother is a citizen of a country where citizenship also passes through the father (as in the UAE, for example, or until recently, in India), the child is rendered stateless. Women like Nargis will be charged with the crime of *zina* and often deemed unfit to parent. Soon, Nargis will be deported, but her son will remain in the UAE as a child without a state or parents.

Nargis begins to cry as she reads the Koran. One of the twelve migrant mothers who share her jail cell rises from her bunk to take the now screaming baby. "Surely Allah doesn't think I'm so bad, that I did so wrong," Nargis says, wiping tears from her face. "I don't think I should be punished like this. I just want to be with my son." Nargis turns to me and the female guard who stands behind me and pleads: "Please don't let them take my son. Please tell them I am a good woman. I am a good mother."

Gender and Migration

The past few decades have seen an increase in the number of women who migrate both within and across borders in search of work, adventure, or a different life. For many of these women, the experience of migration is affected by their intimate lives and relationships, which contour their immobility and mobility. The increasing feminization of migration has productively led to calls for understanding gendered migratory patterns[2] and the commodification of intimacy and intimate labor.[3] Much of the literature, however, focuses solely on the circumstances or conditions of migrant labor. This exclusive focus on the female migrant as worker has eclipsed the multidimensionality of migrant women, erasing their sexualities and multifaceted identities. This erasure is given further credence through laws and policies in places such as the countries of the Gulf Cooperation Council (GCC), where only female migrants are contractually bound to celibacy during their work contract periods and punished for breaking rules enforcing their sterility (Ong 2007). In an important recent volume, *Migrations and Mobilities: Citizenship, Borders, and Gender*, Seyla Benhabib and Judith Resnik make an impassioned call for remembering that migrants are not "disembodied individuals (or by default men) but are adults or children traveling with or leaving family members behind. . . . The mobility of some has consequences for or corresponds to the immobility of others" (Benhabib and Resnik 2009, 4). Scholars including Jacqueline Bhaba, Linda Kerber, Sarah van Walsum, and Nicole Constable argue for the value of placing children at the heart of analyses on gendered migration and citizenship. In another body of work, Rhacel Parreñas and others have focused on children of migrant women who have been left behind in their home countries while their mothers seek work abroad. I take these important analyses as a starting point from which to question our understanding of the intimate lives of intimate laborers.

Migrant women increasingly constitute the majority of migrants to the region, as the demand for intimate labor in the Gulf is on the rise. But migrant women who become pregnant while in the Gulf region are immediately imprisoned and charged with the crime of *zina*.[4] These women give birth while incarcerated and spend up to a year with their babies in prison. Many are then forcibly separated from their children when they are deported, rendering the children stateless in the host country. Migrant women who are often brought to the Gulf to perform (re)productive labor—labor such as caregiving and cleaning, usually performed in domestic environments, that supports productive labor—are seen as immoral if they engage in sexual activities during their time in the Gulf (and this is written into their contracts), and thus are seen as unfit to parent their own children. Some migrant women have recently been protesting these laws by refusing their forced mobility and fighting deportation without their children.

There also exists a growing literature on the families of migrants that looks at children left behind, reunification, and the challenges of transnational families.[5] Some—but not all—of this literature (exceptions include the work of Rhacel Parreñas, Geraldine Pratt, and Jacqueline Bhaba) tends to focus on the results of absentee parenting or family reunification, making children the central focus of concern. This is mirrored in larger national discourses in major migrant-sending countries such as the Philippines and Malaysia, where nationwide panic is building around concern for children who are raised without their mothers. This is likely related to the place that children occupy in society and the perceptions of innocence and victimhood in regard to children. While the plight of children left behind is certainly important, equally pressing are the challenges faced by women who either were mothers before migration or become pregnant in the host country. However, very little discursive attention has been focused on the lived experiences of mothers. Instead, migrant women are painted as "aliens" or as schemers. Even in national debates about "anchor babies" in the United States, Canada, and Ireland, migrant women who become pregnant are viewed as deviant or in some way trying to "scam the system."[6] Discussed less often are the salient facts that (1) many women who migrate do so during their most fertile, reproductive years; (2) migrant women, like other women, have sexual and reproductive desires; and (3) female migrants are often hired to perform reproductive labor, while discourses in both home and host countries paint migrant women as "loose women" or "unfit mothers."

Migrant women's sexualities have been obscured both discursively and politically, which corresponds to and contrasts with the hyperregulation of women's bodies and reproductive capacities. Migrant women in the Gulf are contractually bound to celibacy, and any deviation from this—even a suspicion that a female worker is engaging in sexual activity, and even if it does not result in a visible pregnancy—is grounds for termination, deportation, and often incarceration. Women face criminal charges for breaking their contracts and are subject to heavy fines (while women who migrated illegally are subject to even more serious penalties when arrested for suspected sexual activity). To compound their already precarious legal situations, migrant women are also charged with the crime of *zina*. In a powerful article titled "Criminalizing Sexuality: *Zina* Laws as Violence against Women in Muslim Contexts" (2010), Ziba Mir Hosseini outlines the ways in which *zina* has been used to regulate and criminalize female sexuality, leading to both physical and structural violence. In the case of migrant women in the Gulf, the deployment of *zina* laws reinforces the regulation of migrant women's sexuality that is codified through labor laws as outlined by the *kefala* system. This guest worker program (which will be further detailed below) contours all migrant work in the UAE and Kuwait and is structured such that the employee is entirely dependent on the employer, who acts as sponsor, or *kafeel*. The sponsor, on whom the employee is dependent for legality while in the country, regulates all movements of the migrant. The *kefala* system outlines strict rules for working hours, responsibilities, days off, and access to health care, but offers limited rights protection for labor migrants. Other scholars have emphasized the structural violence inherent in the *kefala* system.[7] But many women, even those who migrate informally or abscond in order to circumvent the *kefala* system, still experience the violence of discursive and political regulation of their bodies. Specifically, through a combination of *kefala* and *zina* laws, women are subject to what DeGenova and Peutz term a "deportation regime," wherein women's deportability (deportation or possibility of forced removal) is tethered to their sexualities (De Genova and Peutz 2010). Furthermore, as the cases of Diana and Nargis illustrate, *kefala* and *zina* laws collide with incongruent citizenship laws to render children either stateless or forcibly removed from their mother's care. The mothers are sometimes deemed "unfit" to parent their children, either by the court or by labor attachés in sending and receiving countries.

Both discursively and legally, women are portrayed as hypersexual and in need of regulation. In sending countries, anxieties about migrant women's sexualities manifest in the form of rumors or the emasculation of men who stay behind—a clear illustration of the domino effect of migration on the intimate lives of migrants and their loved ones (Osella and Osella 2012). In receiving countries, laws to criminalize migrant women's sexualities respond to and perpetuate discourses about the need to control migrant women *because* of their sexualities. Frequently, employers cite these discourses as reasons for not allow-ing their female employees out of the house unaccompanied. Female employers also perpetuate this fear by categorizing migrant women as a threat and seek to control them through the regulation of their movements, activities, and bodies.[8] In response to these anxieties, laws and policies aim to strip women of their sexualities by forcing celibacy and punishing deviance (Ong 2007). Part of the punishment for many women involves forced separation from their babies, as they are deemed immoral and unfit to parent given their status as criminals. This is achieved through forcibly separating women who give birth in jail from their babies as well as forcibly deporting them without their children.

What is interesting to note, however, is that migrant women are deliberately imported to perform intimate labor. They are brought in to parent the children of citizens, to care for the elderly, to provide intimate services to customers, and generally to provide love. They are tasked with the most important repro-ductive labor of raising the future leaders of the nation, yet deemed immoral and unfit to parent at the same time. Their own intimate lives are eclipsed in an attempt to reduce them to their labor alone, which functions to flatten their identities and erase their abilities to parent their own children.[9]

Migrant women, however, have pushed back against this erasure. In the absence of the ability to negotiate their economic/political citizenship rights and agency vis-à-vis their sending or receiving state, many women turn to the sphere of the intimate to define their subjectivities, focusing instead on their intimate citizenship. The family then becomes the institution through which the self is explored and operationalized. Women who are mothers articulate a sense of empowerment through sacrifice for their families. Many experience migration as an economic strategy for upward mobility and an exercise of agency in the face of larger state and globalized pressures. However, as noted by many scholars, structure and agency do not operate as a binary but rather as continuously cyclical processes.[10] Women migrate to support their families as an empowering strategy while at the same time feeling constrained by their families and a sense of familial duty, producing the simultaneous sense of im/ mobility. This is compounded by rhetoric in their home communities about migrant women being "bad mothers" (Parreñas 2005a) or "loose women" (Osella and Osella 2013). In India, for example, women who migrate are seen as morally depraved (Osella and Osella 2013), and their husbands and family members back home are ridiculed for having allowed them to leave the home community (Gamburd 2008). This is also the case in Iran, where the community heavily regulates women's sexualities, and migrant women's sexualities are seen as the most deviant of all (Mahdavi 2008). In the Philippines, the discourse about migrant women as "bad mothers" and criticisms of women who leave their children to care for other women's children (Ehrenreich and Hochschild 2003; Parreñas 2008a) have collided with state rhetoric about migrants in general as "heroes of the nation" (Mahdavi 2011). To respond to this conflicting rhetoric, Filipina migrant mothers have organized messaging campaigns calling migration the ultimate maternal sacrifice (Agunias 2010)—providing one example of migrant women turning to their intimate lives to assert and explore their agency.

Motherhood both affects and is affected by experiences of migration. Migrant women note that they are simultaneously immobilized and mobilized through their bonds of love and familial ties. But they find creative expressions of agency through their own intimate lives, which can be read as a type of "infrapolitics," a term used by James C. Scott (1990) to capture the realm of invisible, hidden political struggle to which severely subordinated groups turn when direct political confrontation is impossible that is quite salient in the case of many of my interlocutors.[11]

Regulate, Discipline, Punish

Migrant workers are often subject to two levels of policing and disciplining, with these two levels sometimes being incongruent. The first level involves state laws, including labor laws (and lack thereof) as well as the sponsorship, or *kefala*, system.[12] The second level involves the *kafeels*, or sponsors, themselves, who often do not abide by state laws. *Kafeels* take the form of large corporations or private employers in the home, and while there are laws against retaining passports and not providing days off as well as rules prescribing the humanitarian treatment of workers, many sponsors take it upon themselves to discipline their employees. Many employees do not agitate for their wages or report abuse out of fear of the harm that might come to their families, deportation, or detention, which allows these employers to continue to violate migrant workers' rights, resulting in trafficking-like experiences.

The Kefala System

Having emerged in the 1950s to regulate the relationship between employers and migrant workers in the GCC countries, the *kefala* system's economic objective was to provide GCC governments with temporary labor as a means of regulating labor flows in and out of the country. This allowed them to accept large numbers of temporary workers during economic booms and to expel them during less prosperous periods. Migrant workers receive an entry visa and residence permit during a temporary contract period, usually two years, once they have been sponsored by a *kafeel*. The assumption within the *kefala* system is that workers are temporary contract labor, which is reflected in the GCC's official use of the terms "guest workers" and "expatriate manpower" to refer to migrant workers. This notion comes from the Bedouin custom of granting strangers protection and temporary affiliation to the tribe for specific purposes (Longva 1999).

Although labor migration to the Gulf region began in the late 1930s, the practice of *kefala* was not formalized in its first decades; the Aliens Residence Law of 1959 in Kuwait, which was amended in 1963, 1965, and 1968, did not mention it. It was not until the law was amended in 1975 that *kefala* was included in the legal text. However, prior to that, in 1969, the universal visa requirement became an established rule, which resulted in the need for all migrant workers to be vouched for by their citizen employers. By the 1980s the *kefala* system had become a general requirement; foreigners in Kuwait or the UAE who migrated from a country outside the GCC states had to be sponsored by either a Gulf citizen or a private or state institution.

The *kefala* system has built into it different responsibilities/protections depending on the category of worker. Notably, domestic workers (both male and female) are held to the same responsibilities as other workers but do not have the same rights.[13] Domestic workers are seen as working in the realm of the "private" or "intimate," and thus their employers are not subject to the same types of labor inspection or standards that, for instance, employers of construction workers must adhere to. Ever since 1965, the demands for domestic workers in Kuwait and the UAE has increased exponentially, as the state saw a huge increase in its oil revenues and domestic workers immigrated from India, Sri Lanka, and the Philippines to meet the increasing demand for household labor.

Because of the increasing state dependence on nonnationals, some government officials felt the need to create a migration scheme wherein the migrants would be dependent on citizens. Thus, a migrant worker's legal residence in Kuwait or the UAE is tied to his or her sponsor, or *kafeel*, who is financially and legally responsible for the worker. These *kafeels* grant permission for foreigners to enter the country, monitor their stay, and approve their exit. Not surprisingly, the quality of a migrant worker's experience in the GCC is directly tied to the quality of his or her sponsor. Many migrants have good employers, and thus their work experience abroad is positive. Some migrants never come in contact with their actual sponsors, dealing instead with middlemen who are often co-ethnics. Other migrants have physically or emotionally abusive sponsors. Since the quality of *kafeels* is variable, the situation for many migrants can be precarious. Workers may be trapped in situations of abuse and forced labor because if they abscond, they will immediately be rendered illegal and subject to arrest. And since the *kafeel* is responsible for all aspects of the foreigner's stay, even if a worker escapes from an abusive workplace, the employer can withdraw sponsorship, making the worker vulnerable to arrest and deportation for residing in the country illegally. Because the system requires that migrants only work for one sponsor, migrants who engage in what is known as "visa trading," or moving within different spheres of employment, are also subject to arrest and deportation.

The *kefala* system collapses the employer and sponsor into one category, creating a situation in which a labor dispute with an employer that ends with termination of employment or with the employee fleeing renders this employee an illegal or undocumented worker. Thus, while "either party can break the contract at any time," doing so forces the worker to provide his or her own funds for a return ticket, an already high price that is often further augmented by the debts that "laborers occur [*sic*] . . . in order to finance their out-migration" (Longva 1999, 21). Many workers who choose to break employment contracts attempt to stay in the country as long as possible, working as illegal aliens—a better option for them than returning home empty-handed. While there are some aspects of the labor law that would allow the worker to take his or her employer to court for violating the labor contract, this law "does not take into consideration the fact that while the trial is pending, the plaintiff is unemployed and forbidden to work for anyone else" (Longva 1999, 22). Additionally, according to the Aliens Residence Law of 1959, an alien can be deported as the result of a judicial or administrative decision if "the alien has been convicted and the court has recommended deportation, if he/she has no means of sustenance, (or) if the Ministry of the Interior objects to his or her presence on national territory for 'security of moral reasons.'"[14] This presents yet another obstacle: when labor disputes arise between migrant workers and their employers/sponsors, the workers are at a distinct disadvantage in that they can be deported if accused of "moral wrongdoings." Indeed, collapsing the employer and sponsor into a single category—as the structure of the *kefala* system does—would seem to lie at the root of the problem.

Female migrants in many parts of the world face severe hardships such as coping with abusive employers, working illegally with limited rights, and working unregulated hours with very little recourse if they are abused or if their pay is withheld.[15] The conditions enforced by the *kefala* system in the Gulf countries, however, make the experience of intimate laborers (who make up the majority of female laborers in the UAE) somewhat more difficult. Under UAE labor law, domestic workers are required to abide by the *kefala* system, so their residence in the country is entirely dependent on their sponsor, or *kafeel*, who is also their employer. They are dependent on this person not only for residence but also for assistance in accessing services (such as health care, etc.).[16] More problematic aspects of the General Provisions section of UAE Federal Law No. 8 of 1980 (also known as the Labor Law, as referenced by the Human Rights Watch Report on the UAE in 2007) (United Arab Emirates 1980) that structures the lived experience of migration include Article 3, which states that "the provisions of this law shall not apply to the following categories . . . domestic servants employed in private households, and the like . . . farming and grazing workers"; and later, under Article 72, seafarers are added to the list of migrant workers not protected by any labor laws. Thus, while domestic workers must abide by *kefala* procedures, they are not protected by any labor laws. They, like other migrant workers, are also unable to participate in labor unions, thanks to the UAE law banning the creation of such organizations (according to Articles 155 and 160 of UAE Federal Law No. 8). Laws in the UAE do not recognize foreign domestic workers as part of the labor force (R. Sabban 2004).[17]

Middlemen and recruiting agencies exacerbate the already challenging situations migrant workers in the Gulf face as a result of the sponsorship system. Some licensed, others informal, they can facilitate a type of debt bondage wherein migrant workers feel they cannot break their contracts with employers out of fear of these recruiters. In the cases of some migrant workers, these recruiters work with employers in sending or receiving countries, but for the majority of my interlocutors, recruiters had no contact with sponsors beyond securing their employment. Some women indicated that they had lost contact with their recruiters but remained fearful of not repaying their debt because of the possible negative ramifications for their family. The lack of synchronization between recruiters and employers is significant and is supported by examples from other countries. As Ray Jureidini notes, "In the case of domestic workers, we can identify abuse of migrant workers by middlemen in transit and abuse by employers at their work sites, but there is little evidence of a systemic conspiracy between middlemen and employers" (Jureidini 2010).

That recruiting agencies do not work with employers or the government also reveals a lack of organization and, more important, a lack of regulation of these middlemen. While some of these agencies are licensed by the UAE or Kuwaiti government, they usually are not closely monitored (R. Sabban 2004). Indeed, many middlemen are unlicensed in both sending and receiving countries and thus are not regulated or held to standards of human rights promotion. In his study of human trafficking in Lebanon, Jureidini observed that many women were imprisoned and abused by agencies and recruiters in Lebanon, a finding supported by Rima Sabban in her survey of domestic workers in the UAE, who noted that women were regularly threatened, beaten, and deprived of basic necessities such as food and running water when living in recruitment agencies (Jureidini 2010; R. Sabban 2004).

In addition to the challenges presented by recruitment agencies is the issue of debt bondage, which many recruiters promote and which imposes major restrictions on the movement of migrant workers. Despite its being in contravention of the International Labour Organization (ILO) Private Employment Agencies Convention, Article 7 (1), many agents charge workers for placement or other services in the form of high fees that can often take months if not years to repay (International Labour Organization 1997). This was a significant issue for many of my interlocutors, who indicated they had paid high fees to recruiters in order to facilitate their migration and now found themselves in undesirable working conditions they could not leave owing to the high level of debt they had accrued. Furthermore, as Sabban notes, "most recruiting agencies hide information from foreign female domestic workers about their rights" and prefer to side with the employer in cases of dispute (R. Sabban 2004). As an outcome of Sabban's extensive study, she recommends—and I agree—that there be more stringent monitoring of these recruitment agencies, on the part of both sending and receiving states. One strategy in regard to crafting the strongest possible response to these recruiters promoted by the Migration Policy Institute, one of the major international think tanks working on migration, would involve bilateral agreements between states that would eliminate the need for unlicensed recruiters, who often can be particularly abusive toward women (Agunias 2010). While fears due to middlemen recruiters weigh heavily on the intimate laborers with whom I spoke, these fears were exacerbated by perceived or real threats of deportation and feelings of expendability and interchangeability.

Adding Layers

The laws of the UAE and Kuwait regarding abortion and pregnancy outside of marriage further complicate the situation for many workers. While female domestic workers in particular do not have rights or access to women's health or family planning services, their pregnancy can be cause for immediate termination of their contract and subsequent deportation. In accordance with Islamic law as interpreted in the GCC, abortion is strictly prohibited unless it is necessary to save the life of the mother or if the baby will be born with serious genetic defects and likely will not survive. The government of the Emirati state of Dubai, for instance, is quite clear on its stance toward pregnant women, as shown on the Dubai government website:

> It is of utmost importance for a woman to be married if pregnant in the UAE. At the hospital when you go for your first check-up, you will need to show an original marriage certificate along with copies of your passport and visa. If you are unmarried and pregnant, you should either get married or expatriate unmarried expectant mothers should return to their home countries for the delivery. Also note that abortions in Dubai are illegal unless there are medical complications and the abortion is sanctioned by the hospital. (Government of Dubai 2013)

Pregnancy outside of marriage is not permitted. Although migrant women who become pregnant while in the host country are encouraged to return to their home country to deliver their children, if they can not finance their own return travel they may be held in detention. Several of my interlocutors did not have passports or working papers, which made returning home difficult. Some women do not wish to return to their home countries for reasons including fear of family stigma, fear of returning without money to pay back their family or their own debts, or a general preference to remain abroad. In such cases, the women immediately become undocumented and their children are put in a precarious position. Women who are domestic workers are imprisoned both for *zina* and for breach of contract, and some women's return home is delayed by their incarceration.

Tropes about race, class, and gender as articulated in the UAE and Kuwait are important in marginalizing or privileging migrant workers and their narratives. Racial hierarchies play a role in the construction of local discourses about migrant women's sexualities and reproductive capabilities. Migrant women (especially women from certain socioeconomic backgrounds) as mothers fuel concerns about demographics and racial purity, concerns that are often reflected in state policies concerning reproduction and family reunification for noncitizens. As is clear from the language of the laws, unmarried migrant workers are encouraged (and this encouragement is enforced) to return to their home countries to have their children in order to remain in accordance with sharia law. Women who are pregnant and wish to get married in the country are encouraged to do so; yet often they are unable to retain their employment and/or cannot live with their new spouses if their living arrangements are tied to their employer. For married couples who are not citizens, the criteria for filing for a residency permit for a baby are numerous and accompanied by high costs and bureaucratic red tape. A close look at the requirements reveals the challenges in obtaining such a permit if the relationship with the employer-sponsor is tenuous, as well as those in procuring a passport for the baby. If these requirements are not met and the parents fail to file the necessary paperwork for their newborn child within 120 days of birth, the child will not be permitted to leave the country and the parents or legal guardian must pay a fee of AED$100 (equivalent to USD$25) for each day over the 120-day period.

In actuality, most women are not able to finance their journey home, nor are they always aware of laws pertaining to *zina*. Many are arrested and imprisoned before they have a chance to file for paternity or complete the necessary paperwork for their family. Navigating the bureaucratic red tape of citizenship can be a tricky process for many women. Experiences at sending-country embassies also vary: while some women report receiving assistance at their embassy and white papers for their children to travel home with them, others report no assistance and in some cases further incarceration. This was something I personally witnessed when spending time at various embassies in Kuwait. While the embassy of the Philippines was vested in providing assistance to migrant women and allowing them to remain at their shelter with their children, the Indian embassy was unable to provide much assistance. To be fair, citizenship transfer laws in the Philippines allowed for children of Filipinas to become citizens right away, thus facilitating the procurement of papers for women who were able to avoid or break out of incarceration. The Indian labor attaché's hands were tied because he could not easily extend citizenship benefits to the children of Indian women, owing to controversies back home over migrant women's sexualities and suitability as parents.

Lived Realities: Women's Stories

Nargis

Nargis, introduced in the opening anecdote, initially migrated from Nepal to India when her mother ran away from her father, taking her three children with her. Nargis and her mother worked informally, first in the beauty industry and later as domestic workers for an Indian family who asked Nargis and her siblings to move in with them. Shortly after Nargis turned eighteen, she started to catch the attention of the male head of household, who began making advances. Nargis's mother saw what was transpiring and decided it was time for her daughter to move out of the house. "She thought it would be safer for me if I left," said Nargis. "For me, that was not, that was not what I wanted. I didn't want to be sent away. But my mom told me that if I stay I make problem, I do bad for everyone in the family."

After some consultation with friends, Nargis's mother decided to send her to the Middle East, because she had heard that in the Gulf, in particular, migrant women could make large sums of money as nannies and domestic workers. "My mom said it was a dream. She thought her prayers had been answered. She said if I go to the Gulf, the Arab peoples, they . . . pay too much, then I can send money home for the whole family. And then mom can pay back her debt, and maybe brothers can go to school, or we could someday return to Nepal. At that time, yes, I'm scared, but I'm thinking this is good, my life will be good."

Like many others, Nargis was unable to arrange migration through formal channels. She was living in India illegally, and her mother was desperate for her to migrate as soon as possible. And so they relied on an unscrupulous middleman recruiter, who charged Nargis 2,000 dirhams (equivalent to USD$500) to migrate. Nargis's mother borrowed from her employer, putting the family further in debt. "But mom always was saying that I'm her best investment. I'm the family investment. So, they took the money and I went," Nargis said. The recruiter had promised Nargis's mother that Nargis would be making at least that sum (USD$500) per month and would be able to pay back her debt quickly. Without seeing any type of contract, Nargis and her mother agreed, and Nargis was sent to Dubai just before her nineteenth birthday.

When she arrived in Dubai, her recruiter told her that no matter what happened, she was not to abscond. "He said if I'm runaway maid, very bad. He said then he find my family and make them pay. He said I ruin everything like that. But that day when he said that, I'm becoming more scared, you know? Because, why he is saying that? Are bad things going to happen?"

Nargis was placed in the home of a very religious family from Saudi Arabia and made to work long hours for a fraction of the pay she had been promised. She was asked to care for their four children as well as the elderly father of the female head of household and was told to clean the stables and care for their five horses as well. Because the family was religious, Nargis was told to wear *hijab*, completely veiling herself from head to toe for the first time in her life. Nargis remembers this as a very difficult period for her.[18] "This was the worst time in my life. In India, it wasn't always good. Sometimes we lived on the streets. Sometimes we begged for food. But we were together (with her family). And we had freedom. We choose even when we beg for food. But in Dubai, it's bad, I work too much. Too much. All day, all night. I'm wearing *hijab*. It is hard for me to cook, clean, babies, all with *hijab*." During the month of Ramadan, Nargis's employers required that she fast along with them.

After some months had passed, Nargis began asking her employers more about Islam. Delighted to hear of her interest, the female head of household took Nargis under her wing and insisted that she convert. After her conversion, Nargis was granted more privileges, and her pay was doubled. She was also consistently given one or two days off work each week to attend mosque. Sometimes she would go to religious events with her employers. It was at one of these events that Nargis met Hakim, a young Emirati man from Ras-Al-Khaimah. After six months of courtship, Hakim convinced Nargis to quit her job and move from Dubai to Ras-Al-Khaimah to live with him. "I was in love with him. He was so special. And he made me feel special. And I want to be with him."

"Pathway switching," whereby migrant women can switch visa status from worker to wife or vice versa, is not permitted in the UAE (nor in many other countries). For this reason, Hakim had to convince his family to "hire" Nargis so that they could be together in the same household. He promised Nargis that he would eventually work to help her move from a worker visa to that of a wife and that someday they would marry, but Hakim never came through on his promise. When Nargis moved in with Hakim's family, her new employers treated her as only a servant. "Hakim's telling them, be nice to her. But no, they treat me very bad. They make me sleep on the floor. Clean all day. And I'm getting very

sad because my heart breaking." Still, she looked forward to the occasional evenings when Hakim would sneak her into his room and they could be together.

After a few months of living with Hakim and his family, Nargis became
pregnant. When her belly began showing, Hakim's parents demanded an answer. "I told them, this is your grandchild in here," Nargis explained, gesturing
to her stomach for effect. "But my madam is too angry, she starts beating me.
Hakim is seeing, but he can't, he doesn't do anything." When Hakim's father
learned of the news, he took Nargis straight to the police station. She has not
seen Hakim or her employers since then. She remained in detention, released
only for a few short days to give birth, after which she returned to her cell
with her son. She was told that she would remain in jail, awaiting her trial, and
then would be deported. The child, however, would have to remain in the UAE.
Hakim has, to this day, not acknowledged paternity.

As she recounted this part of the story, tears streamed down Nargis's face.
She tried to shield her face from the baby, who also began to cry at the sight of
his distraught mother. "That day they tell me I can't . . . I can't . . . I can't take
Riza with me . . . that day I want to die. My heart breaks," she said between sobs.

Because of incongruent citizenship laws in the sending and receiving countries, Nargis's son is stateless. She will be on trial and forcibly deported for the
crime of *zina* and for violating a contract that Nargis has still never seen. She
is not sure if she will be sent to Nepal or India and has been awaiting contact
from either of these embassies for many months. Along with over a dozen other
women who share her jail cell, she prays for the chance to remain in prison so
that she can stay with her child.

Nataly

Nataly, who was born and raised in Madagascar, always knew she wanted to be
a mother. Growing up she used to play her mother's role with her younger siblings when their mother would spend months and even years abroad working
to support the family. Nataly's mother had migrated across the globe to countries such as Italy, Sweden, and Lebanon to work as a domestic worker. Nataly's
father had abandoned the family when she was ten years old. The rumor was
that he had moved to South Africa to work in the mines and now had a new
family occupying his time and attention.

When Nataly was eighteen, her mother was injured and could no longer
work. She was sent home from her most recent posting in Lebanon, returning
with bruises, broken ribs, and a broken ankle. Nataly cared for her mother and

siblings during this time. She hoped that her mother had saved enough money to support the family for many years, but after one year the money ran out. Nataly decided she would migrate, as her mother had done.

"I remember when I told my mom that I was going abroad, my mother cried. She was so worried for me, especially after what she had been through. She didn't want me to go, but she also knew that if I didn't go, all of us would starve." Mother and daughter decided together that Nataly would go to the Middle East, specifically the Gulf, as they had heard that salaries were highest there. Nataly's mother had never had a problem finding work abroad and was able to migrate through formal channels with the help of the Ministry of Labor. But this was all changing. When Nataly approached the Ministry of Labor, she was told that they were no longer allowing young women to migrate to the Middle East. She was turned away and told to seek employment in Madagascar or to wait some months until they could find her a job in Europe or East Asia.

Discouraged, Nataly left the ministry, only to meet a recruiter a few days later. "That guy was all dressed up, and he took me to a fancy office in the center of town. It was a nice office, maybe forty or fifty people working there, I remember, and he told me that he could help me go to Kuwait if I wanted to. *Bien sur* [of course], I said I wanted to." Working through this recruitment agency, Nataly went to Kuwait and was placed in the home of a local Kuwaiti family.

To her surprise, Nataly's employers were very kind to her. "I couldn't believe my luck! My mother had prepared me for the worst. The worst. She had experienced a lot of bad things, and she told me that bad things happen in the Middle East. She told me Arab people are bad, but not this family, they were good. I was so happy." The only drawback was that her employers refused to pay Nataly directly. When she contacted her recruiters to ask about her overdue wages, she was not able to get a clear response. One person told her she would have to work off her debt before she would see the money. This concerned Nataly, who was worried about the well-being of her family back home.

Over time, Nataly became very close to the eldest son of her employers, Afzal. He would sometimes take her to the movies on her days off, and the two started sneaking into one another's rooms in the late hours of the evening after the rest of the family had gone to sleep. Nataly remembers Afzal as being kind, courteous, and gentle. "And he smelled good. It was too easy to fall in love with him."

But when Nataly became pregnant, Afzal and the rest of the family changed their attitudes toward her almost overnight. At first, Nataly tried to hide her pregnancy, even from Afzal. Given her slender frame, however, the obvious protrusion of her belly was not easy to hide. Afzal was the first to notice. "He put his hand on my belly and asked, 'Is this what I think?' When I nodded, he was so angry with me! He started yelling at me, asking me how I could have let this happen. Then that night he stopped speaking to me, forever." Her employers hadn't noticed the change in Nataly's figure, but they had noticed the change in their son's behavior. Afzal, who often wanted to take all his meals at home and took Nataly out almost every weekend, was suddenly absent most of the time. This led Nataly's employers to question her regarding his whereabouts. Nataly could not satisfactorily answer her employers' questions and eventually ended up confessing her pregnancy. This was unacceptable to her employers, who turned her over to the police, reporting her for the crime of *zina* and breach of contract.

"They took me to the police and said I was a bad woman, that I had done bad things and brought shame on the household. And I felt so bad, they had been so good to me, and I felt that I had dishonored them and myself too. . . . I just wanted another chance." The police took Nataly to a detention center, where she met over a dozen other pregnant women. The police explained to Nataly that she would be held in the center until her due date drew closer. She had regular medical examinations, and when it was time for the delivery, she was taken to a local hospital and gave birth to a baby boy she named Afzal after his father. She tried to contact her previous employers and the baby's father, but they never returned her calls.

A week after she had given birth, Nataly was sent to a different detention center. This time her suitemates were other Malagasy and Ethiopian women who had babies. The babies were allowed to live with them in the center, but minimal supplies were provided. During this time Nataly was vaguely aware that she would have to go to court and possibly face deportation. What she did not know, however, was that if she were deported, the baby would remain in Kuwait as a stateless person.

"I remember one night another woman named Narindra was crying in her cell. The baby was crying too, so I went over to help them. I asked Narindra what was wrong and she told me she was going to be sent home, but with finger [fingerprint—indicating deportation], but that the baby was being sent to an orphanage. She couldn't take the baby with her. And then I also started crying, because I didn't know," Nataly sobbed.

Nataly and others in the detention center were afraid of deportation because it meant they could not return to the region and might never be able to find work abroad again. One day a representative from the Malagasy government came to visit the women in the center. He was accompanied by a local activist, who had asked to meet with all of the Malagasy women who were being held. When they had convened, he told the women that several women who had been deported from the detention center previously had approached the Ministry of Labor to report the situation of women being held in detention against their will. Because of the efforts of these survivors, in collaboration with several faith-based initiatives, the government of Madagascar had become vested in helping the women go home without the shame of deportation. He offered all of the women amnesty in exchange for testimony about their recruiters and their working situations abroad.

Several of the women took the official up on his offer, but Nataly refused. "I said I didn't want to go home if I can't take Afzal [the baby] with me. I'm not leaving without my son, I told them that. I said I would rather rot in this jail, twelve women and how many babies to one room. All of it, I would take that, but I would not go home, no way." Still, she felt conflicted. On the one hand, she worried for her family back home, especially given that she had not been paid for these many months of her labor, and her mother and siblings could barely survive. On the other, she felt that she could not leave without her son. Nataly's story, however, touched the government official, who used her case to begin lobbying for new laws regarding children of Malagasy women.

Most of the women who did not have children were repatriated, and a few Malagasy women who did have babies left their children behind and went home. Nataly was one of eight Malagasy women who refused to go back to Madagascar. She remains in jail with her son, awaiting trial.

ı ı ı

When forty-seven migrant domestic workers returned to Madagascar in body bags from Lebanon in 2009 (the women, who had migrated to Lebanon, had faced repeated abuse; and while some had died from the abuse, others had committed suicide), the Malagasy government rushed to pass laws that would prohibit the migration of Malagasy women to the Middle East. These laws took the form of antitrafficking legislation and were to be enforced by the Ministry of Labor and the Ministry of Population. The laws officially banned women from migrating as domestic workers to any country in the Middle East and effectively closed off avenues of migration for many women like Nataly. Nataly's mother had been among the thousands of Malagasy women abused in Lebanon in the early 2000s, and Nataly then had to suffer from working with an unscrupulous recruiter because of these laws.

The Malagasy state, however, remained vested in protecting its citizens abroad. When it became clear that many women were still migrating to the Middle East, activists partnered with survivors and the state in 2014 to rework the laws that criminalized migration to the region. Members of the Ministry of Labor and Ministry of Population traveled to numerous detention centers throughout the Middle East, looking for women like Nataly. Inspired by the stories of the women they met, they worked to develop new laws that were more in line with the needs of their population.

Shereene

Shereene is a Sri Lankan mother of two children who has not seen her second child in over four years. Seven years ago, Shereene made a very difficult decision to support her (then) one child after her husband had incurred significant debt when he absconded from his work abroad. Saddled with the heavy debt that her husband owed his recruiter, Shereene realized that she was now the breadwinner, responsible not only for her daughter and herself but also for her mother, who had recently fallen ill and could no longer work in the garment factory that had employed her for more than thirty years. She was hesitant to leave her daughter but also knew that she could not find employment at home that would allow her to support her entire family. "I know to leave is not good. I don't want to leave my girl, but if I stay, no good work. I don't want to work in a factory like my mom. Long hours. Little money. I want to make [a] lot of money, too fast."

Worried about leaving her daughter in the care of her husband, who in addition to his gambling problems had also taken to drinking, Shereene moved her daughter in with her mother. She had heard from friends and family that there were many recruiters looking for women willing to migrate to the Gulf to work as nannies or domestic workers. Though Shereene knew that they already owed a sizable debt to her husband's recruiter, she decided to take on additional debt, reasoning that she would be able to repay all of the family debt as soon as she had gainful employment. "It is hard. I am scared because people taking my money, more debt. But my daughter, she is my jewel. She is my future. I have to take care of her. Make a good life for her." For Shereene, migrating abroad to support her daughter was a sacrifice that increased her agency. She described the process of making this decision as one where she "felt really in control for the first time in my life."

Shereene paid the recruiter and was placed in the home of a Jordanian family in Dubai. She was hired as a nanny and charged with raising the four children in the household. Shortly after her arrival, Shereene realized she was pregnant. She had not had much sexual contact with her husband, but on the eve of her departure, she explained, she wanted to make sure that "his needs were met." Like many other women who migrate abroad, Shereene was worried about her husband's fidelity to her while she was away. This worry was confirmed for her when, not three months after her departure to Dubai, Shereene received word from her mother that her husband had left her for another woman.

"When I realize I have baby, I am scared. Because I want to work. I want to work hard and make money. But if I am pregnant, how I am doing this?" Shereene made a decision to hide her pregnancy for as long as possible from her employers.

During this time, the male head of household began making sexual advances toward Shereene. Though he did not assault or rape her, his increased attentions to Shereene caught the attention of the female head of household. By the time Shereene was six months pregnant, she could no longer hide her pregnancy from the watchful eyes of her female employer. When her employer realized Shereene was pregnant, she became very angry, accusing Shereene of seducing her husband. Shereene tried to explain that she had become pregnant from her own husband back in Sri Lanka, but her employer did not believe her.

She was immediately taken to the police, who put her in jail. After having her baby, her trial began. Shereene described the process of being in court as traumatizing, confusing, and unjust. Her translator did not do an adequate job of representing her case. She was charged with breaking her contract and *zina*. Furthermore, she was deemed "immoral" and "unfit to parent" her own son. She was deported shortly after the trial; her son remains in the UAE to this day. "I didn't even get to say goodbye to him," Shereene sobbed.

But Shereene has not given up her fight to get her son back. Upon returning to Sri Lanka, Shereene became an activist for the causes of migrant women. She started an NGO to help returning migrant women, as well as initiating education campaigns to help future migrant women know their rights. This activism, however, was costly for her, and Shereene was threatened with lifetime imprisonment. Afraid for her and her daughter's safety, Shereene sought asylum in the United States, which was granted to her. Today she owns a small alterations business and is supporting her daughter. Much of her time, however, is dedicated to activism, and she has appeared before the United Nations on many occasions. She is now working with UNICEF to assist other women in her situation and continues to work to find and reunite with her son.

"Bad Mother"

Several of the women in my study were deported without their children to countries where their children *were* eligible for citizenship. In countries such as the Philippines, Ethiopia, and Madagascar, citizenship can technically pass through the mother. However, some of these women were deemed "unfit" to parent their own children by judges in the Gulf. Specifically, they were told that they were "immoral," "irresponsible," and "undeserving" of their own children. As these women were entrenched in legal and court processes they hardly understood, their children were legally taken from them by judges and lawyers.

The responses of these state officials mirror some discourses in the sending countries, while contradicting other discourses in the Gulf and beyond. In the Gulf, women from certain countries (including India, Indonesia, Ethiopia, Madagascar, and the Philippines) are imported to perform the intimate labor of raising the children of citizens and other Gulf residents. They are specifically chosen for their ability to care for children and tasked with caring for the children who will be the future of the nation. Women from certain parts of the world such as the Philippines or Indonesia even command higher prices for their intimate labor precisely because they are seen as more "desirable" caregivers because of their ethnic backgrounds and stereotypes about Southeast Asian women as being more "loving" and "caring." It is ironic, then, that these same women who have been caring for the children of citizens are deemed "unfit" by other citizens to parent their own children.

This response on the part of the state, however, is not restricted to the receiving countries of the Gulf. In many of the sending countries, female migrants who leave their families to make ends meet are viewed as a threat to the fabric of morality that binds the nation together. The role of mothers in "birthing the nation" has been explored extensively in literature on reproduction, state violence, and motherhood (Kanaaneh 2002; Das 1990). Women are seen as an embodiment of the nation, particularly in their capacity and responsibility for giving birth to, raising, and caring for the nation's sons and daughters. In some countries (such as Iran, Japan, and Singapore) women's education has been promoted as a necessary component of their motherhood, while in others (for example, Israel, Iran, and many Gulf countries) the value placed on women's fertility and ability to produce "desirable" citizens is manifested in the form of pronatalist policies (Najmabadi 1998). What then of the mother who must migrate in order to support her family? Not only is she shirking her familial duties, but she poses a threat to the nation by turning over her mothering responsibilities to others (presumably less capable) in her desire to make a better life for herself and her family. These discourses of migrant mothers as a "threat" contrasts sharply with the reality that without these women their families might not survive, even as they contribute significantly to the overall economies of sending countries.

Discourses and policies portraying migrant women as "threats" and "bad mothers" collide with home and host country narratives from female employers and migrant families about the necessity for gendered intimate labor. Female employers in the Gulf frequently acknowledge their dependence on migrant women's labor in the home. Some female employers I interviewed referred to their domestic workers as "caring," "great care givers," and "model mothers." This was echoed by some family members at home in the sending countries, who described migrant women as the hope of their families and their greatest investment. However, policy makers at home and abroad frequently challenge these narratives. This frustrates women whose children have been taken from them, while others are angered by rhetoric pertaining to their decisions coming from home countries. Many women seek to draw on their own experiences to transform rhetoric about migrant mothers to accommodate lived realities.

Almaz

Almaz migrated from Addis Ababa to Kuwait via the Comoros Islands in 2010. She had heard from cousins and friends that work in the Gulf was plentiful and lucrative. After her father passed away, leaving her entire family in significant debt, Almaz, then eighteen years old, decided to support the family by becoming an overseas worker. Like many other women, she approached the Ministry of Labor in her first attempt, hoping to migrate through formal channels. When it became clear to her that this route would take longer and be filled with more bureaucracy, she elected to migrate via an informal recruiter who would send women first to the Comoros Islands. She had no guarantee that she would actually make it to the Middle East from the Comoros but said, "I had to try."

Fortunately, her migratory journey was safe, and after spending two weeks in the Comoros she was sent to Kuwait to work for a local family. "I was scared, but then I'm feeling lucky. Too lucky," she said. She felt fortunate to have migrated safely and been placed in the home of a family who treated her very well. She was tasked with caring for their three children, ages seven, five, and two. "But one thing was, only problem was me not Muslim," explained Almaz. Her employers had apparently requested a Muslim domestic worker; however, they were accommodating when they learned that Almaz was a devout Christian. "At first no, but later then church okay," she said, referring to the fact that the family eventually gave her regular time off to attend church. As Almaz made more frequent trips to church, she began getting more involved with other Ethiopians who were living in Kuwait. Sometimes her church friends would invite her to parties. One evening she attended a party at a local Ethiopian restaurant run by two men who had migrated to work as cooks in Kuwait City. At this party Almaz met a young man named Dabir, who, as it turned out, had gone to school with her older brother. Almaz and Dabir hit it off right away, and he invited her to have a drink with him in the back room of the restaurant. Almaz agreed, a decision she regretted almost immediately.

Almaz doesn't remember much about the incident, just that Dabir was insistent that she have sex with him but that she did not want to. She kept telling him that she did not want to, but he forced himself on her. She remembers passing out immediately afterwards and waking up in a taxi driven by another Ethiopian migrant. Someone had given the taxi driver the address of her employers, and he woke her when they arrived at the house. Bruised, sore, and distraught, Almaz managed to climb the stairs to her employers' house and sneak into her room just before dawn.

A few months later, Almaz realized she was pregnant. At first she hid the news from her employers, but when it became increasingly obvious, Almaz was honest about the incident. Her employers were understanding and told her that they would arrange a ticket for her to return to Ethiopia to have the baby. "They tell me like that it will be more safe, but I'm not listen," she said. She begged them to allow her to stay in Kuwait City to have the baby and live with them. As her employers were contemplating her request, Almaz went to church to pray. At church, however, one of her fellow churchgoers noticed her belly. She confronted Almaz, demanding to know the details behind her pregnancy. Unsatisfied with Almaz's explanation, she called the police, who arrived at Almaz's employers' house that evening. It is unclear why this fellow churchgoer called the police, especially because it seemed obvious to Almaz later on that she knew that that Almaz would likely be arrested. In a conversation I had with Almaz in 2015, she speculated that this woman had likely been a very devout Catholic who believed Almaz had sinned and thus should be punished for her "sins."

She was taken to jail, where she was charged with *zina* and breach of contract and imprisoned for over a year. After giving birth she began a seemingly endless series of meetings with lawyers and judges. She remembers feeling confused and scared during the long court sessions, which resulted in a judicial decision to deport her but keep the child in the country. Her interpreter told her that the judge had decided she was "unfit" to parent the child. "He is telling me I am bad mom. That is what breaks me. 'Bad mom.' Me."

Once deported, Almaz was outraged that the judge had unilaterally taken away her son. She felt that she had not committed a crime, and could not understand why her punishment was so severe. Worse, after hearing what had happened to her, Almaz's family disowned her, reasoning that she was now "damaged." Almaz felt afraid and alone. She wanted to return to Kuwait to move back in with the family she had been working for. "I'm missing my madam and baba, and, of course, the kids. I love the kids," she said. "And I want my baby, I want back to Kuwait for my baby, but no, because they do fingerprint, and say no more back Kuwait."

Upon returning to Ethiopia, Almaz worked with her local church to start a shelter for women returning from migratory assignments. She knew that many women had experiences similar to her own, and she wanted to create a safe house for these returning women. Many of the women in her shelter today have returned with their babies but, like Almaz, have been exiled from their families. Almaz works with her pastor to raise awareness about situations such as her own and continues to fight for her son to this day.

Lola

"When I got the job offer at the hospital in Dubai, I don't know, I was so happy, but also so sad," said Lola, a thirty-year-old mother of two from the Philippines. Lola was born and raised in what she calls a "migrant family." Her mother migrated to Italy to work as a domestic worker when Lola was eight years old, at which point Lola and her sister were sent to live with their maternal grandmother. Her father took a position working on a fishing boat off the coast of New Zealand a few months after her mother's departure. Though she describes missing her parents during her childhood years, she notes that she never felt deprived of love. "Yes, they were far away, but they called a lot, and I knew my grandmother loved me. She told me all the time that my parents loved me too, and that they had left because they loved me. That part was harder to understand until I changed schools and met some friends like me."

A few years after her mother moved to Italy, Lola was transferred to a private school, where her tuition was paid for by her mother's remittances. At her new school, Lola met several other young women whose mothers were Overseas Filipino/a Workers (OFWs) as well. Lola notes that this was a turning point for her. "When I met these other girls, all of their moms were gone, well, it became a bit easier for me. I still missed my mom so much, and I was angry at her, but I stopped thinking she was just a bad mother and I was grateful for the opportunity she gave me by sending money home so I could go to school."

Lola graduated from her school with honors and went on to pursue a degree in nursing. During her time in nursing school she met and married Filippo, who was pursuing the same degree. They had two children and were both able to get jobs at the same hospital in Manila. But when Filippo began drinking and gambling, he lost his job, and the family became entirely dependent on Lola's income. This put a strain on Lola, as well as her daughter and son, who were pulled out of the private school that the family could no longer afford. Filippo's gambling habits further drained the family of their resources, and they had to move from their three-bedroom apartment in Manila to a one-bedroom house outside of town. Lola could no longer make the commute to the hospital where she had been employed and was unable to find another job closer to home.

Things changed for Lola when she received a call from a well-known medical recruiting company in Dubai. "On the one hand, I was so happy. This new job paid four times what I was earning in Manila, and I wouldn't even have to pay my travel fees like many OFWs do. Plus, the job was a dream of a lifetime. I would get to get out, get away, travel, and send money home for my kids." She added that she felt a perverse type of excitement at the chance to escape her husband and all the challenges of living in a shantytown on the outskirts of Manila. She was also anxious to return her children to private school, reasoning that they should at least have the same opportunities that she had had growing up.

"But, like I said, I was sad, too. It meant that I had to do to my kids what my mom had done to me. It meant that I had to become a bad mother." When deciding whether or not to take the job, Lola called her mother to discuss her dilemma. "I remember that call so well," she said, beginning to tear up. "I called my mom and I said, 'Mom, what do I do?' And I remember she said to me, 'Lola, what *can* you do? You must go. You must support your children. This is sacrifice, but it's sacrifice for your children. And you, you will be happier if you go. Yes, you will miss your kids, like I missed you every day of my life, but they will understand one day, just as you do now.' I remember it so well. But I also remember her warning me, telling me that everyone would call me 'bad mother.' And so I knew, I knew I would have to go. There was nothing for me if I stayed there, no jobs, nothing. And if I went, yes, I could change my life and give my kids the opportunities I had."

Lola migrated to Dubai and took a position as a nurse in a new hospital in town. She worked hard and remitted her earnings to her mother, who was caring for her two children. The children changed schools and enrolled in private school, and her mother was able to buy a new house closer to town. Lola described her move to Dubai as a transformative experience. "It made me feel stronger, more bold somehow. Now I was in charge of my life and my family's future. I missed my kids so much, just as my mother said I would, but I was successful."

After her first year in Dubai, Lola gathered up the courage to ask her husband for a divorce. "I would never have done that if I stayed home in the Philippines. I would never have divorced him, I would stay living with him. And he would stay and keep draining me, pulling me down like a weight. But now, I can go on with my life. I know when I do move back home, we will have a chance." Though the dissolution of their marriage had relieved Lola, she explained that the children did not see the divorce as positive. "That was the hard part. The kids felt like I had abandoned them, that I had left and that I had changed into another person. They thought that if I could divorce their dad, that I could leave them too. And that made things difficult."

When Lola's son, Carlo, ran away from his grandmother's house, Lola was beside herself. Her mother called to tell her the news that Carlo was missing, and Lola described feeling powerless. "I wasn't there, and there wasn't anything I could do. He [Carlo] was mad at me, and he was doing this to punish me. It was terrible," she said, her voice trembling. Finally, Lola's son did return home, with several bruises and two broken ribs. Carlo's grandmother took him to the hospital, but when Lola called to speak to him, he refused to come to the phone. Lola immediately took time off from work and booked passage back to the Philippines, but on her arrival Carlo would not even look at his mother. Carlo's doctors made Lola feel even worse by blaming her for the incident. "It was horrible," she said, her voice almost a whisper. "The doctor came in and saw me. He just looked at me and shook his head. And I remember, I remember what he said, he said that this wouldn't have happened if women like me stayed home and took care of their kids. He said it was my fault. He said that women like me were ruining the future of the Philippines." Lola's mother tried to comfort her daughter. She reminded Lola of the many slogans and media campaigns pointing to OFWs as the "heroes of the nation." But this only angered Lola, who said, "My mom said to me that motherhood means going abroad nowadays, but this is something I don't understand. How can we be heroes but bad mothers at the same time?"

ı ı ı

For women like Lola, both the experience of migration and the discourses around motherhood and migration are simultaneously empowering and frustrating. In migrating, Lola had expanded her opportunities and provided for her children. She had also gained the necessary strength to push back against her increasingly abusive husband. But she often wondered why she needed to migrate and make the difficult choice to leave her children behind in order to exercise her agency.

Overseas Filipino/a Workers who are in the same situation as Lola have been active in organizing to challenge communal and state rhetoric about motherhood. Through organizations such as the Scalabrini Migration Center, Migrante, and others, migrant women have organized to tell their stories of motherhood and sacrifice, seeking to change narratives about migrant mothers. Flor, an activist who has started her own organization in the Philippines, is working with seven other Filipinas to write a play based on their experiences. Their hope is to educate their communities and ultimately the state about the complex realities of their lives.

"I think once people understand what we went through, why we became OFWs, what we did for our children, then it's not a mystery anymore and they don't have to be angry with us," said Flor, pointing to a rough draft of her script. "Then, when they understand, that is when things can change. That is when we can go to the government and demand more protection. After all, who hasn't wanted to make a better life for their children? That is what this play is about. It's about celebrating migrant mothers, not punishing them."

Conclusion: Intimacy and Im/Mobility

All of the women whose stories are shared in this chapter made decisions in large part because of their family members and loved ones. Their physical mobility allowed for economic mobility back home, even if it resulted in emotional immobility or instability in familial relations. Their intimate relations and relatives were a major part of the choices these women made, every step of the way. Whether compelling mobility in search of better opportunities or motivating self-imposed immobility in the form of refusing deportation or returning home without their children born in the host countries, for these women im/mobility resulting from their intimate lives was in the forefront of their minds. Their migratory experiences were profoundly affected by their intimate relationships—including new relationships in the host country as well as prior relations back home. These bonds of love were often both mobilizing and immobilizing, for the migrants as well as their transnational families, sometimes at the same time.

Through their migratory journeys women are able to explore their subjectivities, renegotiate intimate relationships (new and old), and seek out various forms of mobility. These new experiences in the host country can come at a high price, in that they may inspire or lead to forced or self-imposed immobility or to forced mobility, sometimes without their children. But the resilience of these women and their determination to draw on their intimate lives and experiences to change their situations and the situations of other women like them must not be underestimated. They draw strength from their bonds of love, and while these bonds and the state regulations they are up against impose a backdrop of inflexibility, migrant women and their kin demonstrate an extraordinary capacity for creative flexibility in their mobility and in the decisions they make.

3

INFLEXIBLE CITIZENSHIP
AND FLEXIBLE PRACTICES

WHEN LUCINDA WAS JUST FIVE YEARS OLD, her mother left the Philippines to work as a domestic worker in Bahrain. "I don't know exactly why my mom left, but I think it was because my dad drank a lot and was always losing his job, but at that time, I didn't understand why she left my brother and I all alone." Lucinda is a twenty-five-year-old woman who was working as a domestic worker in Kuwait City when I met her in 2013. Because Lucinda's father had a habit of drinking and disappearing, sometimes for days on end, her mother decided it would be best to leave Lucinda and her brother, Pedro, in the care of their maternal aunt who lived in a neighboring village.

"The first year my mom was gone," said Lucinda, "gone to Bahrain, it was good. It was okay." Her mother sent money home regularly and her aunt sent the children to school. After a year of being gone, her mother came home for Christmas. "Then I saw her [mother] on the boat," said Lucinda. "And I remember eating the towel, I mean biting the handkerchief, because I was so nervous. I mean, I'm not seeing my mom in one year, and I remember wondering if she would still love me and just hoping, praying she would stay home and not leave again." But, unfortunately, her mother did leave again. "My dad was so bad to my mom. He kept telling her, 'You are a stupid person. You will be nothing,' he would say to her. Then one day, he said to her, 'I hate you. If I am not a successful man, I will kill you.' Then that night I said to my mom, 'Okay, Mom, I know now you have to go, go and be okay, and make your life better.'" Her mother left shortly thereafter for an assignment as a domestic worker, this time in Kuwait.

"At that time, it was bad when my mother went to Kuwait. Something was wrong, her madams were bad and she didn't send money for two years. At that time, my aunt beat me and treated me like a maid. She was so terrible to my brother and me, she made us sleep outside or on the floor, didn't give us food. She just wanted to have us so she could collect the money my mom was sending home." Lucinda pulled at the thread of her ripped jeans in order to hide the growing hole in the denim. "But they never let me, my aunt and uncle, they never let me talk alone to my mom when she called." Lucinda explained how she often wanted to tell her mother what was happening. "She didn't call too much. But when she did, my aunt or someone was standing there to make sure we didn't say anything bad to my mom."

After two years of abuse from her aunt, Lucinda, at the age of seven, decided to run away and live on the streets of Cavite, just outside Manila. She vividly remembers the night she made the decision. "It was one night when my aunt was hitting my brother. She was beating Pedro because he had found some candies and was eating them. She beat him so hard he was bleeding. When I came to help my brother, my aunt started beating me too. That night I knew I cannot stay here anymore. It was so hard for me to leave my little brother; that was the hardest part. I held him all night and told him I would come back for him. I kissed his head and said it was going to be okay. Then I left."

When Lucinda ran away, she said, she was terrified but at the same time felt proud. "I knew my mom had to go away to work and make money, so I thought, it's the same for me, I must go." Demonstrating her entrepreneurial spirit, Lucinda began digging through trash heaps and selling the food she found to other children on the street. She would still go to school during the day and sell candy or medical supplies, such as bandages and lotions, to passersby in the courtyard. "I didn't drop out of school for many reasons. The first was that I wanted to go to school to become smart so I can make something from myself. The other reason was that I wanted to be near to my brother, to make sure he is growing okay. But it was hard. For a long time, he was angry with me asking me 'Sister, why did you leave me with them?' but he forgive me in the end." Lucinda showed me a faded picture that she had photographed with her cell phone of herself as a child with her arms around a little boy. She swiped through the pictures on her phone to show me a more recent picture of her brother, now a grown man, holding a large fish. "He is a fisherman now, and we are close, but he still doesn't talk to my mother."

For the next seven years Lucinda continued living on the streets, occasionally returning to her aunt's home but leaving again once the abuse of her brother resumed. Her mother had absconded from her initial employers and was working informally in Kuwait. "She said she left that job and started working cleaning lots of people's houses, working so hard. Sometimes she send a big money home, but some months no. The worst thing is that the money she sent home never made it to us, her kids. Can you imagine? She is working so hard in Kuwait, living a bad life for us, for her kids, but back home, she doesn't know that my aunt and my grandfather are taking the money for themselves."

Even though Lucinda was living on the streets, she was able to remain an honors student for most of her elementary and middle school years and thus was determined to finish school. After some years, however, her aunt stopped contributing money to her schooling, impeding her ability to attend school. Her father came in and out of her life, and at one point she was able to persuade him to pay for another year of her schooling. "He was a drunk, but a good man. But I can say that now, for a long time I hated him. He would tell me that I'm stupid too, but I would say, 'No, dad, you are wrong. I am in school to make something of myself, so please keep me in school, I am not stupid and I am going to be somebody.' And that worked because for a little while he helped me to stay in school."

By the time Lucinda turned fifteen, she had not seen her mother in eight years. Her mother could not leave Kuwait because she had absconded from her employers five years earlier and would have had to pay heavy fines for overstaying. Lucinda had spent most of her nights living on the streets, suffering from regular abuse—both muggings and beatings on the street as well as abuse from her maternal relatives at her aunt's home. While the challenges were many, Lucinda had still managed to parlay her entrepreneurial spirit into establishing a one-woman business selling medical supplies that had been discarded from hospitals to locals in the village. This work brought her to Manila, where she met a recruiter who was looking for women to work as cleaning staff in the hospitals of Kuwait.

"At that time, I am thinking I am so lucky! I find someone who can take me to Kuwait to go and see my mother, to go and find her and hold her, and be with her. I don't care what work I am doing there, I want to go and I want to be with my mother. Of course I know that it won't be easy. I know that my mother didn't get paid two years. I know that maybe I will get stuck there. But

I know that I must go, that I must be with my mother. That I will do anything to be there with her, and I am not coming back to the Philippines without her."

It was bittersweet when, at the age of eighteen, Lucinda arrived in Kuwait. She was able to find her mother, but the reunification was difficult. Her mother had remarried, this time to an Arab migrant from Bahrain, and had another child in Kuwait. "It was tense between us at first. I didn't realize I am still angry with her for a lot of things until I see her. And she was feeling guilty. So, at first we are fighting a lot." To add to the challenges she faced with her mother, her employer in Kuwait refused to pay her wages for months on end. At a certain point, Lucinda contemplated giving up and returning to the Philippines. "But I tell myself, 'No, no, Lucinda, if you give up then he [her dad] wins. Then he is right, I am a stupid person.' So I decide, I'm going to stay, I'm going to find new work, I'm going to work hard, and I'm going to be with my mother. I am going to stay with her until she is ready to come home."

Lucinda absconded from her work at the hospital and was able to find work as a domestic worker for a series of local families with the help of her mother and church friends. The first family she worked for treated her well and paid her salary promptly. The second family, however, was abusive toward her and frequently threatened to turn her in to the authorities, since they knew she was an illegal migrant. Over time, the male head of household began abusing her, beating her every night and threatening rape on more than one occasion; but Lucinda was resilient. After six months with the abusive family, she absconded and found another family who needed her services and began working at a café on the side, hoping to earn enough money to return home more quickly with her mother.

After four years, it became clear to Lucinda that her mother had no intention of returning to Manila. At this point, Lucinda was faced with a difficult choice: remain illegally in Kuwait and be close to her mother or return to the Philippines, where she would be legal, and try to find employment there. "Neither option seemed good to me, especially because by then my brother had already left to work as a sea man and there was nothing left for me back home." So Lucinda decided she would stay in Kuwait, where she found a family who would sponsor her and help her get legal working papers. Once she became a legal migrant, she enrolled in night classes and is currently pursuing advanced training in computer science. When I last spoke with her in January of 2015, she had found a job as a data manager in a local hospital in Kuwait City and had just given her notice to the family for whom she had been working.

ı ı ı

Discussions about migrant workers in the Gulf, especially those working in the domestic sphere or spheres of intimate labor, tend to paint migrants as one-dimensional by focusing on the types of labor or circumstances of migration. The trafficking debate in particular reduces women to their experiences of abuse, contributing to portrayals of migrants' lives as filled with violence and abuse. Essentializing domestic workers as products of their abuse rather than emphasizing the complexities of their choices further challenges the agency of those who struggle to negotiate their potential courses of action, make decisions, and control their own lives. Migrant domestic workers already face significant challenges and precarious situations working in the private sphere of the home and living in a country in which they cannot fully exercise the rights of citizenship. Some scholars, including Jacqueline Bhabha, have theorized different forms of statelessness, such as economic statelessness, wherein a person cannot fully exercise his or her rights to economic sustainability (Bhabha 2009). It could be argued that Lucinda experiences economic statelessness both at home and in the host country, given the heavy restrictions on her income-earning and survival strategies. And yet it is Lucinda's intimate relations that contour her decision-making processes and sense of belonging and citizenship both at home and abroad. Deborah Boehm has thoroughly explored a type of citizenship that is constantly evolving and negotiated across borders (Boehm 2012). In her book *Intimate Migrations: Gender, Family, and Illegality among Transnational Mexicans*, she details the effects of intimate lives on migration and on the formation of subjectivity. In this in-depth study of Mexican migration to and from the United States, she specifically chronicles the challenges that transnational Mexican migrants face in negotiating their identity and citizenship in the face of heavy restrictions from both home- and host-country laws and illegality. She refers to these challenges as a type of "inflexible citizenship."

Inflexible citizenship is counterpart to the notion of "flexible citizenship" put forth by Aihwa Ong in her book *Flexible Citizenship: The Cultural Logics of Transnationality* (1999). Ong has written extensively on the subject of "flexible citizenship," a modern-day outgrowth of globalization and the expansion of global capitalism. She defines it as a type of citizenship that is tied to freedom of movement across borders and the ability to negotiate political, social, and economic rights. Flexible citizenship refers to an important by-product of globalization: the multiple-passport holders, jetsetters, and cosmopolitans who can utilize this status to exercise physical mobility with ease, receive the promised benefits of citizenship, and take advantage of the benefits of capitalism. Christine Chin argues that a service class has emerged alongside that of the flexible citizens, designed to move along a particular cosmopolitan circuit that parallels the flows of capital perpetuated by the flexible citizens. While Chin focuses on the sex workers who move along this highway, it is equally important to consider other types of intimate laborers, such as domestic workers, nannies, and care workers, who move along this "global circuit" for the same reasons (Chin 2013). All of the individuals whose stories are presented here fall into this category; all have migrated within this global circuit of cosmopolitan cities in order to follow and meet the demands of new capital and the flexible citizens who wield it. And thus their experiences are doubtless shaped by the states within which they move and their desire to negotiate economic, social, and legal citizenship in these spaces.

Neha Vora has also explored Ong's notion of "flexible citizenship" in her work on Indian middle-class migrants in the Gulf (Vora 2013). Vora argues forcefully that many Indian migrants in Dubai attempt to negotiate their flexibility in renegotiating their sense of self through migration. Here, I build on the important work of Ong, Boehm, Vora, and scholars of statelessness such as Bhabha to explore the inflexible citizenship experienced by my interlocutors in both their home and host countries, as well as the flexibility they employ in rethinking their subjectivities and notions of the self, belonging, family, and citizenship. Many migrants struggle with a type of inflexible citizenship linked to structural forces in the home and/or host countries that challenge their ability to attain the full citizenship rights of economic, social, legal, and humanitarian protection. Macrostructural forces such as globalizing capital markets and debt repayment programs in places like the Philippines make accessing employment or education at home difficult for people like Lucinda. Moreover, when Lucinda or her mother migrates, she is unable to access the protections afforded by citizenship rights abroad. In this way, they are challenged by inflexible citizenship or citizenship schemas that are not flexible enough to meet their needs. While the state(s) present(s) many layers of challenges that render their citizenship inflexible, migrants themselves must (and do) remain flexible in moving through the labyrinthine structures they are confronted by. Migrants also demonstrate extraordinary flexibility in negotiating their sense of family and belonging while at home and abroad.

In particular, a focus on the family and migrants as members of families complicates the received narratives of migrants as simply victims of globalization or of their circumstances that is so pervasive in human trafficking rhetoric. When looking at migrant domestic work, the story of someone like Lucinda could be glossed as yet another instance of a migrant domestic worker (MDW) who experiences debt bondage and remains in her challenging employment situation in order to repay her debt. Confining Lucinda to this established narrative however, hinders policy makers, employees of NGOs, scholars, and others from considering her motivations and hesitancies in migrating, her negotiation of relationships, her efforts to support herself and her family, and more. Casting her as a slave or someone experiencing contract slavery or categorizing her as illegal or an absconder is overly simplistic and obscures the intimate interplay between legality and illegality (Boehm 2012). Rather, if we understand the many levels of challenges she has experienced and the creative (flexible) strategies for survival she has employed, in addition to her dedication to her family, her story becomes more than just another catalogue of abuse or violence. To focus on ways in which she is forced to choose between family and self, from her familial turbulence to her strategies for survival first as a child and now as an adult, is to recognize her agency and flexibility in the face of regimes of inflexible citizenship.

Attention to the intimate lives of intimate laborers grants them agency and resists the temptation to flatten their identity by focusing on the type of labor they engage in or the circumstances of their migration. It is imperative to look at the role of family to question the effect of kinship ties and familial duty on the ability to control mobility, which complicates the received force/choice dichotomy that is so prominent in discussions of human trafficking and forced labor (Bales 2012; Farley 2003).

This chapter focuses on the effects of migration on the intimate lives of migrants and their kin. I look at the children of migrants, many of whom have migrated to work or to reunite with parents abroad and some of whom were born in the host country. These families are struggling to define and redefine their understandings of family, citizenship, and belonging across borders. Building on the work of Boehm and Vora, I look at how intimate lives are shaped by migration in the particular context of the UAE and Kuwait. Through the experiences of migrants and their kin, I explore the challenges posed by inflexible citizenship as well as the flexibility they employ to create types of mobility in the face of what may seem like immobility.

Inflexible Citizenship:
Reunification and Citizenship Laws

Both Kuwait and the UAE have fairly stringent laws pertaining to migrant re-unification with families and citizenship transfer. While these laws present migrants with significant challenges, many families have overcome the obstacles interposed by the state and managed to bring family members to or give birth to children in the host country for generations. I begin with a description of reunification laws because most of my interlocutors whose stories follow faced these types of challenges. In a later chapter, where the children of migrants who struggle with legal statelessness are introduced, I will detail the citizenship laws for each country.

Kuwait

Kuwait implements an inflexible family reunification policy for foreigners in order to curtail labor migration and reduce the number of migrant workers living in the country. Kuwait's policy of family reunification is conditional upon the salary level of the migrant worker, such that a minimum income level is required prior to allowing families to accompany workers. In December 2004, the Ministry of Interior lowered the minimum income required for non-Kuwaitis to be granted family visas to KD$250 per month and required workers to live in Kuwait for at least three years; prior to this, the salary cap for family visas was KD$450 per month for government employees and KD$650 for private-sector employees (N. Shah 2007). A majority of migrants earn less than the specified income and must therefore leave their families behind in their home country.

In addition, migrant workers in Kuwait must purchase health insurance for themselves and each member of their family residing in Kuwait, thus increasing the cost of living as a unified family. Private-sector employers, who employ 92 percent of migrant workers in Kuwait, usually do not cover insurance costs, making the stay of family members in the country too costly for the majority of migrant workers (UN/POP/EGM 2006).

Like all non-Kuwaiti citizens, every child born to non-Kuwaiti parents must have a sponsor. On the basis of the birth certificate, the child is issued a dependent residence visa. Within one month of birth, the parents must obtain a civil identification card in order for the child to become part of Kuwait's electronic population database. In the large majority of cases, the father sponsors the child, since he is the one most likely to be employed, be eligible to bring his wife to Kuwait, and have his children in the host country. In some cases, the mother may be the sponsor, if she is employed and entitled to bring her minor children with her; however, in most instances, she is not allowed to sponsor her husband. A male child can live in Kuwait under the sponsorship of his father or mother until he is twenty-one and a female child can do so until she gets married. Once a male child reaches the age of twenty-one, he can continue to live in the country if he is registered as a student and has a student visa or if he is employed and has a work visa. He is not entitled to a dependent visa from his father or mother. Migration rules do not entitle children born in Kuwait to non-Kuwaiti parents to become citizens, regardless of how long they have lived in the country. Thus, a substantial proportion of persons born in Kuwait have been living in Kuwait as foreigners, even though this is the only country they have lived in most of their lives.

United Arab Emirates

In the UAE, family reunification laws vary depending on the relation between the migrant worker and the family member accompanying him or her. When it comes to family sponsorship, a migrant worker must either be a spouse or a first-affinity relative to the relative accompanying him or her in order to qualify as a sponsor. For example, if a child, son-in-law, or daughter-in-law meets a minimum salary requirement, holds a valid residency visa, and can provide sufficient accommodation supported by appropriate documentation, he or she is able to sponsor his or her parents and parents-in-law (Immigration Specialist 2012). Sponsors must receive a monthly salary of at least AED3,000 plus accommodation allowances or a monthly salary of AED4,000 without any accommodation allowances (Suter 2005).

Children born in the Emirates to foreigners do not have rights of local citizenship and automatically assume the nationality of the parents. According to the Ministry of Interior, Emirati mothers married to non-UAE citizens will not be able to get citizenship for their children if they were born before their mothers became citizens. However, if the father is a national of the UAE, the child will usually be granted local nationality and may later become a national of the UAE and obtain a local passport. It is also important to note that in a law passed in 2011, an Emirati citizen married to a non-Emirati man may obtain citizenship for her child, and this has been successfully implemented since the passage of this law (Issa 2011; US Department of State, Bureau of Democracy, Human Rights, and Labor 2012).

While there is no age limit for sponsoring daughters as children to (re)unify the family, a son must be under the age of eighteen to be sponsored as a child. Once he reaches this age, he may legalize his stay only as a student or sponsored employee. If his sponsor is a relative of second affinity, he can apply for a visit visa by seeking the approval of the deputy minister for residence and immigration. In cases of polygamy, up to two wives can be sponsored if the husband earns at lease AED10,000 per month and has two tenancy contracts in his name (Immigration Specialist 2012).

Inflexible Families

Gautam grew up near Tamil Nadu in India. One of six children, Gautam remembers doing much of the child rearing after his mother died giving birth to his youngest sister. "We were many children, all girls and me, and my dad started drinking and gambling when my mom died," he explained. When Gautam's older sisters were eighteen and sixteen, respectively, their father decided to send them to Kuwait to work as domestic workers, since he had heard they could make a good deal of money working abroad. As many other scholars have described, the "grapevine," or rumors about opportunities within migration, shapes decision making for many would-be migrants.[1] After his sisters' departure, Gautam assumed his position as head of household at the age of fourteen. He learned to cook, clean, and care for his three younger sisters.

"When my father see I can cook, he is thinking he sends me to work, also like my sisters. I am thinking I don't want to go, I don't want to leave my little sisters. But I'm thinking I want to be free from my father, I am very angry in that time with him. He drinking all the time, spending my sisters' money. But I know I must go, no choice for me." When Gautam turned sixteen, his father negotiated a contract for him to be sent to Kuwait, like his sisters, to work as a cook in a Kuwaiti home. Gautam never saw the contract but was told that he was going to be borrowing money from his sisters' remittances to migrate and would pay them and his father back within the year.

Instead of going to Kuwait to work as a cook, however, Gautam was sent to work as a shepherd on the Iraqi border. "I was very afraid there. I don't like Iraq. I am thinking I am a cook, why I am sent to work with animals?" After working for four months as a shepherd with no pay, he was finally sent to Kuwait City and placed in the home of a local family. Once again, his host family did not pay him. Although he was frustrated and wanted to agitate for his overdue wages,

Gautam was afraid that he would be sent back to the Iraqi border, or worse, sent home empty-handed after having spent his sisters' hard-earned remittances. "I don't want to stay in that house, that I know soon. But I want to stay in Kuwait City so I can see my sisters. I don't want to go home, see my angry father beat my little sisters. I want to make money to pay back my sisters, to send money home for my little sisters. I want to work hard, to make money, so we be free." He took a breath. "I want to be free from my father, but free for my sisters. I stay here to work, I want to find another job, make money, so my sisters and I can be free. I will go back to India, but not until I can be free."

When I met Gautam in 2013, he had absconded from his work with the family who had not paid him over six months of wages. In total, he had been working ten months, four as a shepherd and six as a cook, without receiving any pay at all. Though he wanted to return home to India, he had absconded and become a "freelancer" to support his sisters, knowing the risks this would entail. While he lived daily with the fear of being deported or sent back to the Iraqi border, his sense of familial duty outweighed these fears and motivated him to stay in Kuwait. The day I met him, he was in the office of the Indian labor attaché, attempting to recover his working papers so he could find new work. The labor attachés were sympathetic to Gautam's situation but encouraged him to return to the family from whom he had run away, to agitate for his wages. They explained that they could facilitate contact between him and his sponsors, but Gautam did not want to return to the family. He reflected on his current situation of being an absconder and now needing to enter the informal economy. He wanted to find new work that would pay him quickly so that he could work for a few years and return home. He explained that he would do whatever was necessary to be with his sisters. "Everyday I'm thinking about my sisters. I am thinking even I can go work as a shepherd, which is very hard for me, but I can do it, just for them. I won't go home now, but when I do go home, I will go with my sisters, and that day, we will never leave India again."

ı ı ı

Ava's story was similar. She had left the Philippines in 2011 at the urging of her mother after her father died and left the family deeply in debt. Ava graduated from college with a BA in sociology. She had wanted to begin nursing school, but her mother told her they did not have enough money to pay for her to further her education, nor did they have enough to send her younger brother to college. "I thought it wasn't fair that I would get to go to college, but not my brother," she said. A petite woman in her mid-twenties with long brown hair that she wore in braids, Ava talked often about how much she missed her mother and brother. "I love my brother more than anything, anything in the whole world. So, even though it's hard for me to go clean homes and leave my home, I decided I will do it."

Ava paid 16,000 pesos, around USD$350, to secure her migratory journey and gain employment as a domestic worker in Kuwait. She was placed in the home of a local family and had to learn very quickly about managing household affairs. "I tell you, I was supposed to be a nurse. I didn't know cleaning. I had to learn how to clean the toilets, how to clean the kitchen. And my madam, she not like me too much. She is asking me all the time, 'Why I get a stupid maid? Why you don't know how to clean?' and she is getting angry with me a lot." Her face grew sad when she spoke of her employer.

After four months in Kuwait, Ava finally managed to convince her employers to allow her to obtain a cell phone. Her employer told her that the money for the phone would be taken out of her paycheck. "Always she tells me that, with everything. She is always telling me, 'I take that out of your paycheck Ava, I take this out of your paycheck.' Like even the sanitary things, pads and toothpaste, you know? I am smart, I remember when I take my contract, she supposed to buy me those things, but no. Sometimes she doesn't buy at all. First month, no toothpaste. Second month, no pads. I am getting blood everywhere and she is getting angry with me for making a mess. I tell her, 'You don't want mess, buy me pads.' She says 'Okay, but it's coming out of your paycheck.' But then what paycheck?" The day she got her cell phone, she called her brother back home to see if the money was being deposited into his account. Much to her chagrin, she learned that despite working day and night for four months, sleeping on the floor of the children's room, not a single dollar had been deposited into the account.

"That day I'm crying too much. I cry for me, yes. But more for my brother. What he do? I am working here, but no money. My mom no money, so my brother no college," she said, her eyes filled with tears. Ava wanted to leave that day and return home. "When I hear his voice, when I hear my brother's voice, I am missing him too much. I am wanting to go home, hug him, tell him I will find a way. But if I go home, then what? No work at home, no money. I think, don't be stupid Ava, you must stay here, you must find a way to make money."

While in Kuwait, Ava had met several other OFWs during the occasional Fridays she was given off to attend church. Several of these friends had absconded from their work as domestic workers for local families. While some had entered the sex industry, others had found employment working as nannies, cooks, or domestic workers for nonlocal families. Technically, noncitizens cannot sponsor employees in Kuwait (though this is not the case in the UAE, thus contributing to the comparatively higher desirability of the UAE as a migratory destination over Kuwait), and therefore they often work through agencies and middlemen when looking for help inside the home. Some families, however, had begun posting advertisements and spreading the word by way of informal networks, such as church gatherings or through community leaders. Because they did not contract the work through agencies, they claimed to offer higher wages. When Ava told her church friends of the situation with her brother and her desire to return home, her friends encouraged her to stay in Kuwait but go "freelance." One of them even said that she knew of a Jordanian family who were looking for a nanny and would pay well.

Ava recalled her uncertainty about the decision before her. On the one hand, she wanted to return to the Philippines to see her family again and be near her brother. On the other, she wanted to support her brother and make her family proud. She, like many migrants I have met over the years, did not want to return home empty-handed, leaving her family further in debt. "I also am afraid, I hear stories about bad things happening. My madam, she yells at me sometimes, but she not hit me, not yell a lot. Sometimes, she is very good with me, and the kids I love, they very good. But I know I must make money, for my brother." One night, she recalls, after putting the kids to bed and hugging them, she took pictures of the little boy and girl with her cell phone. She had grown to really love the children and knew she would miss them, but she felt she would have to take a chance with another family, one who would pay her well, in the hope of being able to return home to see her brother more quickly.

Ava became illegal the day she ran away. At first things went very well for her. The Jordanian family who were her new employers were very kind to her. They taught her how to cook and clean, and she got along well with the two little boys who were her charges. She was even given her own room and one day off per week. For the first nine months she worked for the family, she was paid KD$75, roughly USD$330, per month, which she regularly sent home to her family. The male head of household, whom Ava referred to as her *baba*,[2] often complimented her on her cooking and regularly told her how grateful he and the family were for her assistance. One day, however, the female head of household took notice of her husband's attention to Ava. "I think she is angry when my *baba* nice to me, because after she hear him say 'thank you,

Ava,' she tell me my pay will now be KD$10 less per month, down to KD$65, but I don't know why."

After this, things went from bad to worse for Ava. When the male head of household was away, Ava's madam began abusing her. "She make me clean without gloves so my hands hurt. She pour Clorox in my hair to make me hurt and smell bad, and then she put Clorox even in my shampoo!" Ava asked her madam why she was treating her so badly. "What I do? I am thinking. She tell me I am not fast, I clean too slow. She tell me I cook bad. She tell her sons to throw things at me, to hit me. And she know I am not legal so it is not easy for me to go and complain."

Because Ava was still being paid KD$65 per month, she remained with her increasingly abusive madam, hoping to save enough money to return home and repay her debt. After six months of daily harassment by the madam and her children, however, Ava felt she could no longer remain in Kuwait. "I work hard, I send a lot of money home to my brother, but I can't stay anymore. I called my brother and said, 'Forgive me, brother, I hope I give you enough money to start college. I promise I find a way to give you more.'" Tears streamed down her face. Ava ran away from her employers and sought refuge in the embassy of the Philippines, where she had been living for over three months when I met her in 2103. She said she felt safe in the shelter but frustrated because she was away from her family and not earning any money. "They are good to me here, they take me, even though I have no papers, they take me and they trying to fix my papers now." She was hoping to return home as soon as possible and determined not to leave the Philippines again without her younger brother.

ı ı ı

As scholars such as Leisy Abrego and Deborah Boehm have noted, many migrants define and redefine their sense of family through and within migration (Abrego 2014; Boehm 2012). Narratives of sacrifice and familial duty contour migrants' construction of the "family" and function as major decision-making factors throughout the migratory journey. Whether we read these narratives as stories of sacrifice or as tales of the bonds of familial duty, it is important to recognize that while the state(s) plays a major role in structuring the many challenges migrants face, familial ties keep many migrants like Gautam and Ava in less than ideal working conditions. Neither Gautam nor Ava was kidnapped or forcibly taken from his or her home. For both of them, as for many other migrants, it was their family and the needs of various family members that impelled them to migrate, in order to fulfill their familial duties. While both Gautam and Ava faced inflexible economic citizenship regimes, they were constantly exercising their agency (flexibility) as they looked for creative ways to make their situations viable so that they could earn money to send home. Their ties to their families kept their minds and hearts firmly back home in the sending country and prevented them from ever feeling really settled in the Gulf. They were both adamant that their sojourn in the Gulf was temporary only and that they wanted to return home soon.

But while some migrants move between home and host country out of a commitment to familial duty, others are born to migrant parents while their mothers and/or fathers are in the host country. A new generation of migrants are growing up without a real sense of "home"—inflexible citizens of sending countries they have never seen, their mobility and agency thus restricted by the decision of their parents to remain in countries where citizenship is not an option. Many migrants who have children in the host country indicate that they stay in complex migratory situations, often working in subpar positions, out of a sense of duty toward their children. They say they want their children to have better lives and more opportunities than they would have in the sending country. This contributes to a sense of liminality, as some feel their loyalties torn between their "home" and "host" countries. The children, however, complain that they are being raised in situations where they are viewed as second-class citizens. These ties and tensions between migrants and their children further affect the subjectivity and agency of those involved. Many of those with whom I spoke discussed how family ties or familial duty structures the decisions they make, not only about staying or going but also about the type of employment they undertake. As Sabrina Marchetti and Alessandra Venturini have confirmed in their article "Mothers and Grandmothers on the Move" (2014), the age of migrants and their role in their families have an impact on mobility patterns and choices of employment.

Citizens without a Home

Dilip, age seventeen, was born and raised in the UAE but is quick to remind me, "Dubai is not home, only home for now." His father migrated from India to Dubai to work as a manager on a major hotel construction project. At the time, Dilip's mother, Dipti, stayed behind in India to raise Dilip's two older siblings. Dilip's father was hardworking and entrepreneurial. Although he started out living in a labor camp and working as a manager among many others, he quickly rose through the ranks and was able to move into a small studio apartment next door to the labor camp where he had been living with seven other men in a room. After working in the UAE for four years, Dilip's father was able to make enough money to sponsor his wife and two children to join him abroad. "In this way, I knew we are always lucky, many Indians can never bring over their families, but my dad could, my dad did. Like that, we are a success story, all of us together. All of us in the Emirates, no one left behind in India." His mother was quick to add, however, that she did not want to move. "I was happy in India, but it was hard without my husband. So when he said come, I felt, I have no choice, I must come."

Six months after moving to Dubai, Dipti became pregnant with Dilip. After her son was born, she and her husband decided that she would have to find work in order to help support the family. Dilip's father was making a decent wage, but much of his earnings had gone toward processing the necessary fees for family reunification. Now the family needed more money to make ends meet in the increasingly expensive host country. Unfortunately, however, the family reunification visa on which Dipti had traveled prevented her from gaining official employment. Though she had worked as a travel agent back in India, she was relegated to working informally as a domestic worker for various citizen and noncitizen families.

"I don't like this work," said Dipti, smoothing out the wrinkles in her red sari and brushing off the dirt that had accumulated on her clothes during her day's work. "I don't like to clean houses and cook and always cook and cook and cook. I went to school. I want to work in an office, in a respectable job. But here in Dubai, no. It's not possible." Still, she considers herself lucky in being able to bring in a steady income to help her children and family. "I know that I am lucky. My work, it's my choice. I don't live with the families. I go, clean the house, cook the food, and then leave. I come home to my own family. And I don't wear uniform, I still wear my sari. I don't want them to take that from me. I wear my sari, I don't wear uniform, I wear sari so they know I am from India and I am proud. I'm staying in Dubai until Dilip turns eighteen and then we all go, we go home to India, and we don't come back here." Dipti's insistence on wearing her sari to preserve her identity was a common theme among many of my interlocutors. While scholars such as Neha Vora have argued that new forms of identity are created in Dubai, particularly within the Indian community, part of that new identity for people like Dipti is a preservation of the old. Furthermore, having agency over her attire, insisting on not living with her employers, and setting her own work schedule is an important part of Dipti's subjectivity. This insistence could be read either as a "weapon of the weak" or as a strategy to negotiate her own sense of liminality, living in a space that is far from home (Scott 1985).

At the mention of the word "home," Dilip's ears perk up. He has been busy helping his mom clear the dishes from a delicious meal of dosas. The dinner table is crammed into a corner of their small one-bedroom apartment that is filled with brightly colored fabrics, pillows, and cushions decorated in a style that Dipti calls "modern India chic." The heavenly aroma of spices hangs in the air as Dipti and her husband recline into the cushions on the floor, weary from a long day of work. "Mom," Dilip says, his voice trembling slightly, "I hate when you talk about 'home,' always this talk of 'going home.' But where is home? I'll give you a map, you show me my home! You say India is home, but I was born here." It is clear that this is a much-discussed topic in the household, and everyone becomes uneasy at Dilip's outburst. Dipti rises from the cushions to walk toward her sixteen-year-old son, who towers over her. She takes the dishes from him and motions for him to join us on the cushions, while she begins preparing the tea and dessert.

"India is my home," Dipti says, carrying a tray of rose-scented desserts. "It's not perfect, not a perfect home at all, I don't mean that. And there are good things about Dubai." "But you never talk about those good things," Dilip interjects. "You always complain of cleaning houses, being treated badly, like second- or third-class citizens. You complain about the food, how it's tasteless. You complain that our house here is so small. That your brothers and sisters are far away. So, what am I supposed to think?" Dilip's voice rises once again.

"Look," says Dipti, "I know that India is hard for you. You aren't used to it there. It seems dirty to you, and the roads are bad. I see those things. I also see that in some ways I have more freedom here [in Dubai]. I can do whatever I want, no family to answer to, and in some ways it's safer." Dipti tries to calm her son. "But it's not really safe," her son responds. "I never really feel comfortable here, because I know that I'm not wanted here, you always tell us to look over our shoulders. Always waiting for something bad to happen. Watch ourselves. We have stayed a long time, but we weren't supposed to, not if the locals had their way." Dipti nods and a silence hangs in the air as everyone sips their tea.

"I know India is supposed to be my home," Dilip finally says, "but I go there and I feel foreign. I don't know the roads, I get lost all the time. And I don't like the food, I am always getting sick." Dilip's words reflect a sense of liminality shared by many first- and second-generation migrants and immigrants across the world. I tell Dilip that many people share his feelings, myself included as I grapple with a liminal sense of Iranian-Americanness. Dilip nods, but seems frustrated. "Yes, but the difference between you and I, and me and many other people, is that we know eventually, when we turn eighteen we *have* to leave. Or we can't work here. We can't stay here. We are sent home, to a home that we don't know. And then we are stuck there. I have felt stuck here in Dubai all my life. Angry at my parents for raising me in a country where I'm a second-class citizen. But now I'm worried that I have to leave. Where am I going to go?"

After that night, both Dilip and Dipti referred to this thought-provoking conversation many times. Dipti reflected on the challenges she faced as a mother, working in undesirable conditions to provide for her children. "You don't know how sad it makes me when I know that Dilip isn't happy here," Dipti said to me the next morning as we strolled along the Dubai creek near the bazaar. "I sacrifice everything for them. I work on my hand and knees, sometimes I'm not getting paid even, sometimes the madam yells at me so much I think she is going to hit me. And for what? For my children. To give them a better life here. I stay, I tolerate abuse, screaming, working on my hand and knees for them. Of course I want to go home, I miss India. There I am somebody, here I am nobody." She wrung her sari in her hands as she stared out across the creek. A *dhow* (an old-style boat) full of South Asian–looking men arrived and began walking past us. Dipti motioned to the men as she spoke again. "Look at them, probably Indian, probably from my hometown. My brothers. Abused, treated like animals. Yet we stay. We stay for our children. When they are not happy, it is the worst of insults."

ı ı ı

Dipti's narrative of sacrifice is similar to what many of my interlocutors articulated and what other scholars who write about transnational parenting, such as Leisy Abrego, Rhacel Parreñas, and Geraldine Pratt have observed. While some understood their sense of familial duty as a welcome sacrifice and a way to express agency, others experienced the sacrifice as a burden, constraining their agency. For his part, Dilip felt that he was making sacrifices for his parents as well. "I get so mad at my mom," Dilip said when I spoke with him several days later. "She always tells me that she stayed here for me. That she hates it, but she stays for me. But it's me who stayed for her." He had finished school for the day and was going to play soccer with his friends. On his way, he had stopped at the mall to purchase new shoes. His father had given him an extra allowance this week for his help around the house. He decided to use the money to replace the cleats he had worn out many months ago.

"Do you know how many times *I* have wanted to leave?" he said. "I didn't want to live in Dubai always, I got tired of always being different from the Emirati boys. Knowing that we had to be careful, every step we took. Knowing that if we ever got in trouble that it would be trouble for everyone in our families. We knew we even shouldn't play soccer with the Emirati boys because we always had to let them win. And we were better than them, even though they had newer shoes and uniforms all the time. And we are always reminded we don't belong here. I always wanted to go somewhere I belonged. But where? It's not India, but soon I will be sent there because the Emirati government thinks that is my home, but it's not."

The conversation between Dilip and Dipti reveals the complexities faced both by migrant parents and by this new generation of children, born in countries where they do not and cannot attain legal citizenship because of the inflexibility of citizenship regimes in the UAE and other countries where citizenship can only be attained through parents who are citizens. Although there is a large and growing literature about first- and second-generation children, much of it does not pertain to Dilip because he has been born and raised in a country where he will not be allowed to remain. Both Dilip and Dipti, albeit at different points in their lives, feel trapped and immobilized; both feel that their choices are limited. Yet at the same time both experience the frustration of forced migration: Dipti, forced to migrate by the decision made by her husband; Dilip, facing the impending doom of being sent "home" at the age of eighteen, to a "home" that he does not understand and cannot experience as such.

The question of citizenship also weighed heavily on their minds. Dipti articulated a need to maintain her identity, to counter her inability to attain citizenship in the country in which she had been living for almost two decades with an assertion of her "Indianness." Though Neha Vora has argued that Indian migrants in Dubai forge a new sense of "Indianness" (Vora 2013), for many mothers such as Dipti this is not the case. While they do renegotiate their sense of belonging and subjectivity, this is in constant tension with what they have left behind. For the new generation of children, however, the sense of belonging and "home" is complicated by not having experience with and within the "home" of their parents—a "home" that is eventually to be theirs as well.

For Dilip, being born and raised in a place that offered him no protections—legal, economic, social, or otherwise—was disturbing. This lack of legal citizenship, together with its attendant limitations, colored his experience daily. This is something that Vora has explored in depth in her work on Indian migrants in Dubai, looking at how they are able to negotiate economic citizenship in the face of formidable challenges. But for Dilip and others like him, negotiating his economic agency in Dubai seems as impossible as attaining legal citizenship. He feels that his forced mobility at the age of eighteen significantly restricts his economic citizenship. He also feels that his social citizenship is limited by his not being able to fully explore his agency in interactions with UAE citizens. These are challenges that Dipti feels daily as well—challenges that require flexibility but do not allow for flexible citizenship.

Both Dilip and Dipti (and possibly even Dilip's father) experience the environment of Dubai as rife with hostility and challenges to their ability to exercise the full spectrum of agency and citizenship rights. Dipti, lacking the right to choose her type of employment, must remain working in the sphere of domestic work or not work at all. She is in a constant state of anxiety because even though she works and contributes to the society around her, she does so in contravention of the law. Dilip remains anxious about his status as a second-class citizen, constantly aware that the country in which he was born and raised is not his home, that it would expel him if he should make a single misstep and will indeed expel him once he turns eighteen. The place in which they live, the country that Dilip calls "home" and to which Dipti has dedicated countless hours of her time and service, not only will not protect them but remains hostile to their presence.

Dilip and Dipti represent what Paul Dresch has termed a type of "foreign matter" in the eyes of the host country (Dresch 2006). As such, their bodies and movements are the focus of constant surveillance—which can be experienced as hostility—in order to ensure the security of the country's citizens. Migrant workers across the globe experience similar hostility as they struggle within other inflexible citizenship regimes. Furthermore, as parents and their children are immobilized in potentially hostile locales, they experience a collision between the politics of race, ethnicity, and class and the desire to fulfill familial duty. Thus immobilized at their destination by family ties, they must exercise flexibility in crafting a sense of home and family while abroad, even as the threat of being sent to a "not-home" looms large for the next generation of migrants.

From Inflexible Citizenship to Connected Lives

While the migrant workers who move along the global circuits of cosmopolitan destinations such as Dubai, Tokyo, Singapore, and Hong Kong have some things in common with their employers/clients, it is their differences that make my interlocutors "inflexible citizens." This class of migrants, like the flexible citizens they follow, must be flexible in adapting to new environments, new economies, and new encounters with the state. Unlike their counterparts, however, they do not hold multiple passports, cannot negotiate the protections of citizenship from their host country (or countries), and are treated as no more than lower-class citizens in their locales of employment, both the workplace and the nation. It is precisely their inability to access citizenship rights both at home (by obtaining gainful employment) and abroad that necessitates their flexibility in the face of inflexible regimes—their need to be flexible in terms of the type of work they do, the amount of time they spend away from home, and the new family configurations they create. The conundrum posed by an inflexible rights regime combined with the necessity for flexibility produces the most pressing challenges that migrants face. Robust responses to these challenges can be developed through the fine-grained analysis of the choices that migrants must make and understanding the multidimensionality of migrants' lives: their family structures, feelings of familial duty, and efforts to negotiate agency and citizenship.

Scholars such as Aihwa Ong and Christine Chin point to the important division between moneyed and nonmoneyed classes. This class division is made most obvious in the juxtaposition of "global talent" (Dresch 2006)—referring to higher-skilled migrants who are often termed "expats" in the Gulf—with a lower class of migrants who move in order to meet the demands of the global talent by providing them with what Ong (1999) refers to as "the good life." This classism is made all the more manifest because migrants often move seeking upward class mobility (which may or may not coincide with higher wages). The class of migrants termed "global talent," however, depend on a lack of upward mobility (and on lower wages) for low-skilled migrants in order to maintain their "good life." Thus, class immobility in the host country—which does not always correspond to lower wages or lack of mobility back in the sending country—for low-skilled migrants becomes yet another type of immobility with which migrants must contend in the host country (even though some transnational families are able to find class mobility through the remittances of one or more family members). While migration often leads to higher wages in the host country, as in the case of Dipti's family and many other examples throughout this book, this does not always bring about class mobility, as foreigners working in particular industries are deemed "working class" despite their wages or wage-earning potential. Families back in the sending countries, meanwhile, are able to enjoy some degree of class mobility (as has been the case for many of those discussed in earlier chapters), receiving remittances, moving out of their neighborhoods, sending their children to more elite schools, and obtaining higher levels of social capital. For most migrants in Dubai and Kuwait City, however, breaking through a class-based glass ceiling remains an unattainable goal. Often, certain arms of the state are aware of this phenomenon, and in their desire to attract global talent to cities trying to define themselves as "cosmopolitan" they turn a blind eye to the needs and desires of low-skilled migrants and the stark classism inherent in various migrant groupings.

Viviana Zelizer (2005) has argued against a "hostile worlds" approach that divides capital and intimacy into different spheres. By questioning received notions about the commodification of intimacy, Zelizer has pointed to the reality of what she terms "connected lives," which refers to the ways people define their rights and responsibilities when the spheres of intimacy and capital overlap. Her work focuses on the economic aspects of intimate lives, not just within the sphere of intimate labor but also in terms of familial ties and intimate aspects of economic life. In the "connected lives" approach, a focus on the intertwining of economics with family lives, duties, and protections better represents the many "connected" layers of migrant experiences. Looking at how migrants turn to the sphere of the intimate and familial realm to assert their agency can help to animate the lives of migrants whose identities have been flattened by discourses and policies that adopt the "hostile worlds" approach. Migrants are not flat, one-dimensional beings but rather complex, agentive subjects with connected lives who employ flexibility in the face of extreme inflexibility. As the stories related here demonstrate, migrants must make a series of complex decisions from a series of options that is often limited. For many, their own intimate lives structure their economic potential and the choices they make. Only by recognizing these choices—the "connected lives" of multidimensional migrants—can agency be maintained and the complexity of their lives understood.

The intimate lives of migrants are impacted in many ways by the experiences of migration. Some of these migrants, like Dilip and his family, exist somewhere in the liminal space between immigrant and migrant as they negotiate their sense of belonging and home. They demonstrate extreme flexibility in the face of inflexible regimes as they seek to explore and manage their intimate lives while reconstituting the notion of family. Others, like Lucinda, struggle to find their way and make a new home in and through migration but ultimately feel more connected to the host country because of the opportunities available. Still others, like Ava and Gautam, find their hearts and minds firmly bound to their families in the sending country, so that home is always where their families are. For these individuals, their time in the Gulf is experienced as a major interruption in their lives, one that they hope will end very soon. Thus the liminal space between considering oneself a migrant or an immigrant—which is fluid for many people like Lucinda—is connected to migrants' own intimate ties and subjectivities. Many people struggle to define themselves in relation to a home even as they struggle to define "home" in and through migration and the mobilities it offers or prohibits. It is in the liminal spaces of im/migration and im/mobility, together with the flexible responses to this liminality, that the many layers of the migrant experience can begin to be understood.

4

CHANGING HOME/S

There is a growing understanding that migration can help people move out of poverty. But this strategy works better for some migrants, and in some places, than others. The Consortium's research is identifying the factors at household, community, and macro levels which affect migration and poverty.

Migrating Out of Poverty RPC mission statement

For me it wasn't like I was starving at home. I left because I wanted to get away. I had to get away from my family, and mostly from him [intended husband].

Interview with Supriya, Indian domestic worker, twenty-two, Dubai, July 2013

Simple and not simple. If I stay (at home) I am miserable, living with that man, living that life. But when I leave, I am free. Divorce is not an option in my culture. So I left.

Interview with Gladys, Filipina care giver, thirty-seven, Singapore, September 2014

I moved to Dubai because I wanted to explore who I was. I couldn't do that at home in the Philippines; I couldn't fully be me. I moved away to dance, and I didn't look back.

Skype interview with Yudi, Filipino dancer, twenty-two, living in Dubai, October 2014

THE SAME BONDS OF LOVE that may compel some to migrate owing to a sense of familial duty may compel others to migrate in order to escape familial or communal obligations. Some migrate in search of work in order to support their families and loved ones back home. Others, however, feel stifled by their loved ones and elect migration in order to explore their intimate subjectivities. The migrants whose stories are told in this chapter chose to migrate in search of a kind of intimate mobility they could not find at home. While they doubtless migrated in search of economic prosperity and upward class mobility as well, social reasons were first and foremost among the decision-making factors impelling them to migrate. These young women and men describe wanting to migrate not in order to escape poverty or to support their families, but in order to leave their families and communities altogether. They have migrated away from unwanted or arranged marriages, familial pressures, or social contracts that require them to perform within communal expectations. Such migrants may search for love or adventure abroad, hoping to form new intimate bonds away from the watchful and sometimes censorious eyes of their social communities. Others may feel they can only express their sexualities in a space where they will not bring shame on their families. Still others may wish to escape from uncomfortable situations at home, such as the formation of blended families with new step-parents and/or siblings. These migrations in search of emotional and social mobility may also result in upward class mobility for the families back home. This type of migration exemplifies how intimate mobilities put into play the relationship between mobility and immobility in the intimate lives of im/migrants whose migratory journeys take them in search of a new home or sense of home.

The desire to migrate in search of love, adventure, or "freedom" (as indicated in the quotation from Gladys at the beginning of this chapter) can be just as salient a "push" factor as the economic necessity for making ends meet. Thus migrants should not be categorized artificially according to one particular reason or another for their migration; many people migrate for multiple reasons, including economic, social, *and* intimate mobility. The formation of new ideas about home, family, the self, sexuality, and intimacy is an integral part of intimate mobility. Within migration, many individuals find the opportunity to rethink their intimate selves, develop new identities, and reconstitute their idea of "home." The role of migration in encouraging the exploration of subjectivity, masculinity, and femininity may be better understood by paying attention to these complex decision-making processes.

In conversations about migration in the Gulf these intimate reasons for migration have been eclipsed by a focus on rights abuses and the types and circumstances of migrant labor. Specifically, much media attention focuses on human trafficking in places such as the UAE or on the abuse of laborers working under the *kefala* system throughout the GCC. While these abuses certainly take place and certainly merit attention, here we shall look at migrants whose

journeys to Gulf cities like Dubai and Kuwait City have afforded them an opportunity to move away from problematic situations back home, which are not
always tied to poverty. In following migrants as they explore their changing
notions of "home" while physically changing their home, we can come to ap-
preciate the opportunities that migrants may find abroad that were not available to them back in their sending countries. We can also see how family, which
is a source of strength and support for many migrants and for which many
are willing to make sacrifices, may also be felt as a constraint by others—not
because these others feel a need to support their families or keep them safe and
connected, but because to stay home with their family is felt to be unsafe.

ı ı ı

In subtle and not so subtle ways, looking at migrants who seek to move away
from the family or community both advances and problematizes notions of the
social contract. Some political philosophers such as Jean Jacques Rousseau define
the social contract as a type of implicit agreement among and between members
of a society to engage in mutually beneficial cooperation (Rousseau 2002). What
constitutes "cooperation" and what types of power relations are embedded in
this "agreement" are the subject of much scholarly debate among sociologists,
anthropologists, and political theorists. In challenging social contract theory,
scholars such as Pierre Bourdieu question the construction of the social contract
and the resulting aftermath of power imbalance within and between societies or
communities. While the definitions, uses, and expectations of the social contract
have been contested, its existence has not.[1] That there are responsibilities (and
rewards) woven into social relations—familial or otherwise—is salient in understanding migrants' decisions to escape the social contract. The social contract in
the form of familial or communal duties and expectations operates as a type of
constraint for many of my interlocutors, who see more drawbacks than benefits
involved in full participation in the community. Some reject the social contract
altogether and thus migrate in search of a space where their only obligations are
tethered to the sphere of the economic. Others see the social contract as a type of
surveillance, hindering the full exploration and expression of their identities—
sexual, social, or otherwise. They thus seek to evade the surveillance that they
view as intrinsic to the social contract by migrating in search of anonymity or
different sexual spaces where new types of contracts can be formed.

ı ı ı

As Neha Vora and Filippo and Caroline Osella have shown with respect to the Gulf in particular, many migrants forge new (stronger) senses of identity through migration to the UAE. One aspect of the construction of new migrant subjectivities is tied to economic prosperity, but the "money" part of their argument is only part of the construction of identity. Most of the Osellas' interlocutors are not "migrating out of poverty" per se but rather migrating *in* to new positions of power, new identities, and new subjectivities; money is only one small part of a much larger and intricate picture. Vora's work builds on that of the Osellas to explore the concepts of "belonging" and economic citizenship (Vora 2013). She shows that while Indian middle-class migrants may be constrained by economic citizenship, they are still able to forge new forms of social citizenship not available to them back home. In rethinking the ideas of "home" and "belonging" and exploring how migration may offer an important avenue for social mobility, I take the work of Vora and the Osellas, which describes subject formation in the Gulf, and extend it to the intimate lives of migrants in order to explore not just social and economic mobility but intimate mobility as well.

There is also an extensive body of work looking at "marital migration," referring to people who migrate in order to marry (or marry in order to migrate). Scholars such as Sara Friedman, Hyun Mee Kim, and Brenda Yeoh have been writing about marital migration in Asia for the past decade, and their work has been seminal in showing the complexities involved in marital migration, highlighting the many levels of agency that migrants and their partners deploy and engage with. There has also been a smaller though no less influential body of literature focused on sex workers and the role of love in motivating female migrant sex workers who seek to move with partners with whom they become involved. The work of anthropologists such as Denise Brennan and Sealing Cheng, as well as that of sociologist Rhacel Parreñas, provides excellent examples of studies that focus on migrant female sex workers' subjectivities as they engage with partners and potential partners. Here I add to this scholarship, which looks at the phenomenon of migrating in order to get married, by examining the experiences of those who migrate in order to *avoid* marriage.

Migrating Away from Marriage

"I had to leave, I felt I was being strangled at home. Not literally, of course, but I felt that I would not be who I am if I had married the man my family wanted me to marry," said Leela. Leela was born and raised in Mumbai in a solidly middle-class family (as defined by their income and education levels). Her father is a software engineer, her mother a schoolteacher. Leela herself graduated with a bachelor's degree in communication before deciding to migrate to Dubai to work as a domestic worker for a local family in 2011. Her parents did not—and still do not—agree with Leela's decision to migrate.

After Leela graduated from college, her family began pressuring her to marry. "But, they didn't want me to marry just anyone, it had to be someone *they* approved of," Leela explained. At one point during her college years she had met a man named Akash, and the two had fallen in love. When she told her parents of their relationship, they became angry and insisted she end it. "They said because he was of a lower caste or class than us. They said I should be marrying up, not marrying down," she said. Heartbroken, Leela ended her relationship with Akash and after graduating never saw him again. Her parents then began introducing Leela to men they found more suitable. "High-class men," as she described them, who did not always catch her fancy. One evening a young man came to visit Leela and her family. "He had very nice shoes. Very fancy shoes, that's what I remember most. I just peeked my head out and saw his shoes and decided I didn't want to come out of the room," she recalled. Her parents, however, were very impressed with this young man, who came from a considerably higher socioeconomic class than their own. Despite Leela's protests, they accepted his offer of marriage for their daughter. Devastated, Leela decided to migrate in order to escape the familial pressures that followed.

"I told my parents, there is no way I'm marrying that man with the flowery, fancy shoes. That's not me. I want a man who wears sandals. Simple. A good man. I don't want to live a life without love. But they did not want to listen to me." During this time one of Leela's friends who had migrated to Dubai in order to support her family began corresponding with her. Her friend told her of the excitement in Dubai and promised her that life in Dubai brought love, adventure, freedom, and economic prosperity. Inspired by her friend's stories, Leela sought out the same company that her friend had used and found a position as a domestic worker in Dubai. One week before her arranged wedding, Leela made the announcement that she was leaving the country. Her parents were angry, but she had made up her mind. "I knew that if I move to Dubai, my life would change. I would be in control of my own destiny. I would make my own money, and my own decisions. I wouldn't have to be bound by my family. And best of all, I wouldn't have to marry 'fancy shoes,'" Leela said emphatically.

"When I got on the plane, I felt the freedom. I felt I had wings. I felt I was going to finally start to live my life," Leela said. But her arrival in Dubai was anything but smooth. She was placed in the home of a family who withheld her wages and made her work twelve- to fourteen-hour days. At one point her female employer threatened to physically abuse her. Leela was afraid but determined to make the most of her situation. "It was hard at first in Dubai. My madam was so frightening. I was so frightened. But I thought, 'No, Leela, you are not going home, this is you now, you are going to stay and you are going to make it.' 'Make it work,' I told myself. So I did." She stayed with her first employer for three months, during which time she suffered occasional abuse. After three months, however, with the help of her friend and others whom she had met in Dubai, Leela was able to change employers.

Her new employers were much kinder to Leela, and she was given regular time off. During her days off she would wander around Dubai, occasionally visiting temples, the bazaar, or the beach. One day she met Mustafa, a Pakistani bank manager, and the two began spending time together regularly. "When I told my parents back home about Mus, they were even angrier than when I told them I'm leaving, but I didn't care. This is me now. I am finally living my life," Leela explained. Her family felt betrayed by Leela's decision to take up a relationship with a Pakistani man and pressured her to end the relationship. She adamantly refused to give in to their demands.

ı ı ı

Leela's experiences were similar to those of at least five other Indian women I met in Dubai. The familial pressure to "marry up" or use marriage as a strategy for social and economic mobility is not new, nor is it limited to Leela's situation or the situations of women in India. Many women describe facing the same type of familial pressure, even in contexts where arranged marriage is not necessarily common. Iranian, Arab, Pakistani, Malagasy, Ethiopian, Nigerian, and Filipina women I have met during my fieldwork have narrated similar stories. Some, like Leela, were able to resist the pressures of this aspect of the social contract through migration or other creative means. Others (like Sylvie, whose story is below) succumbed to familial pressure only to find themselves plotting an escape from a loveless or abusive marriage.

In Leela's case, her family's strategy for economic and social mobility would have immobilized her emotionally. She felt she would be "stuck," as she often said, and decided that the best way to ensure her own freedom of mobility was to migrate. It is important to note that Leela was not from among the lowest classes in India nor was she plucked out of a village and forced to work as a domestic worker in the Gulf. Instead, she viewed migration to the Gulf, even into low-skilled labor, as a strategy for her own upward emotional and social mobility. As Leela said many times, migration was a major part of crafting a different type of subjectivity and defining herself against her family. Her often-repeated phrases "this is me now" and "I'm finally living my life" indicate the creation of an authentic self within and through migration. This is something that many interlocutors alluded to in reflecting on their decisions to migrate.

ı ı ı

Sylvie had experienced similar types of familial pressure to marry. Born and raised in Antananarivo, the capital of Madagascar, Sylvie was the eldest of three daughters, and her parents were adamant that her marriage be to a man of a particular class and clan in order to set the stage for her younger sisters. "They said I had to marry Philippe [her husband] because if I didn't, then my sisters wouldn't be able to get a good match. So even though he disgusted me, I married him," Sylvie explained. She was married at the age of nineteen, but by the age of twenty-four Sylvie was ready for divorce.

Sylvie described her marriage as the most difficult aspect of her life. Her husband had gambling and drinking problems. When microcredit programs were introduced to Madagascar, Philippe pressured Sylvie to take out a loan, reasoning that women were more likely to be approved than men. "I still don't know why, but a lot of people said that these loaners liked to give to women more than men. So the husbands pressured a lot of wives like me," she recalled. Giving in to her husband's increasing demands, Sylvie sought out and was granted a microcredit loan to start a clothing business. Shortly after receiving the money, Philippe drained her account, spending the money on alcohol and gambling. A few months later, Sylvie found herself in the difficult predicament of needing to start paying back her loan and being pressured to show proof of her business. Because her husband had taken all of her money, however, she was slow to open the clothing stand she had promised to run. To add to her financial troubles, Philippe became increasingly demanding and abusive. "He would tell me I needed to work to bring him money. If I didn't sell anything from my little stand, he would beat me," she said. Fortunately, she was able to work hard, open her clothing stand, and pay back her microcredit loan. Her clothing business started booming, but she was resentful of her husband, who took all of her profits, leaving her with little money to spare.

After a severe beating following an argument with Philippe, Sylvie decided she could no longer live with him. But when she returned to her parents' home to ask for help and support in her decision to leave her husband, she was told to go back to him and "work it out"; her father even threatened physical abuse. Unsure where to go, Sylvie decided to migrate abroad, reasoning that distance would provide her safety from both her husband and her parents. She had heard of work opportunities in Kuwait and Dubai and sought out a recruiting firm for assistance. In a matter of only a few days, Sylvie sold her clothing stand, paid her recruiters, and moved to Kuwait, all without saying goodbye to her husband or family.

"Divorce is not an option for many of us," Sylvie said, reflecting on her decision to migrate. She described her life in Kuwait as "quiet but safe." She worked long hours as a seamstress but said that she enjoyed the work and was happy to live abroad. Though her pay was not high and her living quarters cramped, with seven women to one room, she felt that her decision to migrate had been the "right decision." When Sylvie spoke of Philippe, she always lowered her voice, explaining that no one in Kuwait knew of her husband back home. "I'm not telling anyone that I was married, or that I have a husband back home, I want to keep my options open," she said. Sylvie said that she told everyone that she had migrated to support her parents back home but that she had never disclosed her primary motivation. "I don't want people to think bad of me, if I tell them I left to get away from a man. I want people to think I'm good. I'm doing this to support my family. Even though I'm here because of me." Sylvie's family, initially angered by their daughter's departure, became supportive of her once they began receiving remittance checks. Her decision to migrate became a source of pride for her family back home, who had previously been ashamed of their daughter's failed marriage.

ɪ ɪ ɪ

Migrating away from marriage was a common theme for over a dozen of my interlocutors, who indicated that migration was a better solution to a failed marriage than divorce. Several women echoed Sylvie's comment about divorce not being an option because of cultural, social, and/or familial pressures. Migration then becomes a desirable alternative for both the migrants as well as their families, all of whom can subscribe to the "sacrifice" narrative that the women migrated in order to support their families. This allows families to save face with their home communities, while migrant women, like Sylvie, reproduce this narrative abroad in order to obtain social capital within their new communities. Thus migration turns a failed marriage into a story of success and sacrifice, allowing the migrant to reconstruct her subjectivity, while also allowing for the maintenance of family ties. Additionally, migration gives women such as Sylvie an opportunity for social and emotional mobility and an avenue for reinventing themselves abroad.

Migrating Away from Motherhood

"It isn't nice to say this, but I left because I could not stay home with my kids anymore. I had to go," Gabriella said, her voice almost a whisper. I had known Gabriella for many years, and it wasn't until my most recent trip to Dubai in 2013 that she felt comfortable talking about her family back home. She had always vaguely alluded to migrating for financial reasons: "to make money, to support my family," she would say. But this conversation was different. I had been telling her about my recent book project and the focus on ways in which people become immobilized in the host country because of their families. As I was telling her about my theory that people's intimate lives become immobilized when they are away from their families, I saw a mischievous smile cross her face. When I asked her what she was smiling about, she suddenly became serious and looked over her shoulder before responding.

"It is not like that for me, Miss. It's maybe the opposite. When I left the Philippines, that's when I'm feeling like my life is beginning, like really beginning," Gabriella said. She then spoke of the guilt and shame she felt over being happier living away from her children, even while she missed them. "It is not like I don't miss them, and I love them of course. But I could not stay home to take care of them. Could not be a mom, it just was not for me," she explained. Then, after a moment of reflection, she added, "I mean, I am a mom. I always will be, but I am a better mother when I am away from them. When I am working here to support them."

Gabriella, like many other OFWs I met, left her two children in the care of her mother back in Manila when she decided to move to Dubai in 2008. Between 2008 and 2013 she had made only one trip back to the Philippines to visit her family. I had always assumed that she did not return for financial reasons or perhaps that her employers were not generous with giving her time off. I later learned that Gabriella had one month of paid vacation every year, during which time she often traveled to other parts of the Middle East (she had visited Oman, Yemen, and Lebanon, as well as the Iranian island of Kish during her time in Dubai). Prior to this conversation, I had not known this about Gabriella, and I encouraged her to elaborate on her reasons for choosing to travel locally instead of returning home. "It is not that I don't want to see my children, it's more that going home is so difficult. Filled with so many emotions," she explained. Gabriella mentioned familial pressures to support the family and return home bearing large numbers of gifts and money for numerous family members. She also noted that upon her return, her mother and others in her community made her feel guilty for having migrated abroad, even though they were enjoying the fruits of her labor.

"Going home for me, it, it hurts my heart," said Gabriella. "Everyone wants something from me, and everyone wants to give me advice. And when I am home, I cannot enjoy my children because I'm feeling bad about myself all the time," she added. Gabriella expressed a confusing sense of both guilt and relief about her decision making. She explained that she felt "more like myself" when in Dubai and felt "out of place" back home in Manila. For these reasons and more, it was more appealing to Gabriella to spend her vacation time in the Middle East rather than going back home. When she did return home, she only felt a stronger need to keep migrating and to work harder to renew her contract. As of 2013, she had no desire to return to Manila.

It is not easy to analyze Gabriella's sentiments and experiences, despite the fact that I heard at least four people from other parts of the world tell me versions of this same story between 2013 and 2014. It was difficult for Gabriella to speak of experiencing her family, and motherhood in particular, as a source of constraint, and it is difficult to theorize because it challenges our notions of the family. Yet it is indubitably the case that many women (and likely men, too) experience their families as constraining them in regard to their movements or decision-making capacities. While familial expectations impel some, in order to support family back home, to remain in migratory situations in which they undergo abuse, others, like Gabriella, feel compelled to stay away from home because they experience life at home, or even a visit home, as a challenge to their agency and sense of self.

Gabriella's story highlights the need for a nuanced understanding when exploring the migratory narrative. On the one hand, her story should not be read as corroborating the trope of the "bad migrant mother," since it fails to capture the ways in which she supports her family as well as herself. Migration enables Gabriella to provide her family with many opportunities and to explore facets of her own identity that she feels were stifled at home. On the other hand, her story challenges problematic and racialized stereotypes of Filipina women in particular as "maternal and loving," which are perpetuated in migrant-receiving countries where Filipinas are viewed as being among the most desirable employees in fields of intimate labor. Her story points to the many layers of identity that migrant women embody and highlights the need to contextualize migrants within their intimate lives rather than reducing them to the circumstances of their labor or migration.

ı ı ı

Amina's case is similar to Gabriella's in that both women found themselves caught in what Nicole Constable terms the "migratory cycle of atonement" (Constable 2013, 2014). Constable uses this term to refer to cases in which migrant women in particular feel a need to continue migrating in order to cope with the guilt of migration. She argues that migrant mothers, particularly those who become pregnant overseas, often out of wedlock, are likely to become constant migrants, creating long-lasting situations of precariousness. The guilt and shame associated with returning home from the migratory journey via deportation as well as pregnant or with a child can lead many women to prefer to continue migrating rather than returning to their home country. They do so not only to support their newborn children but also in hopes of putting some space and distance between themselves and the families and communities that heighten their feelings of guilt. As in Leela's case, for these new mothers migration can help to mend relations with their families; the family can save face by creating a new narrative of sacrifice to replace the feelings of shame in the context of their community.

The outcome of Amina's case mirrors what Constable found in her research with migrant mothers in Hong Kong. Amina migrated from Indonesia to Dubai to work as a domestic worker for a local family. She was not forced to move, nor did she "migrate out of poverty." Instead, she desired to migrate to the Middle East in particular because she is a devout Muslim, and she felt that she would be "closer to God" if she could find a way to work in Saudi Arabia. Her hope was that after working in Dubai she would receive a posting in Mecca or Medina.

Upon her arrival in Dubai, Amina became close to a Jordanian associate of her employer's named Hassan, a very devout Muslim who offered to take her to their local mosque. Over time, the two became intimate. Amina said that they performed a religious marriage between the two of them (also referred to as *sigheh*, or temporary marriage), and for this reason she felt comfortable sleeping with Hassan. "He was the best man I knew. I felt that he was the man of my life. It never occurred to me that we would not be together," she explained. When Amina became pregnant, however, Hassan accused her of promiscuity and reported her to her employers. She was promptly imprisoned for breach of contract and the crime of *zina*. While some pregnant migrant women remain in prison long after they give birth, awaiting the results of their trial, Amina's trial was fairly quick and she was sent home to Indonesia after two months of incarceration. By the time she arrived home, she was seven months pregnant.

"Some of the ladies in the jail, they said I was so lucky that I got to go home, but I did not feel this way. I felt I didn't want to go home. I wanted to stay in Dubai, to find Hassan," Amina said. She was convinced that once Hassan saw the baby, he would change his mind and "do a proper marriage" with her, especially given how devout they both were. She was certain that he would come to his senses and realize that the child was no doubt his, and that he would take responsibility for both of them. "But I never got this chance. I'm sent back to Jogja (Yogyakarta), back to my family, with a big belly and many tears." When she arrived, her parents were furious and would not permit her to return to the familial home. With the help of some friends at her local mosque, she found a shelter, where a midwife helped her safely deliver her son. A few weeks after her son was born, Amina gathered her courage to visit her parents once again. "That was a very hard thing for me," she recalled, adding, "I didn't know how to go to my parents' home, but I knew that the shelter is no place for this baby, so I did it for him."

This time her parents were more welcoming. After seeing the little boy, they allowed Amina to move back into her old room, and her mother began assisting her with the baby. But Amina increasingly felt the weight of familial shame as the months passed. "When people would come to visit my family, they would hide me. They took him [the baby] out and said he was an orphan they had adopted, but no one ever mentioned my name, and this was hard," Amina said. One evening when she was getting ready for bed, her parents approached her and asked her what her "plan" was. "They said, 'Amina, how are you going to live your life? How are you going to give your son a good life?' I think they wanted me to go back to school or find work there in Jogja, but I felt I couldn't stay there anymore." After this conversation Amina decided to migrate once again. Though she aimed for the Gulf, the first position she found was in Singapore. She gladly took the opportunity to leave her parents behind. "It was hard to leave the baby, but I knew his life would be better with my parents, and without me," she explained. After three years in Singapore, Amina, like Gabriella, is adamant that she does not wish to return home anytime soon. "I like my life in Singapore, no more feeling bad about myself all the time, much less weight on me."

ı ı ı

Thus the "migratory cycle of atonement" to which Constable refers can often keep migrant mothers migrating. Gabriella's and Amina's experiences are similar to those of over a dozen women with whom I spoke who referred to the challenges of motherhood and the attendant familial pressures as a major source of agentive constraint. These women found that in migration they were able to seek out the space they needed to explore different aspects of their intimate selves, space created when they were able to unburden themselves of the guilt and shame placed on them by their families. Their desire not to return home speaks to an important aspect of im/mobility, namely, *voluntary immobility*, wherein the migrant has no desire to return home yet no desire to become a permanent resident, either. This liminal space, together with its attendant benefits for women like Gabriella and Amina, merits more exploration in the literature on migration.

Coming Up and Coming Out

While some women described the attraction of migration as a way to alleviate shame or familial pressures around motherhood, others spoke of the desire to migrate in order to explore their sexualities and sexual subjectivities. Specifically, several women said that it was only away from the watchful eyes of families and communities that they could engage in nonheteronormative sexual relationships. Others were looking for sexual adventures without being categorized as promiscuous. For these young women, migration provided the space they needed to explore various aspects of their intimate identities.

Meneesha, like Leela, who was introduced earlier, was adamant that she wanted to move away from the familial expectations of marriage. I met her in 2009, when she was struggling with finding a way to come out to her parents. After years of pressure from her parents to marry, she decided to move from

New Delhi to Dubai to work as a seamstress, in order to put some distance between herself and her family. "I didn't know how to tell them, I just didn't know. And I wasn't totally sure. And I missed my chance to explore in uni [university] because I was studying so hard, so I wanted to explore," Meneesha said. She said that on many occasions she wanted to tell her parents that she was more interested in women than men but feared their reactions. When they started introducing her to possible marital candidates, Meneesha panicked. "Then, right before I decided to tell my parents (about her sexuality), I got a letter from this girl, this girl I had known at uni, and she was in Dubai. She was working in a clothes shop and invited me to join her. It felt like the gods were answering me." She decided to take her friend up on her offer to assist in referring her to an agency that could facilitate her migration. The agency, however, charged a fee for its services, money that Meneesha herself did not have owing to the challenges she was facing in finding employment after graduation. She decided to approach her parents and ask for their help in financing her move.

"I told them, 'Look, I know we are having troubles here, so help me go to Dubai for just a few years, then I promise to return and marry.' I don't know why I promised that, it just seemed like the best way to get them to help me." Her parents were hesitant at first, but her mother, tired of arguing with her daughter about everything from her attire to her comportment to her choice of recreational activities, decided it might be a good idea for Meneesha to gain some work experience abroad, provided that she followed through on her promise to marry upon her return. "I think my mother thought Dubai would cure me of whatever she thought was wrong with me, but she couldn't have been more wrong," Meneesha reflected.

Meneesha moved to Dubai in 2009 and began work as a seamstress in a clothing shop close to the place of employment of the friend who had inspired her migration. She was given dormitory-style housing, with eight women to a room furnished with bunk beds and mattresses on the floor. Though her housing was much smaller and more cramped than her living quarters back home, Meneesha described her living situation as giving her more "space to explore." In this female-dominated space, she was able to meet and connect with several other women who were interested in the same type of sexual exploration that Meneesha was eagerly seeking. "It is really great here," Meneesha said. "All the women I meet, they are so open. No one judges, and lots of people are interested. I feel like it's OK to talk about my feelings and what I want, because a lot of people want that too."

When I last spoke with Meneesha, the return home that she and her parents had agreed upon was three years past due. "Sometimes when I call them, they get mad and tell me I have to come home, that I promised and everything. But I'm in no hurry, and I think, I think, maybe they aren't really in a hurry either. It's easier to have me here, and they know that I'm happier here, so we will see what happens," Meneesha said. As of August 2014, she had no plans to return to New Delhi.

ı ı ı

Charmilla, like Meneesha, described her migration to Dubai as motivated in large part by a desire to move away from her family in order to explore what she termed her "sexual side." I met Charmilla in the summer of 2009, just three months after she had moved to Dubai from Karachi, Pakistan. "Maybe it's a bit strange for you, but I moved to dance, and now I dance and move," she said one evening. She had just finished her shift at a local club in Bur Dubai where she worked as an entertainer, or what many Pakistanis back home would refer to as a "dancing girl." Charmilla was born and raised in Karachi in a middle-class family with many political ties: her uncle was a senator, and her father had various political ties as well. For this reason, she often felt herself to be in the limelight. "I felt I couldn't be me. I couldn't do or say anything I wanted to, I was always looking over my shoulder back in Karachi. Plus back in Pakistan, you know, everyone knows everyone, so everyone knows everything you do. It's like all public all the time," she explained, referring to her upbringing. The youngest of six children, Charmilla described her parents as "very strict." She remembered feeling she was constantly being watched by parents, aunts and uncles, and older siblings.

This constant scrutiny was a source of continual worry for her. "It's not like I was a 'bad girl' or something like that, you know? It's just that, well, I liked to have fun. And boys like me. And some girls too. But I couldn't really let loose, I was scared. Even though I wanted to." She began dating when she was in high school, but when members of her family found out that she was engaging in what they described as "improper behavior," such as fraternizing with the opposite sex, they punished and monitored her. "They kept saying, 'You want to bring shame on your family? You want all of us to lose everything we are working for?' But that's not why I was doing what I did. I just wanted to be me. To have fun. To enjoy my life with the people around me. But that just brought misery for everyone. Including me." After high school she announced

that she did not want to go to college but rather aspired to become a professional dancer. She had found a teacher willing to work with her to teach her
traditional Pakistani dances, and she hoped that after some training she would
be able to audition for roles in films. "When I said this to my parents, it was like
someone had been murdered. My mom kept saying, 'How could you do this to
me? What did I do wrong?' And I could never figure out why they thought that
I was doing this *to* them." But she didn't give up on her dreams; she enrolled
in dance classes despite her parents' objections. She promised her parents that
after a year of dance classes she would go to college, and it was because of this
agreement that they permitted her to leave the house at all.

During this time Charmilla had met and fallen in love with a young woman
from her high school named Aidah. This young woman, who was also a dancer,
began spending a lot of time with Charmilla; the two would often sneak into one
another's houses when they thought their parents were away. One afternoon,
however, Charmilla's eldest brother walked in on the two of them in bed without
their clothes on. After chasing Aidah out of the house, he began beating his sister.
When their parents came home, Charmilla's brother told them what he had seen.
Though Charmilla was badly bruised and bleeding from the beating she had
suffered at the hands of her brother, she was locked in her room for the next two
days without food or water, let alone medical attention. On the third day Aidah
returned to sneak back into Charmilla's room. When she heard about the ordeal
that her girlfriend had suffered, they decided that Charmilla would have to run
away. Aidah assisted the now weakened Charmilla to leave her family's house and
seek out their dance teacher. After staying two nights in the dance studio, where
she was able to regain her strength, Charmilla decided to move to Dubai.

"I'm not sure why I chose Dubai, just that I'd heard from my cousins that
people are more free there. I knew that if I could just get myself to Dubai,
that my life, my life could possibly be, you know, I had a chance of living my
life the way I wanted to." Aidah had promised that once Charmilla had moved
to Dubai, she would follow, and the two could resume their relationship away
from the watchful eyes of their families. "I remember Aidah saying she would
move to Dubai and we would get an apartment together on the beach. I remember in those days how perfect that sounded. And all of that, Aidah, and
my desire to be, well, free, all of that made me want to come here," Charmilla
explained, referring to her decision to move to Dubai.

Fortunately, Charmilla's dance teacher had connections with several entertainment agencies in Pakistan that were looking for "local talent" to send to the

Gulf. Charmilla auditioned and was offered the exact job she was hoping for at a club in Dubai. "A lot of people think like being a dancing girl is shameful. They can't believe that it's something I really wanted to do. That it was something I dreamed of." When I asked her to elaborate, she continued: "Because it's like, I can finally dance the way I want. I *like* dancing sexy. I like being on stage. I like the costumes. And that's it. I dance, that's all I do. And I can live my life and be free the rest of the time." Charmilla moved to Dubai in early 2009 and was placed in dormitory-type housing with three other women. One of her roommates, Misha, had a very similar upbringing to Charmilla's; they quickly became very close and romantically involved. They were so involved that when Aidah, Charmilla's girlfriend back in Karachi, wrote to Charmilla telling her of her plans to move to Dubai, Charmilla couldn't bring herself to write back. "It wasn't that I didn't or don't love Aidah anymore, it's just that I'm loving my life now. I love having sex with Misha, and she doesn't mind if I sometimes experiment with guys who come into the club." At this last sentence, Charmilla paused and looked at me. "I don't think that came out right. Can I try explaining what I just said?" she asked, eying the recording device that lay on the table between us at her apartment. I invited her to continue. "I *do* go with the guys from the club and we fool around and stuff, but it's because I *want* to do that. I don't get paid for that stuff. I just like trying it. But it's mostly so I can be sure that it really is girls that I want to be with, you know? And I think it is. I just want to be sure."

When I last spoke with Charmilla in 2014, she was living with another woman, whom she described as her soul mate. She had lost touch with both Aidah and Misha but was still dancing at the club. When I asked if she had any plans to return to Karachi, she was surprised but emphatic. "What? Why would I go back to that hellhole? Karachi is the sewer. Dubai is where the world is going, and I'm part of that. And, Dubai is where I can be me. I love living here. And when people ask me where I'm from now, I don't say Karachi, I say 'Bur Dubai.'"

ı ı ı

In conversations with colleagues who primarily study male migrant workers in the Gulf, several have told me that they have heard similar stories of male migrants who move to the Gulf in search of space to explore their sexualities.[2] Anthropologist Michiel Bass and geographer James Siddaway have both studied men who migrate specifically in search of spaces they perceive as being more "queer friendly" than their home countries, as well as men who find themselves in predominantly male-dominated spaces such as labor camps and then begin to explore their sexualities in these new spaces. Many migrants are able to find sexual spaces in the Gulf that facilitate the exploration of their intimate and sexual subjectivities, spaces that inspire continued migration and mobility in hopes of fostering emotional and intimate mobilities.

Changing HomeScapes

The desire to find a new home is a major motivating factor for some migrants, who seek out new spaces in which to explore and understand their subjectivities while rethinking the notion of "home." For such individuals, the home they are living in does not match their notion of what a home should be, and so they migrate in search of a new home, a new family, and a new space in which to explore different aspects of their identities. Even when formal immigration is not possible, as in the UAE and Kuwait, some of my interlocutors asserted that they had found or fashioned a new home in migrating and found themselves often living emotionally in the liminal space between the statuses of migrant and immigrant. While they knew that they might have to leave when their contract expired or if they were subject to deportation, they still chose to refer to the host country as "home." They were also adamant that they did not wish to return to their sending countries, despite the challenges they were facing abroad.

ı ı ı

Yudi had just celebrated his twentieth birthday when I met him in Dubai during the summer of 2013. Despite his young age, he had been living and working in a nightclub in Dubai for the past four years. He described himself as "an artist and a dancer" and worked events outside of the club when male dancers were requested in order to earn more money on the side. At the age of sixteen Yudi had made the decision that he wanted to leave the Philippines, his natal home, in search of a new home. He cited familial reasons and a lack of inspiration in his hometown as the primary reasons for his decision.

"Well, it was just that, things for me in the Philippines, they didn't seem right anymore. Maybe they didn't seem right for a long time," he explained when I asked him to talk about his migratory decision-making process. Yudi cited his mother's remarriage when he was twelve years old as the beginning of a lot of his "troubles." "Before that it was just me and my mom. And that was hard, but it was good. Just me and her, and that, like that it was okay. But then when she met my stepdad, well, he didn't like me. Or maybe he just wasn't interested in me. And then, slowly, my mom changed too, and she wasn't interested in me either." Yudi vividly remembers a series of incidents when he was thirteen years old. "At that time, I know my mother likes music, right? So I'm teaching myself and practicing hard the guitar. And I was getting pretty good, right? And so one day she came home from work tired—like always. I got out my guitar and started playing for her. But you know what she said? She said, 'Oh, Yudi, stop making that noise, you are giving me a headache!' That is what she said. And you know what? That hurt. That hurt me a lot. You don't forget something like this." He paused and took several steadying breaths before continuing. "So, I, I, was sad. And I went out back with my guitar and I started to cry. And then, then, then, that is when my stepdad came and saw me crying. He grabbed my shirt and said, 'You are crying! You need to be a man!' Or something like that. And then he hit me. And it hurt, yeah, but I was just so shocked he hit me. That was the first time, but then it happened again many times."

For some years, Yudi recalled, he felt "out of place" at home and often dreaded returning home to his mother and stepfather. When he turned sixteen, he decided that he wanted to migrate abroad in search of a new and better life. He chose Dubai because he remembered his mother telling him that Dubai was where she had met his father, a Filipino security guard who was working at a bank where his mother had been employed as a janitor many years ago. When Yudi's mother discovered her pregnancy, she and his father had returned to the Philippines. But Yudi's father did not wish to stay in the Philippines and thus chose to move back to Dubai a few months after Yudi was born. "I don't remember anything about him because, you know, I was just a baby when he left. But until I was like maybe eight or nine he sent letters, pictures, and cards. And I kept a lot of his pictures. They were pictures of him with these tall and shiny buildings in Dubai. And I kept those pictures by my bed and I always thought, I'm gonna find him, you know? And when I find him, I'll find me."

When Yudi told his mother of his decision to move to Dubai to look for work and possibly his father, his mother did not object. "That was hard for me too. I thought, maybe she will say, 'No, don't go.' But she didn't. So, I knew it was time for me to go. Nothing left for me in the Philippines." Using a contact from a cousin of his in Dubai, Yudi sought out a job with a construction company just outside of Dubai. When he arrived in Dubai, like many others, he was sent to live in a labor camp, with eight other men in one room. "That was a shock. I get here and I'm like, 'What? I'm living like this?' And it's so hot. And we work all day. And it's terrible. And worse, I can't find my dad. So, I'm pretty sad those months." He described feeling hopeless at times, but he never considered returning to the Philippines to be an option. "Some of the guys at the house, they would talk about 'going home' all the time. But not me. I was always thinking, this is my new home. No way I'm ever going back to the Philippines. I would rather die first. So, I'm gonna make it work. No matter what, I'm gonna make it work."

After six months of working for this construction company, Yudi met a young Indian woman named Sapna who worked at a club in Bur Dubai. She told him about opportunities for young men who were "good dancers" at the clubs in the district where she worked. Eager to find a different mode of employment, Yudi took the advice of his new girlfriend, absconded from his job at the construction company, and started auditioning at various clubs in Bur Dubai. On his third try, he was hired to work as a dancer in a club three doors down from Sapna's club. He met several other Filipino dancers at the club and moved into an apartment with three of them.

"That time things are starting to change for me. And I'm starting to feel really happy. I am living with my *kababayan* [countrymen] and they are becoming like my brothers. And Sapna is becoming like my family too. And Dubai is becoming my home." When Yudi absconded from his job at the construction company, he had simultaneously nullified his working visa and thus joined the ranks of many other overstayers. Though he did not have legal working or residence papers, he considered Dubai home, even though his existence in the country was precarious. "I know that I can get taken in any day. But I don't think about this too much," he replied when I asked him about his working papers. "But even though maybe I'm not supposed to be here, I feel that I am meant to be here. I feel this place, this place, it fits me. I like the work. I like the money. I like my new family. Now, this is my home." When I last talked to Yudi in February of 2015, he had saved enough money to move into his own apartment and was still happily living and working in Dubai. Though he had not yet located his biological father, he had not given up hope and was determined to continue living in Dubai for as long as he possibly could.

ı ı ı

Margaret, like Yudi, had migrated from the Philippines to Kuwait City and now considered Kuwait her home. At the age of twenty-two, Margaret graduated from university in Manila. Unlike many of her classmates who went on to pursue further training in nursing or social welfare, Margaret decided after graduation to look for work in the Gulf. Her decision was motivated not by economic factors but rather by a desire to "find herself," as she would often say. I met Margaret in Kuwait City in 2013, and by then she had been living in Kuwait for five years. Like Yudi, she was now an "overstayer," having stayed longer than allowed by her initial two-year domestic-worker contract, from which she had absconded after the first year.

Margaret was the youngest of four children. While her mother and father had both worked abroad many years ago before meeting one another, none of her three elder siblings had considered becoming an OFW, preferring instead to work in professional industries in the Philippines. "I remember like my brother always saying like it's our duty to stay in the Philippines and do good work in our home country and make our country proud. He was always saying things like that, and this always bothered me," Margaret said. Growing up, she felt "restless," "out of place," and often like "something was missing." "I couldn't never say what it was. I just always felt like, I need to go. I need to get out there. I need to go somewhere and find me. Find a new me. Because Manila, that's not me. It never felt like my home." Margaret's parents both worked full-time, and as the youngest child, she felt "forgotten." "My parents worked so hard, and I know they did that for us, but for me, it always feels like no one cares for me. And my brother and sisters, they are just like my parents. Working, working, working. No time for fun. And they are angry with me when I want to have some fun."

Margaret liked to go out in the evenings with her friends. She would stay out late, and when she got home, her mother or siblings would chastise her for "not being serious about her future." When she told her family that she didn't want to pursue studies but instead wanted to become a singer, her family became very angry. "For them it's like a betrayal. Because like my mom and dad and everyone is working so hard so we can have a good life. Do good things. Live well. So, me wanting to be a singer, that was terrible. And me enjoying myself with my friends, they couldn't stand it."

Margaret completed her university degree "only to please my parents," she said. But after her studies were completed, she decided that she could no longer stay in Manila. "It's like, I'm living someone else's life there. And I know that it's not right for me. I know that I can go somewhere and do something different, and be something different. I know there is something better out there for me." With the help of her aunt and despite her mother's objections, Margaret found a job as a domestic worker in Kuwait City in 2008. When she initially moved to

Kuwait, she was placed in the home of a Jordanian family with three children. After a few months, the family decided to move back to Jordan, and so she was moved in with a local family from Kuwait. Though she didn't mind caring for children and cleaning house, Margaret continued to feel that something was missing in her life.

"My work wasn't bad. It was fine. And the house was beautiful. And what I'm seeing of Kuwait, I like it. A nice city. But I'm still not having a lot of time for me." A year after moving to Kuwait City, Margaret met several other Filipina workers in town who worked at a local karaoke club in a hotel restaurant near the waterfront. Persuaded by the stories told by these women, she absconded from her work for the local family and joined her friends at the club. "When I'm finding these other Pinoys, and the club, and karaoke, I'm so happy. I'm loving it." She moved in with four other women in a nearby dormitory and began to work every day.

"At first, that work it's good. It's fun. But then the boss wants us to do more than sing. And for me, I'm thinking, that is okay, that's an adventure too. But it was hard," she said, pausing before continuing. "But even though it was hard, I didn't ever want to go back to the Philippines. My mom was calling me, and my sisters too, and everyone is saying, 'Just come back home,' but I'm telling them, that is not my home anymore. As hard as things were getting in Kuwait, it still felt more like home to me than Manila ever had."

After a year of working at the karaoke club, Margaret quit and sought out work as a waitress in a restaurant at another hotel in town. She continued living with her friends, whom she described as her "new family," and was able to find side work for a catering company. "I've done a lot of things, different kinds of work here [in Kuwait]. Some of it has been hard. But still, I'm happy here. It makes sense, so, no, I don't want to go back," she said emphatically. When I last spoke with her in January of 2015, she was working full-time for the catering company and was considering a new managerial job at a local hospital. She did not have legal working papers but was optimistic about her ability to find a job and gain legal sponsorship in the coming months.

Conclusion: Intimate Migrations

Migration is a key factor in shaping the intimate subjectivities of those who migrate. Many people move in search of love, adventure, or a new sense of "home." While some may be moving into vocations that seem less than desirable to an outsider, many migrants themselves see these as offering opportunities for them to explore their intimate selves away from the constraints of their families. Highlighting the decision-making processes that migrants work through presents them as people rather than just the products or circumstances of their labor. Migrants should be understood as individuals, connected to families, communities, cultures, and systems; the context of their lives is as important as the work they do at home and abroad. Migration is often discussed solely in terms of "push" and "pull" factors, with economics being the primary framework: migrants are "pushed" by poverty and "pulled" by the allure of capital and employment; sometimes violence, in the form of war, is also cited as a "push" factor. But rarely are migrants' intimate lives viewed as major decision-making factors, which would require a deeper understanding of migrant subjectivity and a reexamination of the artificial force/choice dichotomy that frames so many discussions of migrant agency.

As the stories presented here demonstrate, the same forces that may impel migrants to act out of familial duty may also impel them to migrate away from their bonds of love. Moreover, some of the same forces that operate to immobilize them may encourage their mobility as they work through intimate im/mobilities by migrating and crafting a new sense of self and home. While familial duty and ties may have immobilized their intimate lives or subjectivities at "home" in the sending country, migration to these Gulf cities provides opportunities for migrants to mobilize their intimate selves. In rethinking their sense of "home," these individuals continue to occupy a space between statuses as im/migrants, seeing the host country as their permanent home even if their legal status doesn't match their emotional state.

The tendency of a great deal of the media and literature concerning the Gulf to focus on migrants who "migrate out of poverty" brings with it the assumption that if given the opportunity, all migrants would return to or stay at "home." In this way, Gulf migration is presumed to be very different from the south-to-north migration to destinations such as the United States and Europe. It is presumed that migrants in the Gulf only move out of desperation, and that those working in "undesirable" industries (such as the entertainment industry) would jump at the chance to leave Gulf cities such as Dubai or Kuwait City. This subtly racialized portrait of migration in the Gulf fuels large-scale "rescue" campaigns in which NGOs and other transnational organizations seek to repatriate migrants working, often against their will, under what are perceived as conditions of distress. But while some migrants may wish to return home and some would have preferred not to migrate at all, it is important to real-ize that others do in fact wish to leave their communities and for other than just economic reasons. It is also possible, as the stories presented here show, for families or communities to prefer for family members to migrate, not only for economic but also for social reasons, allowing them to shift from narra-tives of shame regarding a particular family member to narratives of sacrifice. Moreover, many migrants have reconstituted their notion of "home"; from their perspective, deporting them to their country of origin would be disas-trous. Thus, recognizing the complexity of subjectivity for migrants as well as for their families/communities lays the groundwork for more robust and hon-est policies and outreach strategies that are aligned with the desires of migrants and their families.

5

CHILDREN OF THE EMIR

Now a man of the tribe of Levi married a Levite woman, and she became pregnant and gave birth to a son. When she saw that he was a fine child, she hid him for three months. But when she could hide him no longer, she got a papyrus basket for him and coated it with tar and pitch. Then she placed the child in it and put it among the reeds along the bank of the Nile. His sister stood at a distance to see what would happen to him.

Then Pharaoh's daughter went down to the Nile to bathe, and her attendants were walking along the riverbank. She saw the basket among the reeds and sent her female slave to get it. She opened it and saw the baby. He was crying, and she felt sorry for him. "This is one of the Hebrew babies," she said.

Then his sister asked Pharaoh's daughter, "Shall I go and get one of the Hebrew women to nurse the baby for you?"

"Yes, go," she answered. So the girl went and got the baby's mother. Pharaoh's daughter said to her, "Take this baby and nurse him for me, and I will pay you." So the woman took the baby and nursed him. When the child grew older, she took him to Pharaoh's daughter and he became her son. She named him Moses, saying, "I drew him out of the water."

Exodus 2:1–10[1]

Fieldnotes, June 4, 2013, Kuwait City

Four children are gathered around a table, shaping playdough into various molds resembling animals of all kinds. Bits of red, pink, blue, and green dough have spilled off the table onto the woven IKEA rugs that feature trains and mountain landscapes. The other seven children run around barefoot, pushing toddler walkers that light up and play songs like "Twinkle Twinkle Little Star" at an electronically high pitch. Five adults, all of different nationalities, chase the children around, catching them and cuddling them at various intervals.

Haifa, the woman who runs the Department of Family Nursing and therefore this orphanage, leads me to a couch at the center of the room. As I sit down on the couch, a five-year-old girl with thick, curly hair and a heart-melting smile walks up to me and asks to sit with me. I nod as she climbs onto my lap and introduces herself as Serena before reinserting her thumb in her mouth. She dips her hand into her pocket and produces a sticker before running off. "Serena is a good kid, but she doesn't speak much," Haifa tells me when Serena is out of earshot. As we walk into the adjacent room where five elaborately dressed toddler beds line the walls, Haifa continues to tell me about Serena.

"Yes, we worried about Serena for a long time. She, like most of the children here, are what we call 'foundlings' (Arabic translation for *yetim*). They were literally found in baskets, either outside hospitals, in malls, or on street corners. Their parents are unknown, and the police bring them here. These children become Kuwaiti citizens," Haifa explains, referring to a Kuwaiti law that decrees that the children of unknown parents must be taken in and cared for and are eligible for citizenship.[2] The facility that Haifa runs is truly state-of-the-art, complete with twelve different cottages for children of various ages. The complex is large and features several playgrounds and parks, multiple medical centers with full-time doctors and nurses on duty twenty-four hours a day, computers, and transportation to take the children to and from school.

"Some of the children, the girls in particular, stay here until they are in their mid- to late twenties, and some, like Serena, will be taken to the palace, raised there, and given a good life in the palace, but all of these children are children of the Emir," Haifa says, adjusting her head scarf and wiping the beads of sweat from her brow. "The Emir himself comes here several times a year, and others from the palace come at least once a month. They bring clothes, laptops, televisions, and lots of gifts for the children. He really considers all of them children of Kuwait, no matter what they look like."

As we walk to the larger complex across the playground, Haifa pauses before opening the door. She turns to me and lowers her voice. "We try to make a good life for these children, and many of them are happy. We send them to school, and some of them do very well for themselves." Almost as if on cue, a young woman wearing a Led Zeppelin t-shirt walks up to us. "This is Dunya," Haifa says, motioning to the young woman, who stretches out her hand to greet me. "She is eighteen years old and graduating from high school next week. She is very talented in maths and so has won a scholarship to Kuwait University to study." Dunya blushes. I congratulate her before she turns to Haifa to give her a hug. "Good to see you, Mama Haifa, and nice to have met you," Dunya says, her seven bracelets jingling as she hurries off to join a group of her friends two cottages over.

"Dunya was one of our foundlings. We think her mom was Sri Lankan or Bangladeshi, but because she was found outside the police station, she was brought here, given citizenship, and has working papers. She wasn't raised at the palace like some of her friends maybe because she is a bit darker, but still, she will do well in life. Possibly even better than had she gone back to Sri Lanka." Haifa sighs, looking down the corridor at Dunya. "But in here, in this cottage, are some of the kids you asked me about, the *bidoun* [stateless]."

While the Family Nursing Act of 1977 and the subsequent Ministerial Order No. 97 of 1993 (Kuwait 1993) generously offer citizenship to foundlings, the same benefits are not offered to children born in hospitals to unmarried migrant women. The law is clear; citizenship and services are offered to children in the following three categories: (1) children of unknown parents; (2) illegitimate children where the mother is Kuwaiti but the father is either unknown or the parents are not married; or (3) children of destroyed families (where one or both parents have passed away, been incarcerated, or are otherwise incapable of raising children). If, however, the mother of a child is known and she is unmarried and not Kuwaiti, the child is ineligible for citizenship and becomes stateless if the sending country from which the mother hails does not extend citizenship to the child.[3] In these cases, women who go to the hospital for prenatal care or assistance in delivery are sent to prison, sometimes with their children, other times without. Some of the women are deported, while the children remain in Kuwait; other women remain incarcerated for long periods of time. In some cases the women choose to abandon their child; in others they are forcibly separated.

As Haifa knocks on the door of the cottage, a young woman with dark, sunken eyes answers the door. "This is Meysoon," Haifa says as we enter the cottage. Five young women, ranging in age from fifteen to twenty, are watching music videos and reading magazines. Meysoon makes room on the couch for me to sit next to her. It takes a long time before she is ready to talk to me, but when she does, I am astonished at the frankness with which she speaks. Haifa had told me that Meysoon was born to an Indian domestic worker in a local hospital nearby. The nurses there had told Haifa very little, but what she knew was that Meysoon's mother had been raped by her employer and then sent to jail. The nurses had cared for Meysoon for nine months, waiting to see if her mother would return after serving her jail time, but they had heard nothing from her. They did not know whether she had been forcibly deported and not given access to the child or if she had abandoned Meysoon altogether. The labor nurse on call the night Meysoon was born had chosen Meysoon's name, after her favorite aunt. Beyond this, Haifa did not know anything else. She had only told Meysoon the story of how her name was chosen but had not shared any details with her about her birth mother. On her twelfth birthday (Meysoon is now fifteen), Haifa and the other caregivers at the center told Meysoon that she was stateless, which sent Meysoon into a downward spiral. For the past three years she had stayed solely with the other girls who were in the same situation. She started cutting class, and on her fourteenth birthday she attempted suicide.

"My life hasn't been easy," Meysoon said, not making eye contact. "Mama Haifa and everyone here, they are good to us and they try their best, but for me, what is the point?" She flipped through channels on the television screen as she spoke. "When the other kids travel, I can't go. No passport. When others graduate from school, they can work or do a lot of things, but not me, no working papers. Lots of the girls get married and move out, but who will want to marry me?[4] Some of the girls get to go to the palace and live there, but not me. They don't want the *bidoun*. So I am here. And maybe I will always be here." She turns off the television and rises from the couch. Some of Meysoon's friends have left the cottage; others are in the kitchen making lunch, and she goes over to join them. After a few moments she comes back to me to leave me with a parting thought. "It doesn't make sense, does it? My mom didn't do anything wrong, she went to the hospital to have me instead of leaving me at the mall. And now my life is forever ruined."

Theorizing Integration

Meysoon and Serena are among the many children whose lives have been shaped by the complexities of migration. While scholars have recently become more interested in the realm of intimate labor,[5] very few studies examine the intimate lives of the laborers themselves.[6] The struggles of migrant parents and their children who are raised in places such as Kuwait can be understood in terms of a variety of concepts. For the particular phenomenon that is the focus of this chapter two interconnected approaches prove useful: theories about perverse integration and theories about the legal production of illegality, which together produce a concept I call "perverse intimacies."[7]

In many ways, the theoretical framework of perverse integration can best explain what these children and their mothers face from a legal standpoint. The term "perverse integration" denotes a concept introduced by sociologists Manuel Castells and Mitch Duneier to describe the ways in which formal and informal or legal and illegal economies collide. Informal economies are very often perversely integrated—perverse in that the integration is often illegal but highly lucrative—into formal economies, with the formal depending on the informal (Duneier 1999; Hopper 2002). The term itself refers to the paradoxical opportunities provided within the gray areas of legality and illegality. Duneier uses the example of homeless panhandlers in New York City, showing the ways in which panhandling (which is not quite legal but not always illegal) is the most profitable means of survival for many men suffering from mental illness and economic challenges. Other anthropologists such as Kim Hopper note that the integration into "mainstream" society of persons working in informal (sometimes illegal) economies is perverse for two main reasons: because the state may depend on these economies for the provision of certain goods and services, and because this type of labor functions as a survival strategy for persons who are otherwise unable to work and survive in the formal economy. Perverse integration applies to situations in which individuals are better off turning to the realm of the informal, illegal, or illicit in order to survive.

Blanca Garcés-Mascareñas builds on this concept, using the example of "illegal" migrants in Spain and Malaysia to show that illegal migrants are necessary in order to define the "other" against the state, but more important, because they form a flexible oversupply of labor upon which the formal/legal economy rests. Deborah Boehm, Susan Bibler Coutin, and Nicholas De Genova have all explored ways in which laws produce precarious situations of illegality for those crossing borders (Boehm 2012; Coutin 2007, 2000; De Genova and Peutz 2010). Coutin and Boehm have been explicit in detailing how these legal productions of illegality impact and shape migrants' intimate lives while challenging their sense of agency. Theories of perverse integration together with Manuel Castells's concept of the fourth world further exemplify the intertwined nature of legal and illegal processes and the symbiotic relationship between the state and illicit networks as they impact migrant lives at the level of individuals. Castells holds that "the process of social exclusion and the insufficiency of remedial policies of social integration lead to a key process of perverse integration referred to as the labor force in the criminal economy" (Castells 1999).

Organized crime and illicit activities can also benefit members of the formal economy, rendering them an intrinsic part of the system in many countries. Perverse integration theorists such as Castells and Duneier note that informal or illicit economies are often intertwined with and depended upon by formal or licit economies, making them perverse (in that they are illicit but desirable) and integrated (in that formal economies depend on this labor).

In the case of children like Serena and Meysoon, the theory of perverse integration provides a lens for looking at the incorporation not of economies or labor but of persons, bodies, and the question of citizenship. While these children and their mothers don't always provide services that the state needs, their very existence and the ways in which they navigate the law point to creative survival strategies embedded in the concept of perverse integration. Indeed, this theoretical framework can be applied both to the women who become mothers in country as well as to their children, who become integrated in different ways in the host country. Laws in regard to childbirth out of wedlock combined with laws in regard to foundlings and children born to unmarried noncitizen mothers produce a situation in which the route of illegality or informality becomes comparatively desirable and sometimes, as for Duneier's panhandlers, the only option for survival. According to Kuwaiti law, an abandoned child found in a mall or on a street corner whose parents are unknown will be eligible for citizenship. A child born to an unmarried noncitizen mother, however, will be kept in the country but will be stateless. Paradoxically, then, a situation is created wherein a migrant woman is—perversely—better off having her child at home, abandoning it, and working in the informal economy than she is coming forward, asking for prenatal assistance, and reporting the circumstances that resulted in her pregnancy. If she comes forward, the odds are high that she will be separated from her child, detained, and deported, and that her child will become stateless. By contrast, if she manages to hide her pregnancy and abandon her child, then she will be able to continue working in the country, while her child will be eligible for highly coveted citizenship rights in Kuwait. This paradox leads to the integration of abandoned children into Kuwaiti society either by extending them the legal rights of citizenship or by caring for, financially supporting, and socially sanctioning them.

In many ways, it is very progressive and generous for the Kuwaiti state to extend citizenship rights and care for abandoned children regardless of race, gender, or sexuality. That abandoned children are afforded more rights than children of known migrant mothers, however, is perverse. The children born to migrant mothers in Kuwait or the UAE are also perversely integrated in that they are raised and remain in the country, often illegally or without visas or citizenship papers. Some are taken to the palaces and grow up to become very successful; others remain stateless and are raised in orphanages until they marry. Host country laws about reproduction, citizenship, and marriage thus shape the experiences of both children and mothers. As a result of these laws, in line with Boehm's, Coutin's, De Genova and Peutz's, and Garcés-Mascareñas's understanding of the legal production of illegality, mothers who are working legally in Kuwait are rendered illegal if they are unmarried and become pregnant in country; the children of known mothers become illegal by virtue of the circumstances of their birth.

Bringing together these two bodies of literature—writings on the legal production of illegality and theories about perverse integration and social exclusion—allows us to see, through the lens of the concept of "perverse intimacies," how people's lives, movements, and intimacies are integrated (and challenged) by the host country. The legal assignment of status and hierarchy to the foundlings perversely makes the intimate details of the circumstances of their birth public. The selective and exceptional conferral, particularly upon those highly fortunate children growing up in the palaces, of certain citizenship benefits that extend beyond legal citizenship to include the social and economic citizenship that is based how one is perceived highlights the extent of the perversity.

Foundlings traverse the liminal space between im/migrant and native or local. They can be termed "foreign-born natives," having spent their entire lives in the host country, in most instances cared for by nationals of that country. While they may identify with the host country culturally, many remain as outsiders. Some are well integrated, in that they are endowed with citizenship and become very successful in the country; such instances, however, are exceptional across the globe. Others, not so fortunate, often find creative survival strategies to mobilize, moving physically or through activism in the face of their frustrating immobility, thereby experiencing the perils of im/mobility all at once.

It was initially my goal to find an equal number of "foundlings" in Kuwait and the UAE, and I had hoped to spend time at some of the orphanages hosting these children in both countries. But I was unable to access the orphanages in the UAE and thus unable to interview more than a few such young people in that field site. For this reason, I shall focus predominantly on the experiences of children in Kuwait, but I shall begin by detailing the citizenship laws in both countries.

Citizenship Laws

Citizenship is considered "a foundation of identity, dignity, justice, peace, and security" as well as a basic human right (Blitz and Lynch 2011, 208). Many migrant workers in Kuwait and the UAE, however, do not have the opportunity to enjoy these privileges, since they are not citizens of the countries within which they work. This amounts to having no legal protection or rights, including no right to participate in the political arena, no access to quality education, no freedom to travel, and vulnerability to harassment and violence. Citizenship laws define not only the rights and obligations of citizens but also the manner in which citizenship can be acquired and lost. Citizenship can be acquired through *jus sanguinis* (blood-based transfer), in which the citizenship of the parent—and sometimes the gender of the parent is significant here—is transferred to his or her offspring; through *jus solis* (soil-based transfer), in which birthright citizenship is acquired by being born in a particular country; or through naturalization, the legal process of acquiring citizenship. The UAE and Kuwait do not allow *jus solis*, and naturalization is very difficult. Thus the primary mode of citizenship transfer is *jus sanguinis*, which is typically passed only through the father in Kuwait. This patrilineal conferral of citizenship has led to much controversy, and in the UAE as of 2011, children of citizen mothers are also allowed to obtain citizenship.

Emirati Citizenship

In the UAE, citizenship laws are based on Federal Law No. 17 for 1972 and amended by Federal Law No. 10 for 1975. Citizenship can be acquired by having resided in the Emirates in 1925 or before, by being born to a male or female citizen whether abroad or in country, or by being born in country to unknown parents. Citizenship through naturalization requires migrant laborers from non-Arab states to reside in the country for at least thirty years, with twenty of those years under the Citizenship Act of January 1, 1972. Migrants can become citizens either by the laws stated under Article 1, Extension of Marriage, or through naturalization. Children, regardless of their country of birth, are granted citizenship if they are born to a male citizen or, as of 2011, born to a female citizen. Anyone born in the country to unknown parents may also be granted Emirati citizenship, but it must be established legally that neither parent is known.

Foreign women who marry UAE citizens may obtain citizenship provided they reside three years in the country after applying for citizenship, have given up previous citizenship, and have obtained the approval of the Ministry of the Interior. As in Kuwait, this is not easily achieved, and there are many foreign women who have waited a very long time for citizenship transfers through their spouse.

Additionally, UAE citizenship may be granted to any fully competent person if he or she has been legally and continuously residing in the emirates since 1940 or before and has maintained his or her original residence until the date of implementation of the Citizenship Act of January 1, 1972. The person must have a lawful source of income and be of good character, not convicted of a crime against honor or trust, and proficient in the Arabic language. The wife of a citizen by naturalization shall be considered a citizen by naturalization if she renounces her original nationality. Minor children of a citizen by naturalization shall also be considered citizens by naturalization unless they decide to resume their original nationality within one year following the date of majority. Naturalization will only be granted once a foreigner renounces his or her original nationality.

Kuwaiti Citizenship

The official Kuwaiti Nationality Law was published in 1959 and amended through 1987 (Kuwait 1959). The document includes twenty-four articles detailing the conditions that must be satisfied in order to obtain Kuwaiti citizenship. To summarize, any person born to a Kuwaiti father, regardless of where he or she is born, is considered a Kuwaiti national (following the principle of *jus sanguinis*). Anyone born to a father who is not a Kuwaiti national may be granted nationality by decree upon the recommendation of the emir for any of a number of reasons, including being Muslim by birth, having knowledge of the Arabic language, being of "good character," or having lawfully resided in Kuwait for at least twenty consecutive years. Yet even if these conditions are met, citizenship can remain elusive. Those who gain citizenship through such measures have limited rights, such as not being able to stand as a candidate for any parliamentary body. And Kuwait does not recognize the acquisition of citizenship through birth in its territories by citizens of other countries (*jus solis*). A foreign woman who has been married to a Kuwaiti national for at least fifteen years may also be granted citizenship, though this is not currently the case for foreign husbands. Finally, dual citizenship is not accepted in Kuwait.

The issue of citizenship in Kuwait has been controversial because of the large number of migrant workers in the country. Kuwaiti law considers these migrant workers to be citizens of their countries of origin, and even the children born in Kuwait of long-term migrant workers do not always qualify for citizenship, which depends on the father's nationality rather than on territorial factors. These restrictions and other factors have resulted in over 100,000 stateless people called *bidoun* (literally, "without") who reside and work in the country. Many *bidoun* were born and raised in Kuwait. Some are stateless because their parents or grandparents did not apply for citizenship when the country declared independence in 1961, while others come from families in which the father was foreign (some *bidoun* are foreign men who have married Kuwaiti women) (Toumi 2010). These stateless people are not recognized by the government, have difficulty obtaining official papers such as identity cards and driver's licenses, do not qualify for government jobs, and are among the poorest in the nation. Children like Meysoon (introduced at the beginning of this chapter) born to unmarried migrant women also become *bidoun*.

With citizenship privileges passing through the father, children whose fathers are unknown cannot register in Kuwait (unless they do so with their home embassies, which is often challenging because of the stigma against migrant women on the part of some home country embassy staff). In addition, some citizenship laws in migrant sending countries also pass through the father or are interpreted by embassy staff to mean that citizenship should not be granted to "illegal migrants," and therefore children such as Meysoon are unable to return to their mother's home country because the embassy will not grant them legal documentation. At least two of my interlocutors were seeking Indian passports in order to be sent to India and reunited with their mothers, who were actively seeking their return. The Indian embassy would not process their paperwork, reasoning that the children had been born to women who migrated "illegally" and thus the children were not "deserving of citizenship." They remain, stateless, in Kuwait, without citizenship or working privileges.

Over the years there have been a number of calls for amendment of the Kuwaiti nationality laws in support of migrant workers' rights, as well as gender equality. In April of 2013, the country passed a bill to naturalize 4,000 stateless people—just the beginning of a solution to the problem of the stateless people (France-Presse Agence 2013). Another proposal calls for granting Kuwaiti citizenship to foreign husbands of Kuwaiti women and their children, but this remains controversial and has not been adopted (Toumi 2010). There are also a number of NGOs (such as Trustline and Group 29) that are currently lobbying for the protection of the *bidoun*, but these efforts are still new and the results remain to be seen. Virtually all of these organizations focus their efforts on working with *bidoun* populations that are known to have existed for generations in Kuwait, rather than the children of migrants, such as Meysoon.

Stateless in the City: Perverse Incorporation

While many children who are stateless are raised in state-sponsored orphanages, hundreds of stateless children become perversely integrated, living and working illegally in Kuwait. Some of them remain with their mothers, who have gone underground; others are informally taken in or adopted by co-ethnics who then employ them. Some live in Kuwait for many years; others are caught when something goes wrong. The following are case studies of three such individuals, who are stateless but have been incorporated into the host country.

ı ı ı

I met Cecilia one warm Wednesday afternoon when I visited the informal women's shelter at the Philippine embassy. One of the Filipino labor attachés had been kind enough to allow me to visit the women in the shelter on occasion to talk with them about the reasons for their being in the shelter and their experiences. Most of the women I met were between the ages of twenty and thirty and had migrated to Kuwait to work as domestic workers. When things went wrong between them and their employers and they were abused, had wages withheld, or in some cases both, the women absconded and came to the shelter. A few had ended up in the shelter owing to abuses incurred outside the workplace that had rendered them illegal. A very few had been sent to the embassy by their employers when they were found to be pregnant; in most of those cases the embassy did its best to send the women home before their babies were born. I had just sat down to talk to a woman covered in knife wounds when a very young girl walked up and sat down across the table from me, eyeing the three muffins that another one of the women had brought me. I slid the plate over to her, and she devoured one quickly. I was surprised to see a child in the shelter, since usually the children were sent to a separate space.

"Oh, you met Cecilia?" asked Ellie, the woman I had come to speak to. I nodded and stretched my hand out to shake Cecilia's while introducing myself. She turned away and faced the window. I asked Ellie if I should leave, as I had the feeling I was making Cecilia uncomfortable. "Don't leave, please," Cecilia interjected. "I want you to interview me, hear my story." She traded seats with

Ellie, who stood up and started brushing Cecilia's hair. Cecilia took another muffin from my plate and began telling me her story.

She thinks she is nine years old, although her mom, who was also living in the shelter, had told her she had lost track of the years. When I asked Ellie and Cecilia if I could speak to Cecilia's mother, they shrugged their shoulders. I insisted that I needed her mother's permission to talk to Cecilia, so she ran downstairs, had her mom sign the consent form, and returned. Ellie leaned over the balcony to ask Cecilia's mom if she wanted to be interviewed by me, but she didn't answer. Cecilia and Ellie resumed her story. They were both speaking quickly, and I struggled to keep up but was able to piece together the details from the various stories they told. It turned out that Cecilia's mother, Marissa, had become pregnant a year after arriving in Kuwait from the Philippines to work as a domestic worker. Instead of turning her in to the police, Marissa's sponsors told her she was welcome to have the child at home but that she would be rendered illegal. They had explained to her that children born out of wedlock could sometimes be separated from their mothers, who are detained and often deported. Afraid of this outcome, Marissa had given birth at home (with the assistance of her employer's sister). From that point on neither Marissa nor Cecilia left the house, fearful of being caught by the police. Marissa knew that Cecilia was stateless and was terrified her daughter would be taken away from her. When it came time to renew her visa and contract, Marissa was afraid to do so, fearing that the authorities would find out about Cecilia and arrest her.

As soon as Cecilia was old enough to help around the house, she did so and was rewarded with sweets from her mother's employer. When Cecilia turned seven, however, Marissa's employer began withholding her wages. The children Marissa cared for also grew increasingly undermining and would tease and often hurt Cecilia. Afraid to go to the authorities, Marissa worked for the next two years without pay, while Cecilia suffered from an increasing amount of teasing. At one point Cecilia was locked in the dryer by the two young boys who were Marissa's charges. Another time, Cecilia recalled, the boys took turns throwing shoes at her. When Marissa tried to stand up for her daughter, her employer became very angry and started to hit Marissa. One afternoon her employer came home and poured boiling water on Marissa's leg, complaining that Marissa had not prepared food for the children that was to their liking. The next morning Marissa and Cecilia packed their things and decided to take their chances by running away to the Philippine embassy. They were placed in the informal shelter while their cases were examined, and now, nine months later, they still did not have a resolution. For nine years Cecilia had managed to be incorporated into her mother's employers' home, but that had ended. She was extremely fearful of what would happen next.

Alia's story was similar to Cecilia's, except that Alia had remained informally incorporated in Kuwait for twenty-seven years. Alia was born to an unwed Indian domestic worker who had decided to give birth in the hospital in Kuwait City. As often happens in such instances, Alia's mother was sent to jail, while Alia remained at the hospital and was cared for by the nurses and hospital staff. One of the nurses named Alia and told her what little she knew about the circumstances of her birth. At first the nurses would take Alia to the prison to be nursed by her mother. After six months, however, Alia's mother was no longer in jail and nowhere to be found. The hospital staff did not know if she had been deported or had voluntarily returned to India. Alia's father was unknown, and at the time it was difficult for children in her circumstances to be sent to the orphanage, since the emir had not yet issued a decree allowing for the transfer of stateless children. Without any clear place to send the child, the nurses ended up raising Alia in the hospital.

"I lived in the hospital until I was seven years old," Alia said. "But I helped out the nurses, the ones who would give me candies and treats. I would help them, I would go do things for them, pick up their laundry, get them medicines, get them lunch, and they helped me too." But the nurses would also tell Alia that she needed to leave the hospital, perhaps even go to school. "It was hard, though. I was a little girl, and all I knew was life in the hospital. I didn't want to leave because I had become attached to the nurses, but at the same time, I did want to have a home."

One day an Indian couple came to the hospital for fertility services. When they met Alia, they asked the nurses if they could take her home. They promised to take good care of her and give her a good life. At the time, adoptions in Kuwait were not common, nor did any laws govern child adoption. Today, Kuwaiti citizens may adopt, but noncitizens, such as the couple who informally adopted Alia, are not permitted to do so, and even citizens may not adopt bidoun. Alia remembered that the nurses felt conflicted about allowing Alia to go with the couple. "They kept asking me, 'Do you want to go with them?' And they told me that if I didn't want to go, I didn't have to and I could stay." Alia was unsure of what to do, but the Indian couple came to visit her every day for a week, bringing her presents, clothes, and sweets. After a week of getting to know them, Alia told the nurses she would like to go and have a home. They told her she was welcome back at the hospital anytime and said their goodbyes.

Alia lived with this couple for the next ten years. Though she was stateless, they arranged for her to go to the Indian school after teaching her to read and write. She did not fully understand the implications of her lack of citizenship until the Indian couple's work permits ended and they were preparing to go back to India. "They had often gone in the summers, but one of them would stay behind with me. Whenever they traveled, someone stayed with me, or I was sent to stay with friends. I didn't really understand what it all meant until I was seventeen and they told me they were leaving for good," Alia said. When Alia asked if she could go to India with them, they explained to her that she would have to stay in Kuwait because she did not have a passport.

Alia was unsure of what to do next or where to go. "In those days, I cried a lot, even cried myself to sleep most nights," she said. One day, three weeks before the Indian couple were scheduled to return home, some friends of theirs came over for a visit. These friends had two children, ages two and three, and the wife was pregnant with a third child. Upon hearing about Alia's situation, the wife offered Alia full room and board if she would agree to work for the family as a nanny and housekeeper. Alia agreed and has been living with this family for the past ten years. She is now twenty-seven years old and has never gone outside Kuwait's borders. While she knows she is stateless and thus working illegally, she narrates her situation in terms of familial incorporation. "It's true I am working here for the family, but it's also like I'm one of the family, so perhaps it's not work. Also Kuwait is my home, the only home I have ever known, so I feel happy to stay here."

Both Cecilia and Alia were incorporated informally by families in Kuwait. Though neither of them had been able to obtain citizenship, they had both circumvented laws in regard to their presence in Kuwait through informal channels, thus manifesting the "perverse" (in that it is illegal but also desirable and instrumental in their survival) aspect of perverse integration. Their living and working situations provide an example of legally produced illegality, in that both young women were living and working illegally in the host country not because they did anything illegal but because the contours of the host country's laws were not flexible enough to accommodate the circumstances of their birth. In addition, the incongruence between the home country's and host country's citizenship transfer laws further restricted their movements, keeping them stateless and immobile.

Like Meysoon, Elham was born in a local hospital in Ras-Al-Khaimah (RAK), UAE. Now twenty years old, Elham has returned to work as a volunteer in the same hospital in which she was born. She has never left the tiny emirate of RAK, not even to visit Dubai. From the little that Elham knows, her mother was a Nepali woman who had been a "love case," according to the prison wardens who narrated her story to Elham. Her mother had migrated to Dubai initially to work as a domestic worker. There she had met a young Nepali man working as a security guard at a local business. When he was transferred to RAK, he persuaded Elham's mother to join him, which she did, absconding from her sponsor in Dubai and becoming illegal. Elham's father and mother had moved in with each other in RAK and before long, Elham's mother became pregnant. At some point her mother was arrested, but Elham was not clear on this aspect of the story, as different jail wardens, including the one who informally adopted her and had raised her thus far, had told her different versions.

Elham's mother was arrested and tried for the crime of *zina*. The wardens were unclear about whether her mother had initially been picked up because she was without working papers or whether someone had seen her swollen belly and brought her in. Either way, she was arrested and sent to jail after giving birth to Elham in a hospital. As soon as she was born, Elham was sent to live in the prison with her mother, who remained staunchly by her side for two years, refusing to go back to Nepal without her. Eventually, however, she was deported, and Elham stayed behind, unable to travel with her mother. She was to remain in RAK for the foreseeable future.

Elham's mother, however, had grown very close to several of the prison wardens. Many of the wardens tried to help the women who were in their charge by bringing them food, clothes, and money. The wardens played a significant role in trying to secure funds to send the women home and, when possible, to get the babies home as well. Amira, the warden who raised Elham, was one of the more involved members of the prison staff. A woman in her late fifties, Amira had never married or given birth to any children. She had raised Elham as her daughter but had always been very clear with her that she was not her birth mother, telling Elham stories about her birth mother's bravery and hoping that one day they would be able to travel to Nepal together to visit her biological family. I had the opportunity to talk with Amira only briefly, but she said in our short interview that she was committed to the women in her charge, specifically those who had children. "It breaks my heart that a mother would have to be separated from her baby, no matter what the circumstances of her being pregnant are," Amira proclaimed. "Some of the other guards, they think we should only help those who are love cases, some think we should help the rape cases, but I always thought we should help every mother and child."

When Elham was just over two years old, her mother was informed that she was going to be deported but that the child could not come with her. Distraught, she begged Amira to take Elham in and care for her. "Elham's mother said to me, 'Take my baby girl, protect her like she is your own,'" Amira recalled. Amira had grown close to Elham; she had been working tirelessly to get her travel documents so that she could return with her mother. Many of the wardens were successful in helping the women in their charge; Amira noted that she herself had seen over a dozen babies return home with their mothers. "I have never understood why some could go home and others were kept here. It seemed always to me that if a mother wanted to take the baby home, that she should be able to."

For the first few years that Elham lived with her, Amira continued to work to procure travel documents, citizenship papers, or some type of documentation for Elham. Frustrated at the seemingly never-ending series of closing doors, Amira finally accepted that Elham was likely to be living with her, stateless, in RAK for many years to come. Elham and Amira grew closer as time passed, and Amira was able to arrange with friends of hers at a local school to allow Elham to enroll in classes, despite her undocumented status. After graduating from high school, Elham began volunteering at the hospital in which she was born.

"It hasn't been easy for me, growing up in RAK, knowing I can't leave," Elham explained. She indicated on more than one occasion that she was reluctant even to venture to the other emirates for fear that she would be arrested, searched for documentation, and then imprisoned. "As long as I'm in RAK, I know Amira knows people, has good *wasta* [social capital], you know? She can help me, and I know RAK people. They are good, don't want to give me trouble." What she has heard about Dubai and the neighboring emirates makes her uneasy. "I know lots of people in jail in Dubai, and lots of kids like me without papers living in bad places in Abu Dhabi. I don't want this for me."

Elham, like many other young people in her situation, navigates her encounters with the state in dexterous and creative ways. She knows that some encounters with legal figures and authorities can be negotiated, as long as she remains in spaces in which she has social capital. That she and others like her have been able to remain in the country and have had the opportunity to be educated and work informally, demonstrates the necessary flexibility of the state (not as a monolithic entity but as experienced by people like Elham). That she knows the spaces in which she can live and work demonstrates her own creative ability to be incorporated and to carve out her own type of "flexible citizenship" (Ong 1999).

Moses Redux: Royally Incorporated

This chapter began with the story of Moses because his is a notable story of exception. He was "found" by royalty and, in an exceptional turn of luck, was nursed by his biological mother, affording him a range of rights and privileges. While the foundlings introduced below were not fortunate enough to be raised by their biological mothers, they are truly exceptional in that they have been able to obtain and negotiate a wide range of citizenship rights owing to the good fortune of having been chosen to be raised by royalty. This exceptionalism provides a stark contrast to the experiences of the foundlings whose stories have been told above, who continue to employ flexibility and creativity in navigating their own paths. Thus the stories related below should be read, like the Moses story, as exceptions—but exceptions that tell a larger story of perversity, integration, and the power of social and legal capital.

ı ı ı

The first time I heard about orphaned and sometimes stateless children being raised in the palaces by the emir, I was skeptical. A group of expatriate academics were telling me that they had heard this was common practice, though the information seemed to be in the form of rumors. The more I discussed this with locals, members of NGOs, and even hospital staff, the more these rumors were confirmed. But no one had met anyone who had been raised in the palaces. Rather, they had only heard that children were sent there and that the emir and his family were raising dozens of these children each year. Nurses at the local hospitals said that children they looked after were often sent to the palaces after a few years of being stateless in the hospital. Haifa, who ran the orphanage mentioned at the beginning of this chapter, had also said that some of the children from her orphanage had been sent to the palace to be raised there. But whenever I asked if anyone had actually been inside the palaces to see the children living there or if anyone had met any young adults who had been raised there, the answer was always negative. No one had been inside the palaces or met the adults who grew up there. One day, however, I met Barbara.

Barbara is a British woman who had moved to the Gulf when her husband, who works in the oil industry, was relocated. She had been a teacher back in the United Kingdom and sought out teaching jobs in the various countries to which she and her husband moved. When they moved to Kuwait, Barbara's first job had been teaching English to a group of children called the "children of the Emir." These were not the emir's actual children but rather the orphaned and stateless children who had been incorporated into the palaces. As she narrated the experiences of her fifteen years teaching at the palace, the rumors were verified.

"Well yes, of course the children of the Emir, the 'royal foundlings' as I like to call them, of course they exist," she said in her soft but high-pitched voice. "Every day for about fifteen years I went up to the palace to teach them English." She pulled cracked pictures of various children out of her wallet. The children looked like a diverse group, but all were clothed in the *dishdasha* or burqa, reflecting the local dress in Kuwait. "They are a lovely bunch, and it is great to have the opportunity to work with them inside the palace. They range in age from five to fifteen, boys and girls, and all of them speak Arabic and now English fluently." She noted that most of the children were sent to school; Barbara was just the English tutor hired by the emir to ensure that the children's English would be as good as their Arabic.

"They do have everything they need, these kids. Laptops, phones, games, and plenty of clothes. They are well cared for, but some of them want to go home or want to understand who their parents are." After fifteen years of working with these children, Barbara had decided to work with local NGOs to lobby the government to change its citizenship laws so that some of the children could find their parents. She also worked with women who were detained or deported owing to pregnancy out of wedlock and in some cases was able to manage their cases so they could return home with their children. "Even though the lives of these children in the palace is good, it is still hard for them, and I know it's hard for the mothers who are separated from the kids. It was these experiences that motivated me to do the work I do now." Barbara showed me pictures of women with their babies who, thanks to Barbara's help, were on their way home.

After meeting Barbara, I had the good fortune to meet Mona, a twenty-five-year-old young woman who had once been a "child of the Emir." Mona did not know or remember where she was born, but she did remember spending a short amount of time in the hospital before moving to the palace when she was around four years old (to this day, Mona is unsure of her birthday or actual age, but she gave me rough estimates based on what she had been told in the palace). A tall young woman with thick eyebrows and long eyelashes, Mona now runs a daycare program in Kuwait City. She also sits on the board of a public school nearby and is very active in children's education.

"I think I'm passionate about what I do because I was lucky enough to be well taken care of and I got such a great education," Mona said in perfect English. Though layers of black fabric covered her head, body, and much of her face, Mona's kohl-lined eyes were extremely expressive, and they widened when she spoke of her past. "I was one of the lucky ones. I don't know who my parents are, but because I was abandoned at a hospital, I got Kuwaiti citizenship. To add to that good luck, I was also raised in the palace. It doesn't get much better than that for someone like me."

Mona lived in a large room in the palace with three other girls for most of her life. She recalled rising early for morning prayers and learning the Koran from a young age. She said that while she was asked to help out around the palace, most of her time there was spent becoming educated in different ways. A family member of the emir who was adamant that all the children in her care be well rounded had raised her; she had arranged for Mona and her "siblings" to go to school, have language tutoring in English and French, and on occasion take extra art classes. Mona reflected on this time in her life with mixed emotions. "It wasn't always easy, and when I was a teenager, I was angry a lot. I wanted to know who and where my parents were, I wanted to be like some of my friends at school." But as the years passed, Mona said, she became grateful for the support and attention she received as a "child of the Emir." "We were always told we were special, and that we were lucky. After a while I started to feel that way, and I still do."

At the age of twenty-two Mona met a young man named Faisal. They were married a year later, and Mona moved out of the palace and into an apartment with Faisal. They are now expecting their first child, who will be a citizen like his parents. "I hope my baby is as lucky as I am," Mona said, patting her belly. "She won't be raised in a palace, but we will do our best." She laughed.

Like Moses, Mona's story and the stories of many other "royal foundlings," as Barbara calls them, are stories of exception. Though initially, when they were abandoned, they may have seemed to be doomed, their integration—though perverse—has allowed them access to many layers of citizenship that other legal citizens may not be able to access. Their ties to the royal family give them higher status than many other citizens in the country, and their futures look very different from those of other young people who have been born to im/migrant parents or have been rendered stateless, like Meysoon.

Working Together, Moving Forward

Though it may seem that the future is bleak for young people like Meysoon, Cecilia, and even Alia, many things are rapidly changing in both Kuwait and the UAE that may improve their futures. Most notably, adoption is becoming increasingly acceptable and even being encouraged in both countries. The passage of new Emirati adoption laws (United Arab Emirates 2012) is contributing to this change in the UAE. And adoption is on the rise in Kuwait, owing to a shift in discourse on the part of the royal family, according to Dr. K. Nasreen, who runs the Complex of Social Care Homes within the Ministry of Social Affairs and Labor. "The emir and members of the royal family have come forward to encourage Kuwaitis to adopt orphans, saying it is an act of extreme religious piety and even a religious duty within Islam," she explained to me, highlighting the fact that the language of religion is often deployed by the ruling families to spur nationals to action.

Decree Law No. 82 of 1977, referred to as the Family Nursing Law, was the first legislation in Kuwait to structure the contours of the adoption system. This law sets out a series of requirements for "nursing families," the term given to adoptive families, including:

The child's nurser must be Kuwaiti married to Kuwaiti or non Kuwaiti woman. The nursemaid must be Kuwaiti married to Kuwaiti or non Kuwait man. The nurser (man) and nursemaid must be Muslims. The financial capability for caring for the nursed child (must be determined). The nurser and nursemaid shall be socially matured and free from mental disturbances. The nurser and nursemaid shall be morally matured and having good manners. The nursing family must reside in Kuwait for following up the child. (Kuwait 1977)

Several features of this law and its application are noteworthy. The first is that only Kuwaiti nationals, and of these only those who are in "good moral and financial standing," may adopt. This makes it virtually impossible for the many noncitizens and non-Muslims who would like to adopt children to do so. Other challenges embodied in this law are noted by activists such as Haifa and Dr. Nasreen who work in this area. "A big problem is that the kids who are *bidoun* cannot be adopted. It is prohibited, and so these kids stay here until they can marry," Haifa explained to me while discussing the situation of Meysoon and her friends. Dr. Nasreen also pointed out that though the Family Nursing Law was passed in 1977, the number of families who in fact adopt has been very low until just recently. "It's true that it is an old law," she said. "But it just wasn't as common, we didn't have people coming to us to adopt children. There were the kids who were sent to the palace and then everyone else. But that is changing rapidly. I would say in the last five years or so, we have had many more cases of adoption." She referred to anecdotal evidence suggesting that the number of children adopted from her orphanage last year was more than four times the number adopted a decade ago, although she did not have the exact figures.

In the UAE, the law regarding abandoned children and foster families that was recently passed (Federal Law No. 1 for 2012 Concerning the Custody of Children of Unknown Parentage) takes important steps toward meeting the needs of children of unknown parentage, as well as codifying the act of taking custody of a child as charity. Similar to the law in Kuwait, several restrictions prevent noncitizens and non-Muslims from adopting children who are Emirati citizens or children who are stateless.[8] For those eligible to adopt a child, namely, single Muslim Emirati women, the law requires custodians to "undertake to treat the child well and raise him/her in a good manner, taking care of his/her health, education, protection and growth" (United Arab Emirates 2012)—in this way highlighting the government's efforts to meet the child's needs. The law also encourages those who would take custody of children by mandating that doing so is a "charity and voluntary act that is free of charge" (United Arab Emirates 2012)—perhaps helping to increase the rates of adoption.

In addition to changes in the laws regarding adoption and its increasing popularity, the last five years have seen the proliferation of numerous NGOs, particularly groups and organizations advocating for human rights and for the rights of the *bidoun*. Examples include Group 29 and Human Line, organizations made up of pro bono lawyers and activists who are seeking citizenship rights and legal recognition of Kuwait's growing stateless population. Other groups, such as the Kuwait Institute for Human Rights (established, like Group 29 and Human Line, in 2012), are active in promoting justice in the form of migrants' rights and the rule of law for everyone within the borders of Kuwait. Finally, international organizations such as the International Organization for Migration (IOM) and the International Labour Organization (ILO) are also very active in organizing workshops and symposia in the country on issues pertaining to human trafficking, migrants' rights, and labor issues. Most of these organizations have been focused on the plight of *bidoun* whose parents and grandparents have lived in Kuwait for many generations but who did not access citizenship some generations ago; however, since my time in Kuwait in

2013, these organizations have become more aware of the presence of children such as Meysoon and are now taking an active interest in resolving their cases.

During my time in the field I met dozens of activists and members of civil society in Kuwait who were interested in working on issues such as statelessness, migrants' rights, and trafficking. No organization with which I spoke directly focuses on the situations of migrants' children, such as those discussed here, but the tangential work being done on related issues is likely to extend to this vulnerable population about which little is known. When I related the stories and situations of young people like Meysoon and Alia, the activists I met were shocked and surprised. They, like many other locals with whom I spoke, indicated that they did not know such laws existed, let alone that the laws would create this paradoxical situation of illegality for so many children.

"This is a very sad situation you tell us of," said Essie, a human rights lawyer working with groups such as Human Line. "We didn't know about it, but now that we know, we can do something." Mehri, the executive director of another human rights organization, echoed Essie's response. "I think that is how it is in Kuwait, there are a lot of things happening, but we just don't know. When we know, we can do something about it, and there is the desire to change, but we just don't know. Knowing is power. Understanding the stories is a step to helping. And I think no one wants these young people to suffer." Essie continued: "Yes, it is this way. People just don't know. The ones who make the laws, they don't know that this can happen. And then the people working with the kids, they don't know what to do. It's important to have dialogue so that we can be clear about the problems. And then we can help."

When I last talked to Meysoon in early 2015, she was very happy: she had been in touch with several pro bono lawyers from Human Line and was hopeful she might be able to procure a passport to go in search of her mother. Though she had little information about her mother's whereabouts, the lawyers had also put her in touch with the Indian embassy, which was trying to track down her mother and her address. Working together in this way, NGOs, embassies, and government organizations may be able to bring about policies that are more in line with the challenges of the lived realities of young people in Kuwait and across Asia.

Young people like Meysoon, Alia, and Cecilia were thrust into frustrating situations of immobility by the circumstances of their birth. They exist as liminal im/migrants without a home, exemplifying the most extreme conditions of statelessness that scholars such as Jacqueline Bhabha write about. Yet they understand and recast their notion of "home" in terms of where they find support and where they can be integrated. Though they are not as fortunate as young people like Mona or other "royal foundlings," they find ways to carve out a space for themselves in their homes, even if this process is often frustrating and leads to many dead ends. In doing so, they find ways to explore their identity and sense of self and seek out alternate modes of mobility in the face of their immobilities.

6

TRANSFORMATIONS AND MOBILIZATIONS

"ME, I DON'T DETEST THE GOVERNMENT," said Fabian, a slender Malagasy woman not more than five feet tall, "or really, the governments (*les gouvernmentes*), because the governments often help me. But the people, or really, my employer, it's she who detests me." Fabian wore a scarf on her head because, in her words, "the working abroad made me sick, and made me lose my hair and all and all." Fabian was born and raised in a rural area located in the southern part of Madagascar. After her two brothers were killed during violent altercations resulting from the illegal stealing and selling of zebu (a species of cattle), Fabian's father decided to move to Antananarivo, the capital of Madagascar, in search of safety for his only remaining child. When they arrived in Tana in 2012, as locals refer to the capital, her seventy-five-year-old father could not find work.

One day when Fabian was shopping in the Wednesday market, she spotted a flyer promising high wages for women willing to migrate abroad for work. She took the flyer and found the advertising agency the next day. When she visited the agency, she was told that she would be sent to Kuwait and would be making the equivalent of USD$500 per month, a vast sum of money for Malagasy families, who generally subsist on less than USD$2 per day. She was told she would be given regular days off and would work no more than eight hours a day. "What kind of work, they don't tell me exactly, just that I'm working in the house. That is all," Fabian said.

The agency recruiting Fabian turned her over to their partnering agency in Kuwait. When she arrived, the staff at the partnering agency told her she was on a tourist visa, as opposed to a working visa, and that she should keep a low profile because her migration had been illegal. "That is the first time I'm hearing that I'm there illegally. Later I come to learn that Malagache [Malagasy] women are not supposed to go to the Middle East, for this reason I'm just given a tourist visa, but then I didn't know exactly."[1] Fabian was placed in the home of a Kuwaiti family who insisted she wear a veil that covered her from head to toe, only revealing her hands and face. She was given a very small room where she was made to sleep on the floor and was permitted only three to four hours of sleep each night. The house consisted of five stories, with several rooms on each floor. Fabian did not have much experience with domestic work, so it took her some time to learn how to work and clean efficiently.

"Because I don't always know what to do, and because there is a problem with the language, my madam is getting very angry with me a lot of the time," said Fabian. Her female employer began abusing her soon after she arrived. "She hit me, bite me, throw hot water on me, and pull my hair like this," Fabian said, pulling a strand of her hair from her scarf and making a face to demonstrate the suffering she had endured. Her female employer was frequently dissatisfied with Fabian's work and made her dissatisfaction known. On occasion, when Fabian went to sleep before her female employer, her madam would enter her room, wake her, and beat her. "At first, I didn't know why, but later I come to understand that because if I went to sleep before her, then the husband would ask her to do things. And then he would say, 'Why Fabian is asleep so early? You make her work too hard, you should do some of the house things so she doesn't work so hard.' But that made my madam more angry, and detest me more." When she tried to call the recruiting agency in Kuwait for assistance, they told her she should work harder or she would be arrested. When she called the recruiters in Madagascar, she was told that her situation was now "out of their hands."

When Fabian fell behind on her chores, her female employer began giving her shots twice a week. To this day, Fabian does not know what exactly was in the shots, but after the shots her muscles hurt, her hands trembled, and she could not sleep. "The madam is telling me I must do the shots for more energy so I work better, but my body cannot support the shots," Fabian said, referring to the fact that she began to have epileptic seizures after receiving these unidentified injections.

One evening, the male head of household returned from work to find his wife beating Fabian so severely that Fabian began hemorrhaging. Fabian's male employer then began to beat his wife and locked her in their bedroom. Afterwards, he came to Fabian and offered her money. "He came and said to me 'Fabian, you must leave here, if not, my wife will kill you. She is a very jealous woman, and she will hurt you. You must go.' But I was too weak. He saw then that I'm very sick. So I try to rest some days, but I keep the money he gave me and I keep the idea." One night a few weeks later, Fabian exited the house under the pretense of taking out the trash. "That night, I took out the trash and never came back," she said with a slight laugh, revealing a warm smile for the first time.

She was not sure where to go but was certain she did not want to go to the police for fear of arrest on account of the illegal nature of her migration. When an Ethiopian taxi driver offered her a ride, asking her if she wanted to go to the police or the hospital, she asked him to take her to the South African embassy. "I don't know why I'm saying South African embassy, just I have a feeling that there they can help me," Fabian recalled, smiling once again at the decision she had made some months ago. She arrived at the South African embassy just after midnight, and it was closed. The taxi driver, however, recognized the security guard at the entrance and convinced him to allow Fabian to spend the night in the security booth. She was grateful for the help and glad to have a place to rest, as her health was worsening.

The next day she went inside the South African embassy and was able to speak with the labor attaché, despite not being a South African citizen. "He was so kind and helped me. He took me to the shelter and said that he would look after me, which he did." She was taken to a local shelter that housed over 130 women of different nationalities, most of whom had run away from their employers. There was a caseworker working with them, and the Ministry of Foreign Affairs in Kuwait oversaw the shelter. "There, the shelter, it was okay, but like a prison. Not much to do, eat and sleep, and you can't leave. And you are just sitting there, waiting and waiting," Fabian said. After a few weeks the labor attaché from the South African embassy came to visit her and observed that Fabian's health was still worsening. He told her that he was working on finding her passport and resolving her paperwork so that she could return to Madagascar. "He asked me if I am happy at the shelter, but he can see that I'm getting more and more sick. So he calls Mama Lisa from the church and she comes to take me to another, better place, in the church, where I have doctors." Fabian pulled out a photograph of herself sitting in front of a Christmas tree inside a Kuwaiti apartment with four other African women.

At Mama Lisa's informal shelter, Fabian met several other women in similar situations, many of whom had been waiting months or even years to return home. After six weeks, however, the South African labor attaché came once again to visit her. He told her that he had worked with the Ministry of Foreign Affairs in Kuwait and succeeded in creating an outpass for her and procuring a ticket back home.[2] Her ticket was paid for by the Kuwaiti government, which also issued her a check for back pay she had not received for many months. "They were so kind to me, the South Africans and the Kuwaitis, so kind, they helped me to come home. They were worried for me, you know, because I'm sick, so they really wanted to get me home."

When she arrived back in Madagascar, however, she did not receive a warm reception from the customs and immigration personnel at the airport. She was taken to a holding room by several policemen and questioned for many hours. She was told that she had violated a Malagasy law forbidding Malagasy citizens to migrate in order to work in the Middle East. Because she had violated their laws, the police officer told Fabian, she could face arrest and heavy fines. "But even this police, he could see I am sick, that I need help. So, thankfully, he called my pastor instead of arresting me. Then my pastor came and took me to the church; I am so lucky." Fabian spent a week living in the informal shelter at the church in Antananarivo before going home to her father, who was now very ill. Fabian's pastor arranged for her to have regular medical checkups, but she could not afford the medical care that her doctor prescribed.

Today, Fabian is struggling to pay her own and her father's medical bills. She and another survivor of labor abuse who had also migrated to Kuwait and returned home are working together to open a clothing shop in Tana and have successfully secured a loan from the church. Most important, Fabian's story and those of six other Malagasy women who migrated to Kuwait and faced abuse inspired the drafting of a new human trafficking law in August of 2014. Her return and her ability to explain the damaging difficulties posed by the agencies and her employers as well as the help she received from embassy officials and the Ministry of Foreign Affairs affairs in Kuwait have compelled the Malagasy government to rethink their law. Rather than banning women from migrating to the Middle East, the government now seeks to regulate migration and to ensure the presence of Malagasy officials in each country where citizens may travel to work. Fabian is currently working with her pastor and her fellow survivors to influence the new law being drafted by the Ministry of Justice, which will take into consideration their lived experiences and concerns.

ı ı ı

As this story shows, both migrants and the state may be transformed by migrant-state encounters. Whether in the home or host country, interactions between migrants and local or state officials affect and are affected by migrants' intimate lives. The micro-opportunities made possible by multiple state actors may be obscured when migrants are viewed as being in opposition to a reified and monolithic state. Such a view precludes a deeper analysis of how interactions between migrants and those acting on behalf of the state can create opportunities on both sides of the relationship. It is important to examine closely what happens when migrants interact with "the state" in its various, personified forms. These individual and personified manifestations of the state may include embassy officials, employers, hospital staff, or law enforcement. Migrants also experience other arms of "the state," which might not traditionally be understood as "the state," including NGOs, activists, religious authorities, and even employers in the Gulf. These encounters transform migrants and the states within which they move and live, generating micromobilities and movements. For the state, these micromovements include the creation of support networks, NGOs, orphanages, and occasionally changes in policy. For migrants, migrant-state interactions also present new opportunities for them to negotiate their agency and to mobilize through their frustrating immobility. In addition, these interactions affect those who present migrants with challenges and possibilities along their journeys. Migrants draw on their intimate lives in producing these micromobilities and movements. The possibility of drawing on intimate lives to change the im/mobilities of others together with such small openings—provided, created, or forced—were among the most profound opportunities for many of the migrants and state officials I met.

One of my interlocutors asked me, "But who or what is the state?" Rather than being a monolithic, reified, or static construction, "the state" comprises many different layers of power. It is important to understand "the state" as it acts in response to migration and is encountered by migrants themselves. When talking about migrant interactions with the state, I'm referring to both home and host countries, since I follow migrants through the cycles of interactions they have with state actors, citizens, migrant networks, and home communities. Rather than being one monolithic entity that affects all individuals in the same way, the state is experienced differently by different individuals, citizens and noncitizens alike. Furthermore, migrants experience the state, both at home and abroad, in ways that differ from legal, formal, or academic notions of the state. Various agents of the same state may also work at odds with one another. While some agents of the state may facilitate mobility, others restrict and challenge migrants' movements, compounding migrants' frustrations with immobility. In Fabian's case, for example, while her employer-sponsor sought to limit her mobility, the Kuwaiti-sponsored shelter and caseworker facilitated her mobility and return home.

⦙ ⦙ ⦙

Like migrants, state officials must also remain dynamic and flexible as they respond to the rapid changes—social, economic, demographic, and political—that take place around them. Interactions with migrants affect and sometimes transform these policy makers and state officials themselves, particularly when their intimate or private lives become interconnected with those of migrant workers. Adopting Viviana Zelizer's "connected lives" approach, one can see how migrant-state intimacies reveal the interconnections between social and economic mobility and the lives of both migrants and those with whom they work or form intimate connections (Zelizer 2005). These "connected lives" highlight the interdependence between migrants and various personifications of the state at the microlevel of the intimate rather than the macrolevel that is generally given priority in academic and legal discourse. In these microcosms, migrants, and those with whom they connect, mobilize through various types of immobility, both physical and emotional.

Migrants' lived experiences highlight the simultaneous challenges and opportunities presented by the state. Some agents of the state may challenge mobility by establishing laws, confiscating passports, or limiting contact with family members, while others may be invested in protecting migrants at home or abroad. The majority of the migrants I met said that their experience of "the state" was as some combination of restricter and facilitator of mobility. Similarly, in the host country, migrants point to laws and state apparatuses that may seek to restrict mobility but contain loopholes that allow movement on various levels.

Policies that seek to stringently create and police fixed categories of the status of migrants should arouse the most skepticism. Policies that place migrants in static positions often exacerbate the challenges migrants face by failing to take into account what may best support them and their families in terms of their desires and choices. Boundaries between categories such as formal/informal, immigrant/migrant, legal/illegal, and consensual/forced are more fluid in the lived experiences of migrants and thus challenge this kind of state policy. We should question the efficacy of policies that are designed around these categorical distinctions and analyze the consequences of state policies for migrants' lives. Fabian's migration trajectory illustrates how migrant workers can end up in various categories of illegality or informality; yet these "illegal" and "informal" modalities are essential to the workings of states—as much as if not more than labor that is considered "legal" and "formal."[3]

Migrant families seeking to move various family members across borders face significant legal, economic, and social challenges in obtaining citizenship, reunification permissions, and even migratory visas. In efforts to keep their intimate lives whole, migrants inevitably come into contact with a host of state and nonstate actors. The interactions between them and the resulting incremental changes that result fundamentally transform both migrants and their sending and/or receiving states. Migration may be viewed as a static or permanent process: assumptions may be made on the part of receiving and sometimes sending countries that migrants who move across borders wish to stay in their new homes. This holds true in some cases, like those of the migrants in Chapter 4 who do not wish to return home. But often this is not the case, especially when the notion of "home" shifts again and again as migration impacts the intimate lives and subjectivities of migrants and their loved ones.

Encounters and Transformations

Migrants encounter and interact with the state in a variety of contexts. The case studies below explore these various microcosms in order to better understand the contours of these encounters. Looking at individuals' lived experiences through the lens of these encounters also illuminates the diverse and fluid nature of the state and challenges our understanding of state and nonstate actors. I have chosen these particular case studies from various parts of my fieldwork because each of these persons encountered or represented the state in a different context. In addition, these encounters testify to the "connected lives" of migrants and those with whom they interact, as well as the blurred lines between categories such as formal/informal (Garcés-Mascareñas 2008). The perverse integration of migrants into the economic and social systems of the spaces they inhabit raises further questions concerning the artificial nature of this and other, similar binaries.

Lorena and Her Employer

Lorena moved to Dubai in 2008 at the age of twenty-five, leaving most of her friends and family behind in the Philippines. She had completed a master's degree in education but was unable to find a job at home. She made a difficult decision to migrate to the Middle East in search of employment in order to help support her mother and two younger brothers back home. Several of her cousins had moved to the Gulf and were successfully employed as nannies and caretakers. "But I was not eager to join them," Lorena recalled, describing her trepidation at the prospect of moving to Dubai. "When I got my posting, everyone is saying 'Oh, you are so lucky, Lorena! Dubai! You get to go to Dubai!' But I am not thinking I'm lucky. Lucky would have been to stay home with my family and get a job close to them." Lorena is a petite woman, not quite five feet tall, with long, thick black hair that pools at her waist when she sits. When I first met her, she spoke quite softly, eyes frequently darting nervously around the room. Over time, however, her comportment relaxed and she spoke louder, her movements more animated. She was especially open to talking during visits in which I brought my son or daughter with me to the interview; in the presence of the children, Lorena spoke much more freely.

Lorena's migratory process took several months. She underwent training for domestic work abroad and had to work through a significant amount of red tape before successfully acquiring a job. "All that time I'm thinking, 'Oh no, what if after all this I'm getting there and I'm like the other Pinoys who are getting beaten, or worse, coming back dead?'" Lorena had been reading stories in the newspapers that described in graphic detail the challenges that Overseas Filipino/a Workers (OFWs) faced abroad. "But there isn't work for me, not work for me in the Philippines, so I know I'm having to be brave, to take it, to make it my destiny."

To her relief, Lorena was placed in the home of a local family who were very kind to her. Her employers had three daughters, and Lorena quickly grew very fond of the children. Over time she became quite close to her female employer, who was active in several local charities. "My madam was so kind, so loving, at that time, she is becoming like my mom even," Lorena said. For this reason, even when Lorena's three-year contract had expired, Lorena stayed on to work for her employers. She was able to send the equivalent of USD$800 home each month, which allowed her mother to finance her youngest brother's education. Lorena was so pleased with her working conditions that she did not realize the consequences she might face by overstaying her work permit.

During one of Lorena's visits to a local charity with her employer Lorena met Imran, an Emirati police officer who was very attentive to her. He asked for her phone number, and the two began meeting during Lorena's days off. "And every night we are talking or doing SMS [text message], and we are telling each other about our life and our dreams like that." In late 2012 Lorena realized she had become pregnant. Anxious about her future both with her employers and with Imran, she decided to keep the pregnancy a secret at first. "I know I'm in love with him, and I know he loves me, but I'm worried, what his parents will say? What will happen? And what my madam will say? I don't want to bring shame on anyone, but I know I must tell them."

Lorena's employers noticed her pregnancy first. Her female employer knew of Lorena's relationship with Imran and often cautioned her against becoming too close to him. Lorena said that she never knew why and always assumed that her employer did not like her boyfriend, but didn't realize the extent of her employer's concerns until later. When Lorena's employer confronted her with questions about her changing figure and behavior, Lorena was worried. "I tell her the truth. I tell her I love Imran, and this is his baby. I'm thinking that day I will be out. Sent back to the Philippines, but no, my madam good to me, even then."

Her employer was supportive of Lorena's pregnancy and assisted her with prenatal care. Lorena was also given a lighter work schedule, with more hours and days off. Imran, however, was not as understanding. At the encouragement of her employer, Lorena told Imran of her pregnancy. Expecting joy and possibly a marriage proposal, Lorena was disappointed and fearful when Imran became angry. "He mad then. Too mad at me. He tells me he will put me in jail. Deport me. And I know he is police so he can. And I'm too scared."

Afraid of Imran's anger, Lorena returned to her employer's home uncertain of what to do next. As her due date drew closer, the number of tasks Lorena could perform dwindled. She knew that once the baby was born she would be unable to work as much as she had before. She also knew that returning home unmarried but with a child would have significant consequences: Lorena's family were devout Catholics who would likely ostracize her. It was during this time that Lorena realized she had overstayed her visa and was facing steep fines.

One of the organizations with which Lorena's employer volunteered had connections with the embassy of the Philippines, specifically with the labor attaché. Lorena was nervous, however, that because she had illegally overstayed her work permit, the embassy would turn her in to the police. Furthermore, she was told by several volunteers at the charity that she could easily be arrested by the police in Dubai and charged with the crime of *zina* as well as breach of contract. "I am afraid at every corner. If I stay, problems for me and the baby, maybe I'm in jail. If I go to the embassy, maybe they send me to jail too, maybe in Dubai, maybe back home. Even if I go home, I'm scared of what my family will say, but I'm still wanting to go home."

Lorena's employer was able to speak to the Filipino labor attaché through her contacts at the charity. Ironically, it was only then that her employer realized her own culpability in not renewing Lorena's work contract. By not attending to the necessary paperwork, she had placed her employee at increased risk and in a precarious situation. While it was the case that Lorena could be tried for the crime of *zina* and breach of contract, overstaying her visa added an extra layer of culpability. The attaché was sympathetic and told Lorena's employer that Lorena could stay at the embassy shelter until she gave birth, at which time she would be sent home along with the baby. "My madam told me that was good news. She said I'm not going to jail, not here, not in the Philippines. Just going home." She smiled as her eyes filled with tears.

Lorena moved to the shelter later that week and gave birth to a baby boy six weeks later. The staff at the embassy shelter were very accommodating and assisted her in paying the fines she had accrued for overstaying her visa. The labor attaché also issued a temporary passport for the baby and put her in touch with a local Filipino organization back in Manila that could help the baby secure citizenship. Lorena was overjoyed. During the time she had spent at the shelter she had heard stories about women who abandoned their babies out of fear or women who had been imprisoned and given birth to their children in jail and then been deported without their babies. "Me, I'm just happy I'm going home with him," she said, kissing her son on the forehead. "I know at home it will be hard, but in time, my family will accept, and we will move on. Most important is that everyone stays together, that's all I ask now, just to be with my family." Lorena's eyes brimmed with tears.

ı ı ı

Throughout her migratory journey, Lorena encountered "the state" in many different forms, encounters that both challenged and facilitated her mobility. At home, in the Philippines, she had faced bureaucratic challenges in having to wait months for her employment application to be processed as she incurred increasing levels of debt. When she arrived in Dubai, her employer-sponsor was supportive and tried to facilitate Lorena's mobility to the extent she was able. Lorena's relationship with an officer of the state, however, became precarious and exposed her to another level of risk. Her employer, a human arm of the Emirati state given how the state has legally vested power in citizen employers,

helped her overcome the challenges incurred by her pregnancy, a manifesta-
tion of the mobility and immobility of her intimate life. Her employer, however, also created a situation of illegality for her employee by not renewing her
paperwork. Lorena was able to overcome the immobility that resulted from
her pregnancy because she was assisted by her employer, as well as by the labor
attaché of her sending country. Throughout these different encounters Lorena
was able to find pockets of mobility. She was able to move physically and emotionally, while the fruits of her reproductive labor were able to remain close,
avoiding the alienation that can often occur for women in her situation. These
encounters likely transformed Lorena, inasmuch as they presented challenges
and opportunities within which she was able to move. However, such encounters may also transform various human arms of the state, as can be seen clearly
in the case of Iqbal.

Iqbal and Amitya

Iqbal is, in his own words, "as much Emirati as Jordanian." He was born just
outside of Dubai to Jordanian parents who had moved to Dubai to work in the
booming textile industry in the mid-1970s. Born and raised in the UAE but carrying a Jordanian passport, Iqbal said repeatedly that he felt his national loyalties were torn. "I mean, I know that I'm a foreigner, and once a foreigner, always
a foreigner here in the UAE, but I feel very protective of this country because it
has given me so much."

Iqbal was able to take advantage of education subsidies given to the children of some migrants who wish to study abroad. He received a scholarship
from the Emirati government to attend university in the United Kingdom.
After completing his bachelor's degree in political science, Iqbal moved back
to Dubai and took a position in the human rights branch of the Emirati police
department. Five years into his tenure with the police department, he was promoted to a position in the humanitarian branch of the Emirati government,
where he currently works as a liaison with the United Nations.

"When first they are giving me this job, in this, this, place . . ." Iqbal began,
exhaling swirls of cigarette smoke as he gestured around his office at UN headquarters in Dubai. He would often pause for long periods, taking a drag on
his cigarette—despite the numerous NO SMOKING signs that were present in
every room—and squinting his eyes for effect. Sometimes he would stop so
long midsentence I would assume he had finished talking and would interject
another question or even attempt to finish his sentence for him. I interrupted

him on many occasions, but he never grew impatient. "You mean this office?" I asked. "I'm explaining," he said. "Wait, eh? So by this place I mean this whole operation, all of it." He exhaled another cloud of smoke and leaned back in his chair. There were times when I was certain that Iqbal was trying to look like a villain from a movie, often becoming a veritable caricature of himself.

"So, I didn't know why they give me this job—labor? Migration? What do I know of these things? But I'm learning. And I learned from the strangest way . . . You want to know how?" I nodded. "From my maid," he said, puffs of cigarette smoke wafting out of his mouth. He paused, waiting for my reaction, then leaned back in his chair to continue. "It was my maid who taught me everything. Amitya. She is Malaysian. And it's because of her that I can do my job."

Iqbal had hired Amitya when his wife died and left him to care for their two daughters. "I actually went to Kuala Lumpur to interview ladies; I thought it was really important that I not just be assigned someone," Iqbal said. When he met Amitya, Iqbal felt she would be a good fit. "She was smiling all the time, a small fat woman, but so happy. I thought she will be perfect, and I was right, my daughters adore her, they even call her Auntie Amitya now." Amitya moved in with Iqbal and began caring for his daughters. But she often would talk about her own children back home, remarking how much she missed them.

"I started imagining what it must be like for her kids, like for them it's like their mom died too. So I started thinking, maybe Amitya should go visit them more often." He booked Amitya a flight back to Kuala Lumpur and called his own mother to ask for her assistance while Amitya was away. After two weeks, however, Amitya did not return. Iqbal tried calling and calling, but the mobile phone he had given her had been disconnected. Iqbal then tried calling the agency that he had worked with to hire Amitya. "But you know what they told me? They told me, 'You stupid man, why did you send her home? Of course she is going to run away!'" Iqbal laughed. "But I didn't think that she would run away. I don't know why, I just didn't think it. Then I told some friends in the police department and they all laughed at me, saying I got what I deserved." Iqbal narrowed his eyes as he glanced at the "HUMAN TRAFFICKING" poster on his wall.

"So, I'm thinking, that's it, she's gone, skipped out on me, that's it. I started looking at hiring another maid, someone else. But then, one day maybe two weeks after I hire someone else, I get a call on my cell phone." Iqbal picked up his cell phone for effect. "Guess who it is? It's Amitya. She is crying. She is calling me from a jail in Kuala Lumpur, can you believe it? She is using her one call that they permit her per month to call not her family, but me. And she keeps crying, telling me how terrible it is in the jail for her, just awful." Amitya had been arrested at the airport in Kuala Lumpur when trying to return to Dubai. She was told that she had migrated illegally and that the visa on her passport was invalid. Despite her protests, she was put in jail. Iqbal tried calling the Malaysian embassy in Dubai, but they were not helpful. He called some friends at his old police division, but they too said that nothing could be done. "But I knew I can't just leave her in jail. I wanted to help. She had become like family to me. And I was calling everyone in the police department and embassies, and then suddenly I thought, wait a minute, I work on these things. I work on trafficking. This is trafficking. She is being trafficked in her own country. I work with the ILO and IOM. So I called them, and they helped me go there." Iqbal rose from his chair and started to pace the room.

Iqbal arrived in Kuala Lumpur and went straight to the prison where Amitya was being held. "It was a terrible place. So many women in one room. Just disgusting. The women were in rags and treated horribly; I had no idea that someone could be put in a prison like this just for visa problems, just horrible." Iqbal rolled his *r*'s as he spoke. He worked with a local branch of the IOM to secure Amitya's release, but he was not able to return to Dubai with her immediately. She was placed in what Iqbal called a "holding center," where she was made to live while her paperwork was being processed. "This place was just like a nicer jail, but it was still a jail. And she was stuck there for three months." Iqbal and Amitya spoke every week by telephone while Iqbal worked to arrange a working visa and sponsorship papers. After three months Amitya was permitted to return to Dubai.

"I was happy I could come back and work for sir," Amitya said upon her return. "He did a lot for me, and still does a lot for all my family." Amitya described her time in prison as painful and torturous. "But the worst part wasn't the violence or hunger, the worst part was being in jail just a few miles from my children and not being able to see them." By 2013, Amitya had been away from her children for three years. While she visited every year, she said that the relationship had become strained. She was glad to be able to provide for her family and happy with her employment but often wished she could return home to her family life.

For Iqbal, his experiences with Amitya inspired him to work with both the Emirati government and the United Nations to create pathways of safe migration. He was instrumental in strengthening one of the local shelters, and has more recently been working with the UAE government to broker safe and regulated migration between the UAE and countries in Southeast Asia. In 2013 he organized a conference to bring together various stakeholders to support broadening notions of human trafficking in the GCC countries. For both Amitya and Iqbal, their relationship was mutually transformative and has led to larger transformations that may impact the mobility of others. The following story, of Claudia and Helene, provides another example of multiple transformations occurring through a microcosm of encounters.

Claudia and Helene

"Everyday I used to cry one cup full of tears," says Claudia, raising her teacup in a mock toast. Her pastor, Helene, lifts her teacup to Claudia's, and as the two clink, Helene starts to laugh. "Here's to no more tears," she says. Helene then turns to me and adds, "No more tears for Claudia, and I hope, once our law is passed, no more suffering for any Malagasy women." Claudia breathes a sigh of relief as she picks up her spoon to begin eating. "I'm too happy to be home," she says. "I'm so lucky, from nightmares to dreams. I'm back. I'm secure. I'm in this nice place. And I am with my family."

We are all seated inside Pastor Helene's makeshift office/shelter/church/ school. Two large adjoining rooms serve as multipurpose centers for Bible study, children's lessons, work skills training, and on occasion living quarters for women returning from their stints abroad. The linoleum floor is covered in small cushions and pillows. In one corner two small worn-out rugs featuring train tracks, and animals line the back walls. In another corner, three small couches create what Helene calls a "discussion space." Even though it is winter, the windows are open, and a bone-chilling breeze sweeps in every few moments, causing all the women in the room to pull their scarves and jackets tighter around their bodies for warmth. The paint peels from the walls, which are decorated with children's drawings and pictures of various events, from christenings to birthday parties to outreach missions. The women in the room smile and laugh as they find photographs of themselves to point out to me. There is an aura of calm inside these rooms, making the space feel like a sanctuary. Just to the left of the doorway is a small desk with a laptop that remains switched on. Claudia waits patiently before sitting down at the laptop to show me pictures of her friends and family that have been saved on the desktop.

"That is my son. Three girls and then one boy. I really wanted a boy," Claudia says, pointing to a picture of herself hugging a little boy who appears to be between five and seven years old. They are standing in front of a Christmas tree, the boy grinning from ear to ear. Claudia was showing me the pictures to fill in the details of her story, which she had told me earlier that day as we sat with Helene in the sanctuary.

Claudia made the difficult decision to migrate when her husband began abusing her and refused to give her money for the children. She suspected him of having an affair and reasoned that he wanted to save his money for his new mistress. "*Bien sur* [of course], marriage is difficult," Helene said when Claudia described her marital troubles. "But divorce," said Helene, "it's not an option for most of us. So many people go abroad instead of divorce." Claudia nodded and laughed at this. "So from one bad situation, I found another," she said quietly.

"When my children were going hungry because my husband would not help, I knew that I would have to work to send money home, it was the only way. For money. That's why I left. For love and money." Claudia found a flyer advertising work abroad and followed the address to a local recruiter in Tana. The recruiter promised her high wages and good working conditions. She was told she would be a nanny abroad, somewhere in the Middle East. "At that time, I'm thinking Lebanon maybe. I knew of one lady who had gone to Lebanon, so I'm thinking that's where I'm going, but no, for me it was Kuwait."

When she arrived in Kuwait, Claudia was placed in the home of a large family and tasked with caring for seven children in addition to the elderly parents of her female employer. She was made to wear *hijab* and forced to work long hours, with only three hours off in a twenty-four-hour period. When Claudia grew weary, her employers, like Fabian's, began to give her regular shots that she described as "energy shots." "I still don't know what they were," Claudia began. "But they made me, they made it so I was tired but couldn't sleep. And the worst, the hardest was that it hurt my muscles, my hands and my wrists." She opened and closed her hands and massaged her forearms as she remembered the pain. "Sometimes it still hurts me."

During Ramadan, Claudia was not permitted to eat. After a few months Claudia realized that her wages were not being paid. When she mentioned this to her employers, she was told that she would not be paid until they felt that her work was worthy of pay. Claudia felt depressed, fatigued, and very homesick, especially after receiving this new information. When I asked Claudia to describe her working conditions, she paused to reflect on her experiences. After a long silence she spoke up. "It wasn't all bad. I guess it just depends on your employers, because some people have a good madam, some people no. For me, the problem was long, long hours. And I never did anything well enough for them. They were always getting angry and telling me to do it again. It wasn't all bad though: I had a nice room, and the house was very nice. But the work was so hard. And I missed my children a lot." I later asked Claudia about the seven children she looked after. "Oh, the children, they are the worst!" she exclaimed, becoming very animated. "Actually, it was the little girls, not the little boys. But the little girls, they pull my hair, throw things at me, treating me very bad." One of the other women in the room overheard Claudia's description of her charges and stepped in to echo her friend's sentiments. "The children really are the worst," said Rayina, another woman who had just returned from Kuwait. Helene stepped in to add her thoughts: "What kind of children are they raising? Children who are taught it is OK to treat another human being this way?"

After seven months Claudia felt she could no longer endure the long working hours and the distance from her family, especially without being paid. She had also grown weak and weary from the work and the shots and frequently experienced dizzy spells. One night, around midnight, Claudia jumped from the window of her bedroom on the second floor. She ran outside the compound and began walking away. A few hours later the heat and her exhaustion overwhelmed her, and she lay down in a grassy patch along the road and slept. She had only been asleep for an hour when a Bangladeshi taxi driver woke her, asking if she was okay. "He came and started shaking me, I think he was scared because he thought I was dead," she said, laughing at the memory. "But he was so kind. He asked me where I want to go. I said 'Take me to the French embassy.' But he said, 'It's Saturday morning and the embassy won't open until Monday morning,' so he was kind and he took me to the hospital." Fortunately, the taxi driver knew two of the nurses at the hospital. Claudia had told him she was illegal, so the driver had her wait in the taxi until he spoke with his friends. After a few moments, the two nurses came outside and ushered Claudia into a small room at the back of the hospital. There she was given food, clothing, and the opportunity to rest. "I'll always be grateful for those few days," Claudia said.

On Monday morning the Bangladeshi taxi driver returned to the hospital to pick Claudia up and take her to the French embassy. After a few hours at the French embassy, the labor attaché helped Claudia to be transferred to the local shelter overseen by the Ministry of Foreign Affairs. Claudia's time at the shelter was limited, however, as her employers brought a case against her, charging her with crimes of theft. She was put in prison and told she would remain there until she was able to pay back the cost of the goods she had been accused of stealing. "They said I stole the furniture, but how am I stealing furniture? Where am I putting it?" Claudia asked rhetorically. When the French embassy received word that Claudia was in jail, they alerted colleagues at the Swiss embassy, who called Helene.

Pastor Helene became a dual citizen of Madagascar and Switzerland when she married a Swiss man in the late 1990s. She and her husband began working with the men and women of Helene's congregation in Tana in 2000. Part of Helene's ministerial work includes outreach to young Malagasy men and women living on the streets. She works with them to provide shelter and vocational training. She has recently partnered with the now internationally known Akany Avoko, an orphanage turned social justice organization that seeks to provide for young people without a home, and does much of her work through the organization. Although part of the nonprofit and civil-society sector, Helene, her church, and Akany Avoko have all earned high status in the eyes of government officials, who regularly call on them for legal and practical advice. Helene's days consist of working on the ground at the grassroots level in between meetings at the state level.

One of the women with whom Helene worked in 2008 told her that she wanted to move to Lebanon to work as a nanny. "I'm surprised," Helene said. "I asked her, are you sure? You want to move so far away? You want to go all the way to Lebanon?" The young woman told Helene that she had heard wages in Lebanon were high and working conditions desirable. "I remember she said to me, 'Pastora, if I stay here, I'm going to be a prostitute, but if I go there, it will be different. I can save money to start really a new life.' So, I said, 'OK, go my child.' But I'm always worrying about her and praying for her." A few months after this young woman moved to Lebanon, Helene, having had no word from her, tried but was unable to reach her. Helene contacted the agency that had facilitated the woman's migration, but the agency had closed down. With the help of her Swiss husband, Helene traveled to Lebanon to find the young woman. "It was hard, very hard to find her. And I'm contacting everyone. Finally, I found her, but where? In the morgue. I found her dead body and I brought it back home." Helene lowered her voice almost to a whisper.

"This is the time I'm learning about human trafficking. I'm learning about bad things happening to people when they go abroad. And I'm thinking, this, what happened to this girl, that was trafficking for sure," said Helene. The experience inspired Helene to become active in learning about human trafficking and the plight of Malagasy women around the world. She added trafficking as

an initiative for her ministry and organization and began working with government officials in Madagascar to locate other women undergoing abuse while
working abroad. Helene created partnerships with organizations in Switzerland, Lebanon, India, and Saudi Arabia. She began working actively to assist
women who wanted to return to Madagascar or Malagasy women who needed
help abroad. "I knew that I didn't want to find another Malagasy woman in a
morgue, that's what I knew. I knew I wanted to find the women before they
faced too much suffering."

On one of her trips to Geneva, she received a call from the Malagasy ambas-
sador in Geneva, who told her of Claudia's situation. Helene was not aware that
Malagasy women had also migrated to Kuwait but was eager to assist anyone
who wanted her help. At this point, one of Helene's contacts in the United States
put her in touch with me because he knew of my work on trafficking, labor, and
migration in the Gulf. Together, we began working through a number of different avenues to understand the contours of the situation that Claudia—and as we
later learned, over four dozen other Malagasy women—was facing. Through a
series of conversations with US and French officials at the embassies in Kuwait,
Helene arranged for Claudia's release from prison. Helene contacted an American pastor in Kuwait and asked her to take Claudia in until Helene herself could
make her way to Kuwait. Helene and I also began working with the Ministry of
Justice and the Ministry of Population in Madagascar, who decided to get involved because of the series of cases Helene presented to them. Helene traveled
with several Malagasy officials to Kuwait and was able to facilitate the transfer or
release of forty-two women, eight of whom were able to return to Madagascar
with their babies. To this day, the women that Helene works with view her as the
most compassionate and effective arm of the state working for social change.

Claudia shows me the pictures Helene took while they were all in Kuwait
living at the home of the American pastor. There are seven other women in the
photos, all of them smiling, and Claudia describes that period as one of the best
times of her life. She clicks the mouse to show me a picture of herself with her
four children and husband. She looks at me and shrugs. "So, I had to come
back home to him. And it has been hard coming back, hard with my husband,
but better than before. Now he wants to help. He wants to help the children.
My absence was good and bad. Good because he is helping with money, but
bad because now he doesn't speak to me at all. Still, we are all under one roof."

Helene comes to the laptop as Claudia stands to wrap another sweater around
herself. The wind whips through the room and knocks over some of the food.

Claudia and three other women gather up the tablecloth and begin, calmly, to reset the table. Helene sits down at the laptop and minimizes the photo screen. She brings up a Word document to show me: a new draft of the law being written by the Ministry of Justice, the first of its kind to address the realities of human trafficking from the standpoint of advancing the human rights of Malagasy migrants. Because of our work with the Malagasy women in Kuwait, the Ministry of Justice has given Helene and me the opportunity to revise the law. Though I had initially come into contact with Helene in an advisory capacity, I had become deeply involved with her and the women with whom she had been working. I was interested in documenting the women's stories, but as an engaged anthropologist I could not help but want to use the work we had done to effect some positive change. Helene and I worked together to redraft the law, asking for more protections for women abroad, insisting that they remove bans on migration and instead regulate it so that women are not forced to rely on unscrupulous recruiters, and demanding that all recruiting agencies be held accountable. To our surprise, the Ministry of Justice approved all our suggested changes and took the new draft of the law to parliament, though to this day it has not been passed officially.

Claudia, Fabian, and the other women who have returned from Kuwait are overjoyed that their experiences have helped to effect some possible change. Their encounters with various arms of various states at embassies, shelters, hospitals, and ministries of justice back home have transformed them, while their experiences have also transformed the states. The possible passage of the new human trafficking law in Madagascar is a major milestone that would not have been possible without the bravery of Malagasy women who shared their experiences.

Munirah, Dee, and Aisha

Munirah was born and raised in Kuwait. The eldest of five daughters, she grew up in a wealthy family just outside of Kuwait City. When she finished high school, the Kuwaiti government financed her move to London to attend university, paying for everything from school supplies to apartment furnishings. "When I was in London, a lot of people asked me why I would ever go back to Kuwait, why I wouldn't just stay in London, but I always felt like they didn't understand. Kuwait gave me so much. It's my home, my family is there, I always knew I wanted to go home."

When she returned to Kuwait after finishing law school abroad, Munirah announced that she wanted to join a large corporate law firm. Her parents, however, were not supportive of her decision. "They told me work was good as a side hobby, but lawyers work a lot. I think they were worried that I wouldn't be able to concentrate on getting married, but that wasn't what I was interested in."

Despite her parents' objections, Munirah joined the Kuwaiti law firm she had been recruited for and began working long hours. After some time her mother grew impatient with her and began putting a lot of pressure on Munirah to quit. "She used to yell at me, scream even. She would tell me I was wasting my time, and the more I worked, the angrier she became. But I never considered quitting." During this time Munirah became close to one of the domestic workers who had recently moved to Kuwait to work for Munirah's family. Dee, as Munirah called her, had moved from Ethiopia in search of work in order to support her ailing mother back home. Dee and Munirah were roughly the same age, and Munirah described their friendship as "a warmth inside a cold house."

Dee and Munirah began spending time together when Dee overheard Munirah's mother yelling at her. "My mom screamed at me, slammed the door and left. After that I started crying, but Dee came to me and hugged me. Later that day I saw my mom yelling at Dee. I was overcome with the urge to walk over to Dee and hug her, so I did." This was the start of a meaningful friendship for both women. Munirah would often talk with Dee late into the evening hours, the two women exchanging life stories. One evening, Dee told Munirah about a young man she had met at church during her day off the previous week. She had given him her number, and the two had been exchanging text messages all week.

"I was worried for Dee, I didn't know why, I just knew that a lot of men are scoundrels and I didn't want her mixed up with the wrong kind of man. But when I told her that, she just laughed and laughed. She said, 'You know Munirah *jan*, you know a lot of things about a lot of things, but I know a lot of things about men.' That really stayed with me," Munirah remembered. Before long, Dee was in an intimate relationship with this man, and Munirah would often cover for her friend when she wanted to get away to see him. She would tell her mother that she had asked Dee to run an errand for her or would find ways of distracting her sisters when they asked for Dee.

One evening Dee came to Munirah in tears. "She came to me and said, 'The worst has happened.' And I thought her mother had died or something happened to her family. But no, it was worse. She came to me to tell me she was pregnant." Dee was unsure what to do, but Munirah was certain that her friend's pregnancy should remain a secret for as long as possible. "I'm a corporate lawyer, sure, but I do know sharia law, and I do know what you can get arrested for."

Soon Munirah began researching Kuwaiti laws about children born to unmarried women who were not Kuwaiti citizens. She read the law that states that a child born to a foreign woman whose father is unknown will not be granted citizenship and may, in some cases, be stateless. Further research revealed, however, that an abandoned child, or "foundling" as they were referred to in the GCC, was actually eligible for citizenship. Baffled by this law, she told Dee what she had discovered.[4] "Then Dee started to cry again. She told me that the father of the baby had been deported for overstaying his visa. She said that he refused to come forward to acknowledge paternity. Then when I told her about the laws I had discovered, she was surprised. I think I gave her an idea, but it wasn't what I meant." Tears came to Munirah's eyes.

With Munirah's help, Dee found an informal shelter where she could stay until she gave birth. The host of the shelter was nonetheless adamant that once the baby was born Dee would need to find other accommodations. This never happened, however; when the baby was three days old, Dee sent Munirah a text message. She scrolled through her phone to find her saved messages to show me the text. It read: "Baby outside hopital. I did it. Now I go to police. Help baby girl if y cn. Thanks you my friend." Munirah shook her head, as if still in disbelief. Dee had abandoned her baby girl and voluntarily turned herself in for deportation. Munirah went to the hospital immediately to see the little girl.

When Munirah arrived at the hospital, the police were holding the baby. She ran up to them to ask what was going on. "At first they didn't want to tell me, they said like 'Who are you?' But then I told them I'm a human rights lawyer working with children. I don't know why I said that, it just came out. Maybe my heart knew that I wanted to be a human rights lawyer before I did," she said laughing. She told the police that the child was a foundling and thus should be eligible for citizenship. But the policeman told her that someone had seen a "dark skinned" woman leaving the baby outside the hospital. They had somehow identified this woman as the same woman who turned herself in to the police a few hours later. "'No,' they told me. 'This thing will be *bidoun* because mother was known, and mother and father not Kuwaiti.' I got very angry, I don't know why; I was just very angry that he called her a 'thing,' so I said, 'She has a name, her name is Aisha.' I don't know why I said that. Maybe because that was a name that Dee and I had talked about once, a long time ago, but that's what I told the police. I told them I knew Dee, that I knew the baby. But they still took her to the orphanage, all the time she was crying, and it broke my heart."

Munirah was shaken by her friend's sudden departure and worried about the fate of the little girl. She called the orphanage and asked to see the baby but was denied. Frustrated, Munirah began researching laws about children and statelessness in Kuwait and around the world. It was during this time, in 2012, she founded an organization called Human Line, a nonprofit group dedicated to working with stateless children and the children of foreign workers. She quit her job at the law firm and began working full-time on Human Line. She hired two other pro bono lawyers and a team of activists and entrepreneurs to launch the organization, which was funded by the Kuwaiti government. Six months after opening Human Line, Munirah received a call from the director of the orphanage housing Aisha. "She called me and said 'You can come take the girl if you want,' and I was amazed. 'Just like that?' I asked the lady, and she said, 'Look, do you want her or not?' and I just said 'Yes.' I couldn't believe it, I agreed to take in Aisha in a quick decision like that, just like that."

Munirah's mother, however, was not willing to house the child of her former employee. This prompted Munirah, with the assistance of her two elder brothers, to move out of her parents' home and move in with one of her brothers. Aisha moved in with Munirah and her brother and was given her own nursery when she was seven months old. Though Munirah cannot technically adopt Aisha, because Aisha is stateless, Aisha continues to live with Munirah to this day.

"If I didn't have Aisha, or really, if it hadn't been for Dee, I would have still been at that terrible job, getting yelled at by my mother every day. But now my life is so different. So hard, but so different." Munirah never heard from Dee again, despite numerous attempts to locate her friend. However, her work with Human Line has brought her into contact with numerous government officials, and through this work they are drawing attention to the plight of children like Aisha in order to revise existing laws and prevent women like Dee from having to make such a difficult choice.

Moving Home, Moving On

For some migrants, the move home provides them with an opportunity to move through their immobility. The physical move encourages emotional moving on, mobilizing intimate lives that may have become immobilized before, during, or after the migratory journey. Coming home for many of my interlocutors allowed them to process the difficulties they had faced. Many faced increased challenges at home, too, but some, like Claudia, described just above, were able to turn their experiences into activism. Two other interviewees, Indra and Sharona, experienced encounters with agents of their home states that were transformative in mobilizing them through their immobility.

Indra

"I was always thirsty," Indra said of the time she spent in a jail just outside of Abu Dhabi. "I think Yeshim was a water baby, even when in my stomach." Indra cuddled her now three-month-old son. The baby pulled on his mother's long, braided hair as she nursed him, smiling and gurgling while he gulped. "And you see, he is always thirsty, even now, always wants to drink, maybe that's why I was so thirsty when I was pregnant." Indra patted Yeshim's back to burp him. She lowered her voice before continuing. "I was even so thirsty that I used to drink the toilet water in the corner of the room [jail cell]. The other ladies felt so sorry for me, but I didn't know what to do, just that my baby wanted water, so I drank whatever I could find."

Indra had moved from a rural part of Bali, Indonesia, to Dubai in search of work and adventure. "When I was younger, I was always dreaming of going abroad. I know lots of things happen abroad, and I wanted to go too." The youngest of four children, Indra had heard about work overseas for Indonesian women and contacted a local recruiting agency to learn more. One of the recruiters told her about domestic work openings in Dubai. "I had heard a lot of things about Dubai, and I was excited for this opportunity! So, I borrowed money from my parents, well, and some from friends, and I decided to go. At that time I am maybe twenty or twenty-one years old. Very young."

When she arrived she was placed in the home of a Syrian family who treated her very well. She assisted with cleaning duties, but her main task was to act as caregiver for her employers' then six-month-old twin baby boys. "They were so cute, those two, but a lot of work," Indra said. After her three-year contract with the Syrian family was up, she decided to renew her contract and stay an additional three years. Her original employers were moving to Europe, however, so Indra worked with another recruiting agency in Dubai and was transferred to the home of an Emirati family with four young children. There she was among a staff of five other domestic workers, and her workload lessened significantly. She was in charge of two of the children and assisted with light housekeeping duties.

"I thought the first family was kind, and I thought I'm lucky. But then my new madam was even kinder. And she did not make me work too much, and two days off each week, even more when they traveled, so I had plenty of time off." She was also making good money, which she sent home to her parents and older siblings. Despite feeling content with her employers and her salary, Indra missed home and often thought of returning. "I was happy in Dubai, but still lonely. I missed my family a lot. My family and my home. But I know that I'm sending money, and this is good."

For a short period of time Indra's loneliness lessened, when she began a relationship with another staff member in the household. Manee, a young man from the Philippines, was working as the family driver, and he and Indra became close after a year of working together. They began an intimate relationship, but the relationship ended badly when Manee started having an affair with Annie, the family cook.

One afternoon, while working in the kitchen, Indra fainted and hit her head, causing bleeding at the temples. Her employer took her to the hospital to make sure that the fall had not resulted in long-term damage. While at the hospital, the doctors ran several tests, and Indra was told that she was pregnant. Her employer was in the room when the doctor delivered this news, and she instantly became angry with Indra. "She felt I had done a bad thing to her, and I felt that way too. I was sad. But then I'm scared because the doctor is saying I have to go to jail because of *zina*. The police come the next day and take me to jail."

Indra was placed in a jail cell with eleven other women who were also pregnant or had recently given birth. She was told she would have to stand trial for having broken her contract and committing the crime of *zina*. Terrified, she described her time in prison as "living in a nightmare." When she was told she would likely be deported, her fears increased, because she knew her religiously devout family would not accept her pregnancy and would likely exile her. Fortunately, when Indra was seven months pregnant, her employer came to the prison to drop the charges related to her contract. She negotiated Indra's release and gave her the option of staying with their family to have the baby. "My madam was very kind. She gave me choice. She said I can stay with them to have the baby and work with them, or I can go home and she will help me go home. I am scared at that time, but I miss home. I know that going home will be very hard, but still I tell her 'I want to go home.' So she helps me." Indra's smile radiated across her face.

When Indra arrived in Bali, she was afraid to return to her parents' house while still pregnant. She feared that her father would hurt her or, worse, try to hurt the baby. An official at the airport gave her the phone number of a midwifery clinic in Bali. "When I am coming home, he is helping me. He tells me, 'You are pregnant, but you don't have money. If you go to the hospital, you will not be able to take your baby home until you can pay money for the doctors, but if you go here, they will do it free,' so I'm happy." She arrived at the midwifery center and begged them to allow her to stay there until the baby was born. They were kind enough to take her in, and she gave birth one month later to her son, Yeshim.

After the baby was born Indra called her employers in Dubai to tell them the news. They congratulated her and offered her a pay increase if she would be willing to return to Dubai to work with the family. "I'm thinking it is a lot of money. And maybe it will be a good life for Yeshim and me. But then I look at Yeshim, and I think, no. I want to stay home. I want to be home and I want him to grow up in my home," she said wistfully. After politely declining her employers' offer, Indra gathered up her baby and her courage and returned home to face her parents.

Expecting the worst, Indra was pleasantly surprised to find herself welcomed by her parents. "They see me, and my mom starts to cry. Even when she sees Yeshim. She is so happy that I am home, and it makes me cry, and then Yeshim cries too and soon everyone is crying." Indra and Yeshim moved into her parents' new home, which they had purchased with the help of Indra's remittances over the years. Once Yeshim was old enough to stay home with Indra's mother for periods of time, Indra began working at the clinic where she had given birth, volunteering to help other women who faced similarly challenging situations. When I asked Indra if she missed Dubai, a smile once again spread over her face, "Yes, I do miss Dubai. But it wasn't my home. There were many people there who were kind to me, but I need to come home. To be at home."

Sharona and David

Sharona cried leaving the airport in Johannesburg. She had never left home before, and she was saddened especially by leaving her boyfriend, David, behind. Sharona had graduated from university in Johannesburg but was unable to find employment at home. After several months of looking for a job, a local recruiter approached her about moving to Kuwait to work as a nanny. "He made it sound so perfect. He said Kuwait was clean, and that I would live in a big house, not work too much, and be able to make a lot of money. David and I wanted to get married, but then we didn't have enough money to marry and live on our own, so I thought, I can do this for a few years, then come back, yeah?" Sharona said, her accent a mixture of Afrikaans and Swahili.

"I didn't want her to leave; it was hard for me too," David explained. "I was working hard, I was working as a driver and trying to make money, but you see, here in South Africa, there isn't a lot of work for many of us." David and Sharona agreed that once her two-year contract was over, she would come home and they would marry. After Sharona left for Kuwait, however, many of David's friends cautioned him that she might not return from Kuwait after all.

"People were saying, 'Yeah man, why you think she gonna come back, eh? What you got here for her? Nothing, right?' And I was scared. I was scared she wouldn't come back because everyone said that life in the Middle East is so much better than here in Jo-burg." David leaned his head against the window of the car that had become his office over the years. For the first six weeks Sharona was away, David did not hear from her. He worried that his friends had been right and that he had lost Sharona forever. He took extra driving shifts, dropped out of university, and moved in with his brother to save money in hopes of traveling to Kuwait to find her.

"But it's not like that, eh?" David said, his drawl expanding. "Even if I could afford it, I couldn't just go to Kuwait, but I was going crazy, yeah? I can't find my girl? And nothing from her." After six weeks Sharona finally called David, much to David's relief. She explained that it had taken her some time to get a cell phone and to make enough money to purchase credit. The two began talking every evening. "She would tell me about her work, her day. But I always sensed sadness in her voice." He described their conversations as short but passionate and said he promised her that he would work hard to pay off her migratory debt so she could return home sooner.

"For me, life in Kuwait was fine. My employers good. The money good. Life comfortable. But I missed David. I missed Jo-burg, eh? It's just not the same. Maybe it's pretty in Kuwait, but the dirt doesn't smell the same." Sharona smiled as she spoke of the scents of her hometown. "When my employers offered me to move with them to London, all my friends were jealous. They said I am too lucky. But is it?" Sharona did not want to move to London; even though many of her friends told her that this move would really improve her life and lifestyle, she wanted to return home.

"People," said Sharona, "have this idea that when us Africans leave, when we go somewhere else to work, that we just want to stay there. They think, 'Why would someone want to come back?'" "But it's not a permanent thing," said David. "Sometimes you just want to move for money, but your heart is at home."

When Sharona's employers moved to London just six months after her arrival in Kuwait, Sharona decided to return to Johannesburg, even though she was essentially returning home empty-handed; so far she had only managed to pay off her debt to her recruiter. But David had been working hard, and so the two were able to move into a small apartment just outside of Johannesburg. Soon after her return to South Africa, Sharona heard about a project at her old university, tracking South African migrants, with a focus on migrants who return home from various deployments. Sharona called the project director to tell her own story and inquired about the possibility of working on the study. She was offered a position as an intern with very little pay, but Sharona remains optimistic about the possibilities of mobility in her new position.

"This study that Sharona is a part of is a really big deal, Prof," David explained to me. "Because it's showing people, you know, African people, that it's not a permanent thing when people leave, that coming home is what a lot of people really do want." Sharona agreed with David. "For me, I really wanted to come home. Sure, London could have been great for me, and it's not that Kuwait was bad, but I felt I needed to come home to continue living."

Transformative Mobilizations

Many of my interlocutors were able to move, both physically and emotionally, through various situations of immobility owing to their encounters with various manifestations of "the state." Embassies, hospitals, churches, or immigration staff facilitated the migration home or to another destination for some. Others were able to psychologically process their immobility—and move through it—once they returned home and worked with agents of the state. Similarly, people who might be understood as "the state"—such as Iqbal, Munirah, and Indra's employers in the host country—were transformed by their encounters with migrants. Home-country manifestations of the state—local activists, ambassadors, ministers of justice or population—were likewise transformed and moved to action through hearing the stories of their citizens returning from abroad.

Cases such as these complicate the perceived binary "migrants versus the state" and instead demonstrate dynamic and fluid movements in both directions. While some analyses of migration gone awry might point to the state as the guilty party, such portrayals do not provide room for analysis of the micromovements that take place when migrants work with and within various spaces of their home and host countries. Rather than viewing the state uncritically as good or bad, we have been surveying examples of the state operating in multiple capacities, both obstructing and facilitating migrant mobility.

The mutually transformative encounters between migrants and "the state" have in some cases led to tangible changes, albeit comparatively small ones. For example, Madagascar is now in the process of passing a more robust anti-trafficking law that takes into consideration the lived experiences of women such as Claudia and her friends. Rather than adopt yet another law that tightens borders and forces migration further underground, this new law seeks to make migration safer for Malagasy men and women alike. Owing to Iqbal and his colleagues' efforts, the IOM and ILO in Dubai, previously operating mostly as a logistics hub to facilitate transfers of supplies such as food and blankets, have now become actively involved with the UAE government and are working to structure programs such as the UN GIFT program (Global Initiative to Fight Trafficking), which is now heavily funded by the UAE government ("UN. GIFT" 2014). Finally, embassies such as those assisting the women in this book are working to assist nonnationals in their return migration, as well as actively procuring paperwork for the children of migrants born abroad. Importantly, various embassies in Kuwait and Dubai, including those of the Philippines and South Africa, have changed their rules in order to be able to absorb and shelter the children of migrants (citizens or not) born abroad. Though these may not seem like major changes, such micromovements are salient and send a strong message to migrants who have survived ordeals related to their immobility. They help to mobilize migrants on many levels and serve as a beacon of hope for those who are suffering.

While these mobilizations may not always be viewed or experienced as empowering per se, the transformations that ensue from migrant-state encounters may help to mobilize migrants who feel stuck physically or emotionally. Those who return home may continue to feel immobilized but may also find other sources of mobility through their encounters with the state and move on in their intimate lives. Similarly, those individuals who operate as agents of the state may also find themselves challenged and sometimes transformed. Thus, migrants and other individuals who initially may not have been able to see the world through the eyes of others are presented with an opportunity to reflexively explore this aspect of their positionality. Many migrants find that their lives have changed significantly owing to the mobility that comes from immobility, moving through migrant-state encounters.

7

NEGOTIATED INTIMACIES AND UNWANTED GIFTS

THROUGHOUT THE PROCESS of researching and writing this book, I often found myself thinking about Noor, the woman with whose story it opens. The intricacies of her story and the labyrinthine pathways she has taken to negotiate her subjectivity, intimate mobility, and social and economic rights in the face of multiple challenges illustrate the many ways in which migrants negotiate their intimacies and subjectivities in and through migration. Noor's intimate relationships with her family back in Iran, her boyfriend Waleed in Dubai, and their young son contour her migratory experience. Conversely, her position as a migrant (with all the attendant benefits and drawbacks of the liminal status of an im/migrant trying to settle in a host country where she does not have legal citizenship) affects her intimate relationships with all of her loved ones. Early in Noor's migratory journey, she cites her family back in Iran as the reason she does not wish to return home, fearing she will bring shame on the family as a divorcee. Later, after Noor gives birth to a son out of wedlock and is struggling with her legal and economic status in Dubai, she wants to join her family back home, but is prevented from doing so precisely because of the challenges she faces in that country. Similarly, Noor's relationship with Waleed initially provides an impetus to stay in Dubai, in order to be close to the man she loves and with whom she shares a son. When the relationship ends, however, Waleed and his refusal to acknowledge paternity or give his permission for Noor to leave with their son motivate her to leave. Noor's relationship to her young son also shows how the bonds of love influence the mutually constitutive forces of immobility and mobility. Initially, she wishes to stay in Dubai because she wants her son to be raised near his father, hoping she herself may be able to acquire legal status once her son is recognized as an Emirati citizen. Her optimism turns into its opposite when she is forced to choose between leaving without her son in order to assure her own safety and remaining illegally in Dubai in order to look out for her son's safety and well-being. Throughout this process and over the ten years she has been living in Dubai, Noor has somehow managed to create a sense of home while living abroad, as she and her son traverse the liminal space between immigrant and migrant in their minds, even if they cannot do so legally.

The complex choices Noor has had to make in order to preserve her intimate ties, her subjectivity, and her sense of self illustrate the negotiated intimacies that many of my interlocutors seek and explore in search of intimate mobilities. Her intimate self and intimate relations have impacted her migratory journey, which in turn has been impacted by her intimate relations. Throughout these many years, Noor has employed creative strategies to negotiate her legal, social, and economic presence while in Dubai, strategies that also have been affected by and affect her intimate subjectivity. Many of her decisions were motivated by a desire for intimate mobility—to be close to her boyfriend or son, to be far away from or close to her family. And some of the same forces that have impelled mobility have also led to immobility for Noor and her son.

Perhaps her story seems so powerful to me because it so saliently exemplifies the three main, interconnected arguments I put forth in this book. First, migration has an impact on individuals' intimate lives, and vice versa. The experience of migration, even the decision itself between going and staying, is connected to intimate ties and bonds of love. Likewise, migration has an impact on people's intimate lives. Notions of the "family" and "home" may change in the course of the migratory journey, and relationships between loved ones often undergo significant transformations when one or more of them are abroad for long periods of time. Parents may become estranged from their children or vice versa. Informal familial caregivers (such as grandmothers, aunts, or uncles) raising children back in the home country while mothers migrate may also be affected intimately as their lives are inevitably changed. Additionally, as voiced by many of my interlocutors, a desire to mobilize their intimate selves and thus a desire for intimate mobility shape many migratory choices.

Second, mobility and immobility are actually mutually constitutive forces. The same choices or bonds of love may simultaneously or successively bring about both mobility and immobility—they are really two sides of the same coin. Im/mobility may also operate at the level of economic and legal challenges and opportunities and perhaps may be seen most clearly in the multifarious interactions between migrants and various manifestations of the state. While one arm of the state may be erecting barriers to their economic, social, legal, or intimate mobility, others may at the same time be facilitating this mobility.

Third, immigration and migration are not always clearly dichotomous categories but are often interconnected, with most migrants existing in a liminal space in between statuses. Though very few of my interlocutors could legally become immigrants in the UAE or Kuwait, many of them were born in these countries, while others have migrated and consider these host countries their homes. In their minds they have reconstituted the notion of "home" and found a new form of intimate citizenship in the host country through their intimate mobilities. Though technically migrants (and in some cases overstayers and "illegal" migrants), many individuals see themselves as immigrants who have settled in a new "home." Exploring the intimate factors that affect the migrant experience illuminates the very simple but important point made by Nicole Constable (2014): migrants are people too. Understanding migrants as people rather than reducing them to the circumstances or type of their labor allows for a recognition of the negotiated intimacies and intimate mobilities that migrants seek out and attain in and through migration.

Trafficking, Rescue, Development, and Unwanted Gifts

The human trafficking framework has unfortunately cast a large, dark shadow over the lives of many of my interviewees. Though the question of who "counts" as trafficked remains opaque, human trafficking as a discourse and set of resulting policies impacts the lives of many migrants—whether they would be perceived by agents of the state as "trafficked" or not. Indeed, the question of who counts as trafficked seems to be part of the problem with the framework. In the intense concern with this large and nebulous question, the actual lived experiences of migrants and their loved ones are eclipsed. Furthermore, the answer to this question—whether one does or does not count as trafficked—does not always help those facing challenges. On a macrolevel, the set of policies fostered by the trafficking framework have created problems for all migrants, both those suffering from various types of abuse as well as others.

Policies seeking to restrict the migration and the mobilities of migrants, disconnected as they often are from lived reality, may have the unfortunate effect of doing more harm than good.

In previous writings I have speculated that the trafficking framework has the potential to be empowering and offer rights protections for vulnerable labor migrants. I have argued against throwing the baby out with the bathwater, pointing out the weaknesses of the framework but highlighting its positive potential as well (Mahdavi 2011). Now, after several years of writing about gendered migration and human trafficking in the Gulf, I am not convinced that the trafficking framework can be deployed in a positive way. I have observed too many negative consequences come from a hyperfixation on defining and preventing human trafficking. What is even more disturbing, I have observed the harrowing outcomes of policies and outreach implemented in the name of "rescue" or the "protection" of ostensible survivors of human trafficking.

I was recently invited to share the results of my research with a team of officials at the International Organization for Migration (IOM)—an arm of the United Nations. Upon hearing the stories I presented and the arguments I made, the IOM officials responded in a startling way. "This is why we need to get those people out of the Gulf," said one. Another nodded and added, "That's why I always say, development is the best answer to this. So that people don't have to leave their homes." I was baffled. I had been trying to make the point that many migrants *want* to leave and are not *forced* to do so. Encouraging "development" in sending or receiving countries is a fine, albeit controversial, idea, but it totally misses the point. Moreover, in reflecting on the first comment I was shocked at how this official had failed to grasp the details of the situations in which many of my interviewees had found themselves. "But if you 'get them out,' where are you going to take them? What would you do with someone like Noor who isn't sure she *wants* to go home? And certainly not without her son?" I asked the official. She paused for a moment before answering. "I think you have to send them home. People think maybe migrants are better off abroad, but they aren't, they all want to actually go home," she said. One of her colleagues added, "That's why it *is* human trafficking. That's why these people are all victims, even if they don't know it." I felt as though none of what I had said had been heard.

Trafficking as a framework underwriting both discourse and policies has manufactured a veritable charity industry, in which millions of dollars are funneled into antitrafficking initiatives that focus on "rescue" or "getting people out" or development strategies determined to "keep people home." As the many stories of migrants detailed in this book demonstrate, this framework is usually disconnected from the lived experiences of migrants, their families, their employers, and various arms of the state. Significantly, the industrial charity complex, which seeks only to "save" individuals from nefarious organizations or states, has obscured our view of the changes that are taking place as a result of migrant-led activism and partnerships between migrants, employers, and the state. When you talk to actual survivors of exploitation, they say that they don't want charity. What most of them want is the freedom to physically move between their home and host countries and a safe way to do so in order to match the dimensions and speed of this movement in their minds.

ı ı ı

When hearing the stories of people like Noor or Daisy or Saleema (narrated in Chapter 1), common responses include: "I had no idea this was happening"; "How can I help them?"; "We have to get them out of that situation"; "Where can I donate money for this cause?" All these responses fall under the rubric of charity and, while well intentioned, tend to obscure the interconnectedness of the problems encountered by migrants and their families. Trafficking discourses and responses have framed the issue as necessitating charity. Indeed, the entire antitrafficking movement (whatever side one is on—abolition or harm reduction)[1] has been focused on putting pressure on donors, young students, journalists, and others to "get involved," thus fueling the problematic "rescue industry." But migrants and their families repeatedly insist that what they want is not charity, but justice.

Charitable responses to the situations of people like Noor, Daisy, and Saleema would focus on individuals, reasoning that their predicaments can be traced to individual or moral failings. Some might point to a failure on their part or that of their family members, while others might blame their exploitative employers. The response then would be framed around "rescue," of "getting them out" of their current situations. Whether or not they wanted to be rescued would be irrelevant; many antitrafficking responses don't even ask the survivors if they want help but instead take a raid-and-forced-rescue approach, placing survivors in "safe houses" where they are isolated, are sometimes forced to convert to a particular religion, and have their movements monitored regularly.

There has been a recent turn in the anthropological literature to being critical of humanitarian intervention and the role of "charity" in development (Bornstein 2012; Comaroff and Comaroff 2001; Fassin 2011). Erica Bornstein (2012) has documented how humanitarianism may often come in the form of "disquieting gifts" that privilege the position of the gift giver in a problematically perpetuated, unequal power dynamic disguised as "development." Through in-depth ethnography in India, she shows how charity, philanthropy, humanitarianism, and development are all linked through a process of "gift giving" or "gifting" and asks us to question the complex social, class, ethnic, and racial dynamics bound up in different types of "gift giving." Bornstein uses Marcel Mauss's *The Gift* to examine the micro and macro power imbalances created between giver and receiver in a "gift exchange," pointing to ways in which this type of development needs to be more closely examined. In his book *Humanitarian Reason* (2011), Didier Fassin also focuses on power vacuums and imbalances created in the humanitarian "gifting" process. Fassin's work examines the morally infused impetus behind humanitarian intervention, and critiques the overreliance on "morality" as an attempt to justify the negative outcomes resulting from certain types of development or intervention. Though the literature on gift giving is vast, Bornstein's and Fassin's use of this literature as applied to critiques of development is highly salient when looking at the "gift" of rescue campaigns couched in developmentalist terms. I see many parallels between Bornstein's and Fassin's important work on development and humanitarianism and the morally infused "rescue" campaigns that are an outgrowth of antitrafficking approaches. Like Bornstein's "disquieting gifts," I have observed in my fieldwork that "rescue" often takes the form of an *unwanted* gift—those being "rescued" would rather be left alone, particularly by the rescuers. These gifts, unwanted as they may be, reproduce the same problematic power imbalances to which Bornstein and Fassin point. The entire "rescue industry," similar to Fassin's observations, seems to be rooted in a sense of moral humanitarianism (Agustín 2007); a sort of moral panic about human trafficking would seem to have set in, inspiring these unwanted gifts (Cohen 1972). As Bornstein and Fassin describe, the subjectivities of the receivers of these "gifts" become challenged and flattened, constituting both a reason for and an outgrowth of the unwanted gift of rescue. The result is devastating for the gift "receivers" and their families.

The rescue industry has arisen out of a desire to address the plight of migrants from the perspective of charity. Laura Agustín has traced such impulses back to mid-nineteenth-century England, where groups of middle-class women began coming together to advocate for their own roles in society. A major part of this movement, which Agustín terms "the rise of the social," concerned defining the self in opposition to the other. In this case the "self" of the women's groups was structured around liberal values of morality, defined in contradistinction to an "other" of lower-class working women, many of whom labored in the sex industry. The "social" came about as certain women collaborated to "help" the women they saw as deviant and in need of rescue and monitoring. The problem with the approach of these groups was that the sex workers did not want to be "saved" but rather preferred either to continue working in an industry that was more lucrative than other avenues open to them or wanted some form of systemic change that would allow them class mobility. In the absence of structural change, "those declaring themselves to be helpers actively reproduce the marginalization they condemn." Agustín goes on to emphasize that the "social," which today takes the form of the rescue industry and has moved from a focus on sex work to human trafficking, continues to foster a discourse that legitimates its own work (Agustín 2007, 5). As she notes, "the social invented not only its objects [those in need of rescue], but the necessity to do something about them, and thereby its own need to exist" (107). Moving from the nineteenth century to the present, rescue industries and charitable responses continue to focus on the individual, who may or may not want assistance in the form of charity. Such responses are inadequate at best (rescuing people but then deporting them or not having a sustainable way for them to work or live) and damaging at worst (forced rescue and deportation). More important, they obscure the intimate lives of laborers and the grassroots activism that migrants themselves have taken up—inspired by their own lives—while allowing charity givers to feel good about feeling bad and thereby absolving them of their role in perpetuating these same structures.

When I asked Noor, Saleema, and Daisy what they wanted, all three spoke about issues of justice. "I want to be able to live where I want, make love to who I want, and be with whomever I want," Noor said. "I want to live in a world where people don't have to leave their families behind to make money," Daisy said. "I want to go to law school, study hard, and change the laws that make people like me without a state," said Saleema. None of them wanted to be saved or spoke in a way that suggested wanting their own situations to be changed by others. Rather, they spoke of wanting justice and of wanting recognition of the multidimensionality of their subjectivities and identities. For them, current rescue approaches would be not only inappropriate but disastrous.

Negotiated Intimacies

While human trafficking as a discourse and the rescue industry to which it has given birth have a long history that can be traced back to the eighteenth-century panics over the white slave trade and Laura Agustin's "rise of the social," the moral panic over trafficking has seen a resurgence since the late 1990s and 2000s. This can be evidenced through the passage of an increased amount of legislation on human trafficking at the international level (for example, the UN's Palermo Protocol in 2000) and at the domestic level (for example, the Trafficking Victims Protection Act [TVPA] passed in 2000 in the United States and the US State Department's Trafficking in Persons Report, issued beginning in 2001); and responses to the moral panic on the part of individual countries. Discursively and politically, this framework has not only caused a lot of damage but has erased the complex lived realities of migrants' intimate lives. I propose intimate im/mobilities, pointing to the ways in which migrants negotiate their intimacies in, through, and during migration, as an alternative framework—not necessarily a counterframework—to that of human trafficking. We have seen over the last decade that the trafficking framework is inadequate at best. The concept of intimate im/mobilities provides the flexibility to recognize the negotiated intimacies of migrants, their families, their loved ones, and their lives.

Intimate im/mobilities also allows for a reconfiguring of the relationships between love, money, and migration and invites an exploration of the circuitous nature of these flows through the lens of migrant subjectivity. The time for focusing on human trafficking, of exclusively money-driven migration, as a framework for understanding migration has passed. The discourses created by these frameworks, as well as the policies that have resulted, such as rescue or structural adjustment, have also been inadequate and resulted in challenges to migrant mobility and subjectivity. Exploring both the challenges and opportunities experienced by migrants as well as those with whom they connect provides a more robust picture of migration that takes into account lived realities.

ı ı ı

When I think about my conversation with Noor during the summer of 2013, I reflect on the many layers of our negotiated intimacies. We often discussed how our ideas about love, life, family, parenthood, and work changed in the course of moving through different physical spaces and emotional states. "It wasn't until I moved into Dubai, really moved *into* being here that I started to understand what love is," Noor had said that warm afternoon at the café. For Noor, as for many of my other interlocutors, her negotiated intimacies were found in and through the migratory experience. To recognize her journey is to recognize her as a person and to give her the room she needs in order to continue to negotiate her intimate subjectivities and im/mobilities.

ACKNOWLEDGMENTS

The research for this project would not have been possible without the generous support of several institutions and funding agencies. The Pomona College Faculty Research Fund has been a continuing source of research support, seeing this project through from pilot to page. The Asia Research Institute at the National University of Singapore generously provided me with the space, time, and support to finish the writing of the book. And a Social Science Research Council Abe Fellowship allowed me to complete the fieldwork at a crucial stage.

I have benefited tremendously from colleagues around the world who have given me valuable feedback on various chapters, proposals, and lecture versions of what appears in the book. In Claremont, I am grateful for the small liberal arts college environment that allowed me to work with friends and colleagues across colleges and disciplines. Conversations with Lara Deeb, Erin Runions, Tomas Summers Sandoval, Dara Regaignon, and Anne Dwyer shaped my early thinking on this project and helped to get it off the ground. Erin Runions and Lara Deeb in particular offered not only guidance and counsel but a shoulder to cry on whenever I needed it. In Singapore, I was pleasantly surprised to find a large community of scholars, friends, and colleagues who were all open to reading drafts of chapters and talking through my ideas with me. I am grateful to Eric Thompson, Malini Sur, Brenda Yeoh, Martha Kaplan, John Kelly, James Siddaway, and Maria Platt for giving me such inspiration during the writing phase and helping me cross the finish line.

My students at Pomona College never cease to amaze me. In particular, the students in my "Love, Labor and the Law" class of 2014 challenged, inspired, and supported me to make this project the best version of the research that it could be. The students in my Gender and Women's Studies "Senior Seminar" of 2013 gave me more writing advice than I imparted to them, and their writing processes and my own came together in exciting ways. I was also fortunate to have three students, Ben Kersten, Leyth Swidan, and Robin Pomerecke, who provided research assistance for the book. Joan Dempsey read through the entire manuscript and gave excellent editorial feedback.

I would not have been able to even conceptualize this project if it weren't for the love and support of my fantastic family. My parents, Mahmood and Fereshteh, and my brothers, Paymohn and Paasha, remain a source of comfort for me, even when we are thousands of miles apart. I am most grateful to my husband, Peter Kung, for being there for me in every sense of the term. He read drafts of chapters, listened to versions of talks, and was right there with me during almost every moment of my fieldwork. He was willing to travel around the world so that we could keep our family together, and was the most supportive partner I could ever dream of. I must also thank my two children, Tara and Shayan, for their patience and willingness to make friends in many different countries and for being such good travelers. They are both wise beyond their years, and I can only hope that they will remember all of this travel fondly.

Finally, I will be eternally grateful to my interlocutors, to whom I've grown closer during this project than I ever thought I would. They have seen me through the most difficult period of my life, and I feel honored to have been welcomed into their hearts and homes. Many of them were also generous hosts during my stays in various countries, and I am grateful for their time, love, and energy. I am filled with admiration for the migrants and families whom I have met over the years. They are my greatest inspiration and strength, and I will always be in their debt.

NOTES

CHAPTER 1

1. For a more in-depth discussion of the rescue industry, see the work of Laura Agustín and Gretchen Sodurlund. These authors argue, and I agree, that "rescue" is often experienced as violent by the rescuees, resulting in a situation in which people find themselves trying to run away from the rescuers. Agustín has focused much of her work on criticizing the "rescuers" as lacking in self-awareness and seeking only to advance their own, neocolonial, Western, often religiously informed agendas.

2. For a more thorough discussion of moral panics and trafficking, see Mahdavi 2013; Weizer 2007.

3. For more on kinship studies and anthropological approaches to the "family," see the work of Alfred Radcliffe-Brown, John Barnes, Victor Turner, Claude Lévi-Strauss, and Bronislaw Malinowski. These authors point out the fluidity of notions of "kinship" and highlight that who or what constitutes the "family" is culturally, socially, and historically determined. They note the importance of accepting and understanding how fluid and geographically specific conceptions of the family are. I aim to follow the important work of these seminal anthropologists in allowing my interlocutors to determine and narrate their own conceptions of the "family" and "kin."

4. The challenges faced by migrant families and sacrifices made by various family members have been extensively documented in the work of Leisy Abrego, Cati Coe, Nicole Constable, and Geraldine Pratt.

5. The phrase "migrating out of poverty" entered the academic and political lexicon around the turn of the twenty-first century (see, for example, the Migrating Out of Poverty research program consortium at http://migratingoutofpoverty.dfid.gov.uk/). Many scholars take it for granted that poverty is the primary "push factor," but my work suggests otherwise, complicating this received notion.

6. I enclose the term "push" in quotation marks to indicate that while it is a received term in academic parlance, I do not agree with the overly simplified binary of "push" versus "pull" factors for migration. Instead, I see the process as much more fluid and circular (rather than linear).

7. There will be a more complete discussion of the *kefala* system in later chapters; for an overview of the sponsorship system, see Gardner 2010; Longva 1997; Mahdavi 2011; and Nagy 1998.

8. I am particularly grateful to sociologist Eric Thompson for this insight.

9. See Friedman 2010; Hsia 2009; Piper and Roces 2003; and Yeoh 2013.

10. See Chin 2013; Ehrenreich and Hochschild 2003; and Mahdavi 2011.

11. For more in-depth discussion of the construction of human trafficking frameworks, see Agustín 2007; Doezema 1998; Mahdavi 2011; and Vance 2011.

12. For a more in-depth discussion of the problematic aspects of the "rescue industry," see Agustín 2007; Soderlund 2005; and Vance 2011. For additional discussion of the "deportation regime," see De Genova and Peutz 2010. DeGenova and Peutz argue that deportation, like "rescue," is socially constructed and artificially enforced. They note that the selective enforcement of "deportation" as a regime reveals much about neoliberal market schemes, anti-immigrant sentiment, and neocolonial power struggles across the globe.

13. For further discussion of the role of state structures in promulgating systems of abuse, see the work of Andrew Gardner, Rhacel Parreñas, and Christine Chin. These authors look at how state structures, policies, and economies can be experienced as a type of "structural violence" wherein inequality is propagated and promulgated by "the state." They describe how migrants must employ creativity in order to counteract the damaging effect of structural violence on their lives.

14. For more on the problematic approach of the "rescue industry," see the work of Laura Agustín and Gretchen Soderlund.

15. This estimate is based on conversations with the Ministry of Population and Ministry of Labor in Madagascar.

16. For more on this point, see the work of Nicole Constable and the edited volume by Sara Friedman and Pardis Mahdavi.

17. See Parreñas 2005a; Suzuki 1996; and Yeoh and Lam 2007.

18. See Lan 2008; Parreñas 2001a, 2005a; and Pratt 2012.

19. See Hopper 2005.

CHAPTER 2

1. See Friedman and Mahdavi 2015; Piper and Roces 2003; and Yeoh, Huang, and Cheng 2015.

2. See Benhabib and Resnik 2009; Ehrenreich and Hochschild 2003; and Parreñas 2011.

3. See Boris and Parreñas 2010; and Friedman and Mahdavi 2015.

4. *Zina* is the unlawful act of sex outside marriage. This includes both premarital and extramarital sexual relations. This law is established within sharia law, the religious and moral code followed, in combination with secular law, in the GCC and other countries. Migrant women are affected drastically by the laws on *zina* on account of their lack of citizenship within the GCC. Under sharia law there are two means of proving *zina*: either the person who committed *zina* must confess, or there must be four eyewitnesses who will testify. When an unmarried woman becomes pregnant, however, her pregnancy itself can be used to prove she has committed *zina*. Many migrant women are married but their husbands reside in another country. The use of pregnancy as proof of

committing *zina* ignores issues of rape within the workplace as well as denying women sexual autonomy. Because of the issues connected with using pregnancy as proof of *zina*, it is considered circumstantial proof and is hotly debated.

Within secular law in the UAE, *zina* appears in the Federal Penal Code (FPC, Law No. 3 of 1987). The Penal Code includes sharia law. While *zina* is not directly cited in Article 354, FPC Rape, this article is cited in relation to laws concerning sex outside marriage. Article 354 states that anyone who uses coercion to have sexual intercourse with a female or sodomy with a male will be sentenced to the death penalty. This would seem to protect those who are raped against being convicted of *zina* and (if they are migrants) possibly deported. But this law, combined with pregnancy as proof of *zina*, ignores the complexities and situational power dynamics that may occur within a relationship, especially that between an employer and employee.

5. See Abrego 2014; Bhabha 2009; Constable 2013; Parrenas 2005; Pratt 2012; and Terrio 2008.

6. See Abrego 2014; Constable 2013; Luibhéid 2013; and Pelligrini 2014.

7. See Gardner 2008; and Longva 1999.

8. See Hondagneu-Sotelo 2003; Mahdavi 2011; and Parreñas 2005b.

9. See Marx and Engels 1967.

10. See Bourgois 2003; Butler 1990; and Constable 2013.

11. See Fernandez 2015.

12. As detailed in Chapter 1.

13. For a more in-depth discussion of *kefala* as it relates to domestic work, see Agunias 2010; Ahmad 2012; Gamburd 2008; Mahdavi 2011; and Nagy 1998.

14. See Ahmad 2012; Gardner 2010; Longva 1999; Mahdavi 2011; Nagy 1998; and Sabban 2004.

15. See Hondagneu-Sotello 2007; and Parreñas 2001a, 2005a, 2008b.

16. For further discussion of relationships between migrant workers and their sponsors, see Gardner 2010.

17. It is important to note that in 2012 the UAE did draft a law to recognize domestic workers as laborers; however, this law has yet to be implemented as of the writing of this book. See Salama 2012a.

18. It should be noted, however, that women may also find empowerment by becoming involved with religion while abroad, as scholars such as Attiya Ahmad (2012) have shown.

CHAPTER 3

A version of Chapter 3 appears in *Migrant Domestic Workers in the Middle East: The Home and the World*, edited by Bina Fernandez, Marina de Regt, and Gregory Currie. Their thinking on these topics has shaped my own for many years.

1. For more on this, see the work of Attiya Ahmad, Andrew Gardner, and Caroline and Filippo Osella. These scholars note, and I agree, that "rumors" can often be major factors compelling would-be migrants to seek out migratory journeys that can seem precarious at times. Specifically, these authors point to examples where rumors

and knowledge of migrants' successes in the Gulf have contributed to others from their sending communities seeking out the same opportunities. These rumors are not always accurate, as migrants may go to great lengths to maintain a façade of success after migrating to the Gulf in order to preserve their identities and/or reputations back in the sending countries.

2. *Baba* is the Arabic word for "father" or "daddy." It is not unusual for employers in the Gulf to ask their employees to address them as *mama* and *baba*, which together with employers referring to domestic workers as "part of the family" contributes to a rhetoric that erases the labor being performed. Furthermore, this insistence on referring to employers as parents is experienced as condescending and infantilizing by many migrant domestic workers, who articulate frustration at having to use this unfamiliar nomenclature.

CHAPTER 4

1. A full discussion of the debates around the complex notion of the "social contract" is beyond the scope of this book. I acknowledge that it is a contested term insofar as the definitions and uses of "social contract" are open to debate. Here, I make use of the common definition of "social contract" in order to examine how migrants experience the contract as a source of constraint. A full discussion of the debates over the definition of social contract can be found in the work of Pierre Bourdieu and Jean Jacques Rousseau (as cited in the text).

2. I am grateful for the insights provided by Michiel Bass and James Siddaway in this regard.

CHAPTER 5

A version of Chapter 5 appears in *Migrant Encounters: Intimate Labor, the State, and Mobility Across Asia*, a volume that I co-edited with Sara Friedman, to whom I owe a huge debt of gratitude for her patience, keen insights, and constant support. Much of my thinking about Chapter 6 also came from conversations with Sara over the years.

1. Holy Bible, *New International Version*, Bible Gateway; https://www.biblegateway.com/passage/?search=Exodus+2&version=NIV#fen-NIV-1565b.

2. See Kuwait 1977.

3. In cases where the citizenship of the mother can transfer to the child (as is the case for Filipina migrant women and their children), the expectant mother will be transferred to the care of the embassy of the sending country. This presents a problem for mothers who come from countries that do not have embassies on the ground (such as Madagascar) or whose embassy officials may not wish to extend citizenship rights to children of women they see as "unfit" mothers. I observed the latter in the cases of several interlocutors who were attempting to work with the Indian embassy in Kuwait and the UAE. The labor attachés in these embassies were unwilling to extend citizenship rights to the children of at least five of my interlocutors for reasons that were cited to them as having to do with "morality." Thus the extension of citizenship to the children of migrant women can be heavily dependent on embassy staff. The children of women

who hail from countries where citizenship transfers paternally (such as Pakistan) automatically become stateless. The experiences of my interlocutors with embassy staff were highly variable and frequently determined the ultimate outcome of their fates as well as those of their children.

4. Women can only leave the orphanage if they are married because of the law that prohibits single women from renting or buying houses alone.

5. As defined in Chapter 1.

6. With the important exceptions, of course, of the work of Leisy Abrego, Deborah Boehm, Nicole Constable, and Geraldine Pratt.

7. I am particularly grateful to one of the anonymous reviewers at Stanford University Press for this insight.

8. Noncitizen migrants and non-Muslims living in the UAE may now technically adopt children, but these children must carry citizenship from a "third state." They cannot adopt Emirati or stateless children, and thus most of the adoption that occurs in the UAE takes place through contacts in another country. Because very few noncitizen migrants and non-Muslims are able to adopt children from local orphanages, agencies have been created to facilitate adoption from other countries for noncitizens or non-Muslims living in the UAE. See Chubb 2010.

CHAPTER 6

1. See US Department of State, Bureau of Democracy, Human Rights, and Labor 1994, specifically the Freedom of Movement section.

2. An "outpass" is essentially documentation that allows migrants to exit the host country without their passports. These are usually created by migrants' own embassies, but in this case, because there is no Malagasy embassy in Kuwait, the South African embassy was able to step in and assist Fabian.

3. See Chapter 5 for theorization and discussion of how "illegality" and "informality" can be perversely integrated into the workings of the state.

4. At this point, Munirah did not know that according to Ethiopian law citizenship could technically pass through the mother and so could not advise her friend about this possibility.

CHAPTER 7

1. For an in-depth discussion of the contours of the trafficking debate, see Hoang and Parreñas 2014; Mahdavi 2011; and Vance 2011.

REFERENCES

Abrego, Leisy J. 2014. *Sacrificing Families: Navigating Laws, Labor, and Love across Borders.* Stanford, CA: Stanford University Press.

Agamben, Georgio. 2013. "For a Theory of Destituent Power." Lecture presented at the Nicos Poulantzas Institute, Athens, Greece, November 16, 2013. http://www.chronos mag.eu/index.php/g-agamben-for-a-theory-of-destituent-power.html.

Agence France-Presse. 2013. "Kuwait Passes Bill to Naturalize 4,000 Stateless People." *Al-Arabiya,* March 21. http://english.alarabiya.net/en/News/2013/03/21/Kuwait-passes -bill-to-naturalize-4-000–stateless-people.html.

Agunias, Dovelyn Rannveig. 2010. *Migration's Middlemen: Regulating Recruitment Agencies in the Philippines–United Arab Emirates Corridor.* Washington, DC: Migration Policy Institute.

———. 2006. *Remittances and Development: Trends, Impacts, and Policy Options—A Review of Literature.* Washington, DC: Migration Policy Institute.

Agustín, Laura María. 2008. "The Shadowy World of Sex across Borders." *The Guardian,* November 19. http://www.theguardian.com/commentisfree/2008/nov/19/human trafficking-prostitution.

———. 2007. *Sex at the Margins: Migration, Labour Markets and the Rescue Industry.* London: Zed.

Ahmad, Attiya. 2012. *Migrant Labor in the Persian Gulf.* London: Hurst.

Anderson, Bridget, and Julia O'Connell Davidson. 2003. *Is Trafficking in Human Beings Demand Driven? A Multi-Country Pilot Study.* Geneva: IOM International Organization for Migration.

Ashrawi, Hanan. 2002. Foreword to *Birthing the Nation: Strategies of Palestinian Women in Israel,* by Rhoda Ann Kanaaneh. Berkeley: University of California Press.

Baldwin-Edwards, Martin. 2011. "Labour Immigration and Labour Markets in the GCC Countries: National Patterns and Trends." LSE Research Online Documents on Economics 55239, LSE Library, London School of Economics and Political Science, London. Available at: http://eprints.lse.ac.uk/55239/.

Bales, Kevin. 2012. *Disposable People: New Slavery in the Global Economy.* Berkeley: University of California Press.

Benhabib, Seyla, and Judith Resnik, eds. 2009. *Migrations and Mobilities: Citizenship, Borders, and Gender.* New York: New York University Press.

Bernstein, Elizabeth. 2007. *Temporarily Yours: Intimacy, Authenticity, and the Commerce of Sex*. Chicago: University of Chicago Press.

Bhabha, Jacqueline. 2009. "The 'Mere Fortuity of Birth'? Children, Mothers, Borders, and the Meaning of Citizenship." In *Migrations and Mobilities: Citizenship, Borders and Gender*, edited by Seyla Benhabib and Judith Resnick, 187–227. New York: New York University Press.

Blitz, Brad K., and Maureen Lynch, eds. 2011. *Statelessness and Citizenship: A Comparative Study on the Benefits of Nationality*. Cheltenham, UK: Edward Elgar.

Boehm, Deborah. 2012. *Intimate Migrations: Gender, Family, and Illegality among Transnational Mexicans*. New York: New York University Press.

Boris, Eileen, and Rhacel Salazar Parreñas, eds. 2010. *Intimate Labors: Cultures, Technologies, and the Politics of Care*. Stanford, CA: Stanford University Press.

Bornstein, Erica. 2012. *Disquieting Gifts: Humanitarianism in New Delhi*. Stanford, CA: Stanford University Press.

Bourdieu, Pierre. 1984. *Distinction: A Social Critique of the Judgment of Taste*. Cambridge, MA: Harvard University Press.

Bourdieu, Pierre, and Loïc Wacquant. 1992. *An Invitation to Reflexive Sociology*. Chicago: University of Chicago Press.

Bourgois, Philippe. 2003. *In Search of Respect: Selling Crack in the Barrio*. Cambridge: Cambridge University Press.

Brennan, Denise. 2014. *Life Interrupted: Trafficking into Forced Labor in the United States*. Durham, NC: Duke University Press.

———. 2010. "Key Issues in the Resettlement of Formerly Trafficked Persons in the United States." *University of Pennsylvania Law Review* 158:1581–1608. doi:10.2307/25682360.

———. 2004. *What's Love Got to Do with It? Transnational Desires and Sex Tourism in the Dominican Republic*. Durham, NC: Duke University Press.

Butler, Judith. 1997. *The Psychic Life of Power: Theories in Subjection*. Stanford, CA: Stanford University Press.

———. 1990. *Gender Trouble: Feminism and the Subversion of Identity*. New York: Routledge.

Castells, Manuel. 1999. *The Information Age: Economy, Society and Culture*. Cambridge, MA: Blackwell.

Cheng, Sealing. 2013. *On the Move for Love: Migrant Entertainers and the U.S. Military in South Korea*. Philadelphia: University of Pennsylvania Press.

———. 2010. "Sex Trafficking: Inside the Business of Modern Slavery (review)." *Journal of World History* 21 (2): 363–368. doi:10.1353/jwh.0.0120.

Chin, Christine B. N. 2013. *Cosmopolitan Sex Workers: Women and Migration in a Global City*. Oxford: Oxford University Press.

Chubb, Laura. 2010. "How to Adopt in Dubai." *Time Out Dubai*, April 12. http://www.timeoutdubai.com/community/features/15174-how-to-adopt-in-dubai.

Coe, Cati. 2013. *The Scattered Family: Parenting, African Migrants, and Global Inequality*. Chicago: University of Chicago Press.

Cohen, Stanley. 1972. *Folk Devils and Moral Panics: The Creation of the Mods and the Rockers*. London: MacGibbon and Kee.

Comaroff, John, and Jean Comaroff. 2001. *Millennial Capitalism and the Culture of Neoliberalism*. Durham, NC: Duke University Press.

Constable, Nicole. 2014. *Born Out of Place: Migrant Mothers and the Politics of International Labor*. Berkeley: University of California Press.

———. 2013. "Migrant Workers, Legal Tactics, and Fragile Family Formation in Hong Kong." In *Oñati Socio-Legal Series* 3 (6): 1004–1022. Available at SSRN: http://ssrn .com/abstract=2356926.

———. 2007. *Maid to Order in Hong Kong: Stories of Migrant Workers*. Ithaca, NY: Cornell University Press.

———. 2003. *Romance on a Global Stage: Pen Pals, Virtual Ethnography, and "Mail-Order" Marriages*. Berkeley: University of California Press.

Coutin, Susan Bibler. 2007. *Nations of Emigrants: Shifting Boundaries of Citizenship in El Salvador and the United States*. Ithaca, NY: Cornell University Press.

———. 2000. "Denationalization, Inclusion, and Exclusion: Negotiating the Boundaries of Belonging." *Indiana Journal of Global Legal Studies* 7:585–593. Available at: http://www.repository.law.indiana.edu/ijgls/vol7/iss2/8.

Das, Veena, ed. 1990. *Mirrors of Violence: Communities, Riots and Survivors in South Asia*. New York: Oxford University Press.

De Genova, Nicholas, and Natalie Peutz, eds. 2010. *The Deportation Regime: Sovereignty, Space, and the Freedom of Movement*. Durham, NC: Duke University Press.

Doezema, Jo. 1998. "Forced to Choose: Beyond the Voluntary v. Forced Prostitution Dichotomy." In *Global Sex Workers: Rights, Resistance and Redefinition*, edited by Kemala Kempadoo and Jo Doezema, 34–50. New York: Routledge.

Dresch, Paul. 2006. "Foreign Matter: The Place of Strangers in Gulf Society." In *Globalization and the Gulf*, edited by John W. Fox, Nada Mourtada-Sabbah, and Mohammed Al-Mutawa, 200–222. New York: Routledge.

Duneier, Mitchell. 1999. *Sidewalk*. New York: Farrar, Straus and Giroux.

Ehrenreich, Barbara, and Arlie Russell Hochschild, eds. 2003. *Global Woman: Nannies, Maids, and Sex Workers in the New Economy*. New York: Metropolitan Books.

Faier, Lieba. 2009. *Intimate Encounters: Filipina Women and the Remaking of Rural Japan*. Berkeley: University of California Press.

Farley, Melissa, ed. 2003. *Prostitution, Trafficking and Traumatic Stress*. Binghamton, NY: Haworth Maltreatment and Trauma Press.

Farmer, Paul, Philippe Bourgois, Nancy Scheper-Hughes, Didier Fassin, Linda Green, H. K. Heggenhougen, Laurence Kirmayer, and Loc Wacquant. 2004. "An Anthropology of Structural Violence 1." *Current Anthropology* 45 (3): 305–325. doi:10.1086/382250.

Fassin, Didier. 2011. *Humanitarian Reason: A Moral History of the Present*. Berkeley: University of California Press.

Fernandez, Bina. 2014. "Degrees of (Un)Freedom: The Exercise of Migrant Agency by Ethiopian Domestic Workers in Kuwait and Lebanon." In *Migrant Domestic Workers in the Middle East: The Home and the World*, edited by B. Fernandez, M. de Regt, and Gregory Currie, 51–74. London: Palgrave Macmillan.

Fernandez, B., M. de Regt, and Gregory Currie, eds. 2014. *Migrant Domestic Workers in the Middle East: The Home and the World*. London: Palgrave MacMillan.

France-Presse Agence. 2013. "Kuwait Passes Bill to Naturalize 4,000 Stateless People." *Al Arabiya News*, March 21, sec. News; http://english.alarabiya.net/en/News/2013/03/21/Kuwait-passes-bill-to-naturalize-4-000-stateless-people.html.

Friedman, Sara L. 2012. "Adjudicating the Intersection of Marital Immigration, Domestic Violence, and Spousal Murder: China-Taiwan Marriages and Competing Legal Domains." *Indiana Journal of Global Legal Studies* 19 (1): 221–255. Available at: http://www.repository.law.indiana.edu/ijgls/vol19/iss1/9.

———. 2010. "Marital Immigration and Graduated Citizenship: Post-Naturalization Restrictions on Mainland Chinese Spouses in Taiwan." *Pacific Affairs* 83 (1): 73–93. doi:10.5509/201083173.

Friedman, Sara L., and Pardis Mahdavi, eds. 2015. *Migrant Encounters: Intimate Labor, the State, and Mobility Across Asia*. Philadelphia: University of Pennsylvania Press.

Gamburd, Michele R. 2008. "Milk Teeth and Jet Planes: Kin Relations in Families of Sri Lanka's Transnational Domestic Servants." *City & Society* 20:5–31. doi:10.1111/j.1548-744X.2008.00003.x.

Garcés-Mascareñas, Blanca. 2010. "Legal Production of Illegality in a Comparative Perspective. The Cases of Malaysia and Spain." *Asia Europe Journal* 8 (1): 77–89. doi:10.1007/s10308-010-0249-8.

———. 2008. "Old and New Labour Migration to Malaysia: From Colonial Times to the Present." In *Illegal Migration and Gender in a Global and Historical Perspective*, edited by Marlou Schrover, 105–126. Amsterdam: Amsterdam University Press.

Gardner, Andrew M. 2010. *City of Strangers: Gulf Migration and the Indian Community in Bahrain*. Ithaca, NY: Cornell University Press.

———. 2008. "Strategic Transnationalism: The Indian Diasporic Elite in Contemporary Bahrain." *City & Society* 20 (1): 54–78. doi:10.1111/j.1548-744X.2008.00005.x.

Giddens, Anthony. 1993. *The Transformation of Intimacy: Sexuality, Love, and Eroticism in Modern Societies*. Stanford, CA: Stanford University Press.

———. 1990. *The Consequences of Modernity*. Stanford, CA: Stanford University Press.

Gorman-Murray, Andrew. 2009. "Intimate Mobilities: Emotional Embodiment and Queer Migration." *Social and Cultural Geography* 10 (4): 441–460. doi:10.1080/14649360902853262.

Government of Dubai. 2013. "Complying with Marriage and Pregnancy Laws." *The Official Portal of Dubai Government*. March 6. http://www.dubai.ae/en/Lists/Articles/DispForm.aspx?ID=27.

Hashimoto, Akiko. 1996. *The Gift of Generations: Japanese and American Perspectives on Aging and the Social Contract*. Cambridge: Cambridge University Press.

Haynes, Dina F. 2014. "The Celebritization of Human Trafficking." *Annals of the American Academy of Political and Social Science* 653 (1): 25–45. doi:10.1177/0002716213515837.

Hoang, Kimberly Kay, and Rhacel Salazar Parreñas, eds. 2014. *Human Trafficking Reconsidered: Rethinking the Problem, Envisioning New Solutions*. New York: Open Society Institute and IDebate Press of the International Debate Education Association.

Holdsworth, Clare. 2012. *Family and Intimate Mobilities*. London: Palgrave Macmillan.

Holy Bible, New International Version. Bible Gateway. Accessed March 2014. Available at: https://www.biblegateway.com/versions/New-International-Version-NIV-Bible/.

Hondagneu-Sotelo, Pierrette. 2007. *Doméstica: Immigrant Workers Cleaning and Caring in the Shadows of Affluence*. Berkeley: University of California Press.

———. 2003. *Gender and U.S. Immigration: Contemporary Trends*. Berkeley: University of California Press.

Hopper, Kim. 2005. "On Mental Health and Homelessness." Lecture presented at the Columbia University Mailman School of Public Health, New York, February.

———. 2002. *Reckoning with Homelessness*. Ithaca, NY: Cornell University Press.

Hosseini, Ziba Mir. 2010. "Criminalizing Sexuality: Zina Laws as Violence against Women in Muslim Contexts." Violence Is Not Our Culture: The Global Campaign to Stop Killing and Stoning Women and Women Living under Muslim Laws. Available at: http://www.zibamirhosseini.com/documents/mir-hosseini-article-criminalizing-sexuality.pdf.

Hsia, Hsiao-Chuan. 2009. "Foreign Brides, Multiple Citizenship and the Immigrant Movement in Taiwan." *Asian and Pacific Migration Journal* 18 (1): 17–46. doi:10.1177/011719680901800102.

Human Rights Watch. 2007. "UAE: Draft Labor Law Violates International Standards." *Human Rights Watch*, March 26. Available at: http://www.hrw.org/news/2007/03/24/uae-draft-labor-law-violates-international-standards.

Immigration Specialist. 2012. "Relocating with Dependents: Immigration Challenges in Family Reunification." *Move One Inc*, June 21. http://www.moveoneinc.com/blog/moveone-news/enrelocating-dependents-immigration-challenges-family-reunification/.

International Labour Organization (ILO). 1997. "C181—Private Employment Agencies Convention." Geneva: 85th International Labour Conference, June 19. Available at: http://www.ilo.org/dyn/normlex/en/f?p=NORMLEXPUB:12100:0::NO::P12100_INSTRUMENT_ID:312326.

Issa, Wafa. 2011. "Children of Emirati Mothers, Expatriate Fathers Offered Citizenship." *The National* (UAE), November 30. http://www.thenational.ae/news/uae-news/children-of-emirati-mothers-expatriate-fathers-offered-citizenship.

Johnson, Mark. 2011. "Freelancing in the Kingdom: Filipino Migrant Domestic Workers Crafting Agency in Saudi Arabia." *Asian and Pacific Migration Journal* 20 (3–4): 459–478. doi:10.1177/011719681102000310.

Jureidini, Ray. 2010. "Trafficking and Contract Migrant Workers in the Middle East." *International Migration* 48:142–163. doi:10.1111/j.1468-2435.2010.00614.x.

Kanaaneh, Rhoda Ann. 2002. *Birthing the Nation: Strategies of Palestinian Women in Israel*. Berkeley: University of California Press.

Kerber, Linda K. 2013. "Crossing Borders." *Journal of American Ethnic History* 32 (2): 68–72. doi:10.5406/jamerethnhist.32.2.0068.

Kim, Hyun Mee. 2007. "The State and Migrant Women: Diverging Hopes in the Making of Multicultural Families in Contemporary Korea." *Korea Journal* 47 (4): 100–122. Available at: http://www.ekoreajournal.net/issue/index2.htm?Idx=419#.

Kuwait. 1993. Ministerial Order No. 97 of 1993 amending Art. 3 of MD 95 of 1993 concerning Issuance of Work Permits and Annulment of Cancellation and Transfer in the Private Sector, February 24. Department of Family and Nursing (brochure).

———. 1977. Decree Law No. 82, Family Nursing Act, Article 6. Department of Family and Nursing (brochure).

———. 1959. Nationality Law, 1959; amended by Decree Law No. 40 (1987), Decree No. 1 (1982), Statute No. 1 (1982), Decree Law No. 100 (1980), and Statute No. 30 (1970). Available at: http://www.refworld.org/docid/3ae6b4efic.html.

Lan, Pei-Chia. 2008. "Migrant Women's Bodies as Boundary Markers: Reproductive Crisis and Sexual Control in the Ethnic Frontiers of Taiwan." *Signs* 33 (4): 833–861. http://www.jstor.org/stable/10.1086/528876.

Longva, Anh Nga. 1999. "Keeping Migrant Workers in Check: The Kafala System in the Gulf." *Middle East Report* 211: 20–22. http://www.merip.org/mer/mer211/keeping-migrant-workers-check.

———. 1997. *Walls Built on Sand: Migration, Exclusion and Society in Kuwait.* New York: Westview Press.

Luibhéid, Eithne. 2013. *Pregnant on Arrival: Making the Illegal Immigrant.* Minneapolis: University of Minnesota Press.

Mahdavi, Pardis. 2013. *From Trafficking to Terror: Constructing a Global Social Problem.* London: Routledge.

———. 2011. *Gridlock: Labor, Migration, and Human Trafficking in Dubai.* Stanford, CA: Stanford University Press.

———. 2008. *Passionate Uprisings: Iran's Sexual Revolution.* Stanford, CA: Stanford University Press.

Marchetti, Sabrina, and Alessandra Venturini. 2014. "Mothers and Grandmothers on the Move: Labour Mobility and the Household Strategies of Moldovan and Ukrainian Migrant Women in Italy." *International Migration* 52:111–126. doi:10.1111/imig.12131.

Marx, Karl, and Friedrich Engels. 1967. *The Communist Manifesto (1848).* Translated and with introduction by A. J. P. Taylor. London: Penguin.

Migrating Out of Poverty RPC. "Migration and Poverty." Accessed March 4, 2015. http://migratingoutofpoverty.dfid.gov.uk/research/migrationandpoverty.

Morris-Suzuki, Tessa. 2010. *Borderline Japan: Foreigners and Frontier Controls in the Postwar Era.* Cambridge: Cambridge University Press.

Nagy, Sharon. 1998. "'This Time I Think I'll Try a Filipina': Global and Local Influences on Relations between Foreign Household Workers and Their Employers in Doha, Qatar." *City & Society* 10 (1): 83–103. doi:10.1525/city.1998.10.1.83.

Najmabadi, Afsaneh. 1998. "Crafting an Educated Housewife in Iran." In *Remaking Women: Feminism and Modernity in the Middle East*, edited by Lila Abu-Lughod, 91–125. Princeton, NJ: Princeton University Press.

Naufal, George Sami, and Ali A. Termos. 2009. "The Responsiveness of Remittances to Price of Oil: The Case of the GCC." *OPEC Energy Review* 33:184–197. doi:10.1111/j.1753-0237.2009.00166.x.

Ong, Aihwa. 2007. "Neoliberalism as a Mobile Technology." *Transactions of the Institute of British Geographers* 32:3–8. doi:10.1111/j.1475-5661.2007.00234.x.

———. 2006. *Neoliberalism as Exception: Mutations in Citizenship and Sovereignty.* Durham, NC: Duke University Press.

———. 1999. *Flexible Citizenship: The Cultural Logics of Transnationality.* Durham, NC: Duke University Press.

Ortner, Sherry B. 2006. *Anthropology and Social Theory: Culture, Power, and the Acting Subject.* Durham, NC: Duke University Press.

Osella, Caroline, and Filippo Osella, eds. 2013. *Islamic Reform in South Asia.* Cambridge: Cambridge University Press.

———. 2012. "Migration, Networks and Connectedness across the Indian Ocean." In *Migrant Labor in the Persian Gulf*, edited by Zahra Babar and Mehran Kamrava, 105–136. New York: Columbia University Press.

———. 2000. "Migration, Money and Masculinity in Kerala." *Journal of the Royal Anthropological Institute* 6 (1): 117–133. doi:10.1111/1467-9655.t01-1-00007.

Padilla, Mark, Jennifer Hirsch, Robert Sember, Miguel Muñoz-Laboy, and Richard Parker, eds. 2007. *Love and Globalization: Transformations of Intimacy in the Contemporary World.* Nashville: Vanderbilt University Press.

Parreñas, Rhacel Salazar. 2011. *Illicit Flirtations: Labor, Migration, and Sex Trafficking in Tokyo.* Stanford, CA: Stanford University Press.

———. 2008a. *The Force of Domesticity: Filipina Migrants and Globalization.* New York: New York University Press.

———. 2008b. "Transnational Fathering: Gendered Conflicts, Distant Disciplining and Emotional Gaps." *Journal of Ethnic and Migration Studies* 34 (7): 1057–1072. doi:10.1080/13691830802230356.

———. 2005a. *Children of Global Migration: Transnational Families and Gendered Woes.* Stanford, CA: Stanford University Press.

———. 2005b. "Long Distance Intimacy: Class, Gender and Intergenerational Relations between Mothers and Children in Filipino Transnational Families." *Global Networks* 5 (4): 317–336. doi:10.1111/j.1471-0374.2005.00122.x.

———. 2001a. "Mothering from a Distance: Emotions, Gender, and Intergenerational Relations in Filipino Transnational Families." *Feminist Studies* 27 (2): 361–390. doi:10.2307/3178765.

———. 2001b. *Servants of Globalization: Women, Migration and Domestic Work.* Stanford, CA: Stanford University Press.

Pelligrini, Ann. 2014. "Getting Uncomfortable: Religion, Sex, Politics and Other Things You Should Never Discuss at Family Dinners." Lecture presented at Pomona College, Claremont, CA, March 25.

Peters, Alicia W. 2013. "'Things That Involve Sex Are Just Different': US Anti-Trafficking

Law and Policy on the Books, in Their Minds, and in Action." *Anthropological Quarterly* 86 (1): 221–255. doi:10.1353/anq.2013.0007.

Pingol, Alicia. 2001. *Remaking Masculinities: Identity, Power, and Gender Dynamics in Families with Migrant Wives and Househusbands.* Quezon City: UP Center for Women's Studies.

Piper, Nicola, and Mina Roces, eds. 2003. *Wife or Worker? Asian Women and Migration.* Lanham, MD: Rowman and Littlefield.

Pratt, Geraldine. 2012. *Families Apart: Migrant Mothers and the Conflicts of Labor and Love.* Minneapolis: University of Minnesota Press.

———. 2009. "Circulating Sadness: Witnessing Filipina Mothers' Stories of Family Separation." *Gender, Place and Culture: A Journal of Feminist Geography* 16 (1): 3–22. doi:10.1080/09663690802574753.

Ramos, Norma. 2008. "Addressing Domestic Human Trafficking." *University of St. Thomas Law Journal* 6:21–27. Available at: http://ir.stthomas.edu/ustlj/vol6/iss1/4.

Reijenga, Erwin, Sebastian Brückner, and Erik Meij. 2013. "Migration in the GCC Countries: A Double-Edged Sword." Available at: http://www.rug.nl/frw/education/related/migrationinthegcccountries.pdf.

Rousseau, Jean-Jacques. 2002 [1750]. *The Social Contract and The First and Second Discourses.* Edited by Susan Dunn. New Haven, CT: Yale University Press.

Sabban, Rima. 2004. "Women Migrant Domestic Workers in the United Arab Emirates." In *Gender and Migration in Arab States: The Case of Domestic Workers,* edited by Simel Esim and Monica Smith, 85–107. Beirut: International Labour Organisation.

Salama, Samir. 2012a. "Domestic Workers Get More Protection from Exploitation." *Gulf News,* May 2. http://gulfnews.com/business/sectors/employment/domestic-workers-get-more-protection-from-exploitation-1.1016692.

———. 2012b. "Upbeat Egyptian Expatriates Vote in First Free Presidential Elections." *Gulf News,* May 12. http://gulfnews.com/news/gulf/uae/community-reports/upbeat-egyptian-expatriates-vote-in-first-free-presidential-elections-1.1021717.

Scott, James C. 1990. *Domination and the Arts of Resistance: Hidden Transcripts.* New Haven, CT: Yale University Press.

———. 1985. *Weapons of the Weak: Everyday Forms of Peasant Resistance.* New Haven, CT: Yale University Press.

Shah, Nasra M. 2013. "Second Generation Non-Nationals in Kuwait: Achievements, Aspirations and Plans." London School of Economics and Political Science Monograph Report. Available at: http://www.lse.ac.uk/middleEastCentre/kuwait/documents/Second-generation-non-nationals-in-Kuwait.pdf.

———. 2007. "Migration to Kuwait: Trends, Patterns and Policies." Paper prepared for the conference "Migration and Refugee Movements in the Middle East and North Africa," Forced Migration and Refugee Studies Program, American University in Cairo, Egypt, October 23–25. Available at: http://www.aucegypt.edu/GAPP/cmrs/Documents/Nasra_Shah.pdf.

Shah, Svati P. 2014. *Street Corner Secrets: Sex, Work, and Migration in the City of Mumbai.* Durham, NC: Duke University Press.

Soderlund, Gretchen. 2005. "Running from the Rescuers: New U.S. Crusades against Sex Trafficking and the Rhetoric of Abolition." *NWSA Journal* 17 (3): 64–87. doi:10.1353/nwsa.2005.0071.

Suter, Brigitte. 2005. *Labour Migration in the United Arab Emirates: Field Study on Regular and Irregular Migration in Dubai.* Master's thesis in IMER (International Migration and Ethnic Relations), Malmö University, Sweden.

Suzuki, Nobutaka. 1996. "Investing for the Future: Education, Migration and Intergenerational Conflict in South Cotabato, the Philippines." In *Binisaya nga Kinabuhi* [Visayan Life], edited by I. Ushijima I. and C. N. Zayas. Quezon City: CSSP Publications, University of the Philippines.

Terrio, Susan. J. 2008. "New Barbarians at the Gates of Paris? Prosecuting Undocumented Minors in the Juvenile Court—The Problem of the 'Petits Roumains.'" *Anthropological Quarterly* 81 (4): 873–901. doi:10.1353/anq.0.0032.

Thai, Hung Cam. 2008. *For Better or for Worse: Vietnamese International Marriages in the New Global Economy.* New Brunswick, NJ: Rutgers University Press.

Toumi, Habib. 2010. "Non-Kuwaiti Husbands May Get Kuwaiti Citizenship If Wives Approve." *Gulf News*, April 13. http://gulfnews.com/news/gulf/kuwait/non-kuwaiti-husbands-may-get-kuwaiti-citizenship-if-wives-approve-1.611711.

"UN.GIFT (Global Initiative to Fight Human Trafficking)." 2014. *UN.GIFT.HUB.* http://www.ungift.org/knowledgehub/en/about/index.html.

United Arab Emirates. 2012. Federal Law No. 1 for 2012 Concerning the Custody of Children of Unknown Parentage. Issued on May 24. Available at http://www.elaws.gov.ae/EnLegislations.aspx. English translation available at: http://www.ilo.org/dyn/natlex/docs/ELECTRONIC/92738/108187/F-704910911/federal_law_1_2012_en.pdf.

———. 1980. Federal Law No. 8 for 1980 Regarding the Organization of Labour Relations. Issued on April 20. English translation available at: http://www.gulftalent.com/repository/ext/UAE_Labour_Law.pdf.

———. 1975. Federal Law No. 10 for 1975 Concerning Amendment of Certain Articles of the Nationality and Passports Law No. 17 for 1972. Issued on November 15. Available at: http://www.refworld.org/docid/3fba19484.html.

———. 1972. Federal Law No. 17 for 1972 Concerning Nationality, Passports and Amendments Thereof. Issued on November 18. Available at: http://www.refworld.org/docid/3fba182d0.html.

"United Arab Emirates." In *Encyclopaedia Britannica World Data Online.* Accessed 2015. Available at: http://www.britannica.com/new-multimedia/pdf/wordat207.pdf.

UN Office on Drugs and Crime. 2000. "Protocol to Prevent, Suppress and Punish Trafficking in Persons, Especially Women and Children, Supplementing the United Nations Convention against Transnational Organized Crime." In *United Nations Convention against Transnational Organized Crime and the Protocols Thereto,* 41–51. Vienna: UN Office on Drugs and Crime.

UN/POP/EGM (United Nations, Population Division, Department of Economic and Social Affairs). 2006. "International Migration in the Arab Region." Paper prepared for the United Nations Expert Group Meeting on International Migration and Development in the Arab Region: Challenges and Opportunities, Economic and Social Commission for Western Asia, UN/POP/EGM/2006/14, Beirut, Lebanon, May 15–17. Available at http://www.un.org/esa/population/meetings/EGM_Ittmig_Arab/P14_PopDiv.pdf.

US Department of State, Bureau of Democracy, Human Rights, and Labor. 2012. *2011 Human Rights Reports: United Arab Emirates.* May 24. Available at: http://www.state .gov/j/drl/rls/hrrpt/humanrightsreport/index.htm?dlid=18645.

———. 1994. *Madagascar Human Rights Practices, 1993.* January 31. Available at: http:// dosfan.lib.uic.edu/ERC/democracy/1993_hrp_report/93hrp_report_africa/Mada gascar.html.

Van Walsum, Sarah. 2013. "The Contested Meaning of Care in Migration Law." *Ragion pratica* 2:451–470. doi:10.1415/74941.

Vance, Carole S. 2011. "Thinking Trafficking, Thinking Sex." *GLQ: A Journal of Lesbian and Gay Studies* 17 (1): 135–143. doi:10.1215/10642684-2010-024.

Vora, Neha. 2013. *Impossible Citizens: Dubai's Indian Diaspora.* Durham, NC: Duke University Press.

Wacquant, Loïc J. D. 2009. *Punishing the Poor: The Neoliberal Government of Social Insecurity.* Durham, NC: Duke University Press.

———. 2001. "Further Notes on Bourdieu's 'Marxism.'" *International Journal of Contemporary Sociology* 38 (1): 103–109. Available at: http://loicwacquant.net/assets/Papers /NOTESBOURDIEUSMARXISM.pdf.

Weizer, Ronald. 2007. "The Social Construction of Sex Trafficking: Ideology and Institutionalization of a Moral Crusade." *Politics & Society* 35 (3): 447–475. doi:10.1177 /0032329207304319.

Yeoh, Brenda S. A. 2013. "'Upwards' or 'Sideways' Cosmopolitanism? Talent/Labour/Marriage Migrations in the Globalising City-State of Singapore." *Migration Studies* 1 (1): 96–116. doi:10.1093/migration/mns037.

Yeoh, Brenda S. A., Shirlena Huang, and Yi'En Cheng. 2015. "Transnational Domestic Work and the Politics of Development." In *The Routledge Handbook of Gender and Development,* edited by Anne Coles, Leslie Gray, and Janet Momsen. New York: Routledge.

Yeoh, Brenda S. A., and Theodora Lam. 2007. "The Costs of (Im)mobility: Children Left Behind and Children Who Migrate with a Parent." In *Perspectives on Gender and Migration,* 120–149. Bangkok: United Nations Economic and Social Commission for Asia and the Pacific.

Zelizer, Viviana A. 2005. *The Purchase of Intimacy.* Princeton, NJ: Princeton University Press.

INDEX

Abortion laws, 52

Abrego, Leisy J., 17, 84, 88

Abu Dhabi, 33, 37. *See also* United Arab Emirates

Activists: help for migrants, 59, 60, 61–62; in Kuwait, 161–64; legal changes achieved, 29, 60, 146, 161, 170; in Madagascar, 59, 60, 159–61; male, 155–56, 170; in Philippines, 68; in Sri Lanka, 61–62. *See also* Nongovernmental organizations

Adoption: laws, 138–39, 189n8; of stateless children, 129, 131–32, 138–39, 189n8

Agency of migrants, 32, 46, 47, 77, 86–87, 90, 92

Agustin, Laura Maria, 178–79, 180

Akany Avoko, 159

Aliens Residence Law of 1959 (Kuwait), 48, 49

Anthropology, global, 33–34

Asia: ethnic stereotypes of women, 62, 105; marital migration, 98; women's identities, 25. *See also individual countries*

Bahrain, migrant workers, 36, 71

Bass, Michiel, 111

Bedouin customs, 48

Benhabib, Seyla, 43

Bhabha, Jacqueline, 43, 44, 75

Bidoun (stateless people), 121–22, 128–29, 138, 139–40. *See also* Stateless children

Binaries, 24–26, 77, 123, 148–49

Boehm, Deborah, 22, 75, 84, 123, 125

Boris, Eileen, 31

Bornstein, Erica, 178

Bourdieu, Pierre, 97

Brennan, Denise, 16, 98

Castells, Manuel, 123–24

Charity, critique of, 178. *See also* Nongovernmental organizations

Cheng, Sealing, 16, 98

Children: caretaking by migrant women, 46, 63, 64, 83, 130, 154, 157–58, 165; Filipino street children, 72–73; reproductive labor, 31, 44, 46, 153

Children, separated from mothers: emotions, 6–7; foundlings, 119–21, 124–25, 126, 137, 163; left at home by migrants, 44, 60, 62, 63, 65–68, 71–74, 107, 155, 157; mothers' decisions to migrate, 60, 103–5; perverse integration, 124, 125; as punishment of mother, 46, 62; raised by family members back home, 18–19, 60; transnational parenting, 32, 44, 88. *See also* Deportations

Children of migrants: born in host countries, 23, 30, 37, 170; citizenship laws of parents' home countries, 59; as constraint on parents, 104; as foreign matter, 90; residency permits, 53, 78; reunification with parents, 32, 74, 78–80; student visas, 79, 80; survival strategies, 125; white passports, 30, 53; without home countries, 85–90. *See also* Native-born foreigners; Stateless children

Chin, Christine B. N., 25, 31, 76, 91

Christians, 64–65, 156–57, 159–61

Citizenship: economic, 90, 98; flexible, 75–76, 135; of foundlings, 120–21, 124–25, 126, 137, 163; inflexible, 37, 75, 76, 78, 89–90, 91; matrilineal conferral, 126,

188n3, 189n4 (ch 6); patrilineal conferral, 10, 126, 127, 128, 188n3; rights, 126; social, 90, 98; through marriage, 126–27, 128
Citizenship laws: effects on migrants, 14, 23; of Ethiopia, 62, 189n4 (ch 6); of home countries, 59, 62, 128; *jus sanguinis* and *jus solis*, 126, 127; of Madagascar, 59, 60, 62; naturalization, 23, 126, 127, 128; of Pakistan, 188n3; of Philippines, 62; on reunification, 78–80; of Sri Lanka, 11; of United Arab Emirates, 23, 37, 42, 78, 79, 89, 126–27. *See also* Kuwait, citizenship laws
Civil society, 140. *See also* Nongovernmental organizations
Class divisions: among migrants, 91–92; mobility, 20, 22, 46, 91–92, 96, 179. *See also* Middle-class migrants
Commodification of intimacy, 31, 32, 43, 92
Comoros Islands, migrant workers, 63
Connected lives, 92, 117, 148
Constable, Nicole, 16, 43, 105, 175
Coutin, Susan Bibier, 123, 125
Creativity, 25
Crime, 123–24. *See also* Informal economies; *Zina*

Dancers, 109–11, 112–14
Debt: bondage, 50–51; to family members, 80; to recruiters, 50–51, 57, 60
De Genova, Nicholas, 45, 123, 125
Deportations: fear of, 2, 22, 45, 56, 58–59; grounds, 45, 49–50; of mothers without children, 9–11, 42–44, 46, 61, 65, 121–22, 133–35, 136; of pregnant women, 52, 106; resistance to, 44; social construction, 186n12; of trafficked persons, 14–15
Disquieting gifts, 178
Divorce, 1, 67, 102, 157
Documentary risk, 35
Domestic workers: as family members, 9, 18, 132, 150, 188n2 (ch 3); informal economy, 73, 74, 81, 83–84, 86; male, 80–81, 166; for nonlocal families, 12, 61, 83–84, 116, 165; raped by employers, 11, 42, 121; relations with employers, 18, 188n2 (ch 3); rights, 48; working conditions, 19, 31–32, 55–56,

57, 100, 157–58. *See also* Intimate labor; Migrants; Sponsorship (*kefala*) system; Women migrants
Dresch, Paul, 90
Dubai: fieldwork in, 33, 37; hospitals, 65, 66–68; Indian middle-class migrants, 21, 76, 85–90, 98–101; Iranian illegal immigrants, 1–5, 173–74; labor camps, 113–14; orphanages, 34; policies on unwed pregnancy, 52; prisons, 166; shelters, 155–56; UN headquarters, 153, 155, 170. *See also* United Arab Emirates
Duneier, Mitchell, 123, 124

Economic citizenship, 90, 98
Economic motives for migration, 19, 20, 46. *See also* Poverty
Economic statelessness, 75
Economies, *see* Informal economies
Education: of children raised in emir's palace, 135–37; fees paid by migrants' remittances, 12, 66, 67, 150; university study abroad, 153, 161
Employers: abusive, 49, 51; as extensions of state, 30; labor recruiters and, 50–52; migrants' relations with, 17, 18, 23, 30, 49–50. *See also* Sponsors
Employment: formal, 25; informal economy, 25, 73, 74, 83–84, 86, 123; of stateless children, 129. *See also* Domestic workers; Recruiters; Sponsorship (*kefala*) system
Empowerment: of migrants, 46, 68; through religion, 187n18; by trafficking framework, 176. *See also* Power
Ethiopia: citizenship laws, 62, 189n4 (ch 6); migrants from, 34–35, 41–42, 63–65, 162–64; Ministry of Labor, 63; shelter for returning migrants, 65
Exodus, *see* Moses

Faier, Lieba, 31
Families: defining, 17–18; domestic workers as part of, 9, 18, 132, 150, 188n2 (ch 3); duties to, 19, 46, 77, 81, 83, 84–85; effects of migration, 14, 18–19, 22, 32; influence on migration decisions, 60, 68–69, 77, 84–85; migrating away from, 95–97, 112–